How to Cut Your Risk with the Most Powerful ~~~~~~~~ oods

The Anti–
Breast Cancer
Cookbook

JULIA B. GREER, MD, MPH

SUNRISE
River Press

Sunrise River Press
39966 Grand Avenue
North Branch, MN 55056
Phone: 651-277-1400 or 800-895-4585
Fax: 651-277-1203
www.sunriseriverpress.com

Edit by Karen Chernyaev
Layout by Monica Seiberlich
Cover and Title Page Photography by Connie DeFlorin

Cover Recipe: Black Bean and Pumpkin Soup (page 103)
Title Page Recipe: Penne with Summer Squash, Zucchini and Sugar Snap Peas (page 168)

ISBN 978-1-934716-33-5
Item No. SRP633

Library of Congress Cataloging-in-Publication Data
Greer, Julia B.
  Anti-breast cancer cookbook : how to cut your risk with the most powerful, cancer-fighting foods / by Julia Greer.
    p. cm.
  Originally published: 2008.
  Includes index.
  ISBN 978-1-934716-33-5
1. Cancer–Nutritional aspects. 2. Cancer–Prevention. 3. Cancer–Diet therapy–Recipes. I. Title.
  RC268.45.G745 2012
  616.99'40654–dc23
                          2012034469

 Printed in China
10 9 8 7 6 5 4 3 2 1

TABLE OF CONTENTS

Foreword by Lanie Francis, MD..iv

Acknowledgments..v

About the Author..vi

Chapter 1: All About Breast Cancer..1
  Incidence and Prevalence 1
  A Quick Review of Breast Anatomy 2
  Types of Breast Cancer 3
  Risks Factors for Breast Cancer...3
  Early Onset Breast Cancer and BRCA1/BRCA2 Genetic Mutations.............6
  Triple Negative Breast Cancer 7
  What You Can Do to Lower Your Risk..7

Chapter 2: The Role of Diet in Breast Cancer..................................8
  Weight and Breast Cancer 8
  Nutrition and Cancer Risk 10
  Antioxidants and Cancer: How to Protect Yourself from Breast Cancer.............. 13
  Takeaways 22

Chapter 3: The Recipes..23
  Muffins, Breads and Breakfast Foods..25
  Dips and Sauces 54
  Side Dishes 73
  Soups and Salads 98
  Casual Dining: Burgers, Tacos, Sandwiches and More 132
  Main Dishes 148
  Desserts 185
  Beverages 208

Index..218

Foreword

As a medical oncologist, I frequently hear patients and families inquire about what they or their loved ones should be eating. In fact, this is one of the first questions patients ask after receiving a diagnosis of cancer. The question also comes up as patients continue the cancer journey, through treatment with chemotherapy and radiation. Perhaps surprisingly, it comes up again and again—with recurrence or cure, from dying patients, or from survivors who seek cancer prevention. Food, with all its metaphors and connotations, is deeply woven into the fabric of cancer.

The medical community struggles to counsel individual patients about the role of nutrition in regard to cancer. Information is overwhelming, often contradictory, and at times derived in scientifically questionable contexts. This is not an excuse, however, for not searching for ways to effectively and clearly guide patients through this maze of information. As medical professionals, we should take our role most seriously in this endeavor and look to simplify and clarify current knowledge, then provide resources that are accessible and understandable. With these resources, we pass the baton to our patients, with the hope that they can make positive changes in their lives.

Dr. Julia Greer's *Anti–Breast Cancer Cookbook* is one such resource. More importantly, it provides a framework through which health can be integrated into practical living. This integration comes through making good food and lifestyle choices. In many cases, good lifestyle choices contribute to cancer prevention. This book will not do the work for you. It will not bring healthy anti-cancer foods to your pantry and to your table. It will, however, educate, guide, and inform you. It will coax you to make good choices for yourself and your loved ones. This book will not cure cancer. It does, however, give you the power to contribute to your overall health and well-being by offering ingredients and recipes that are known to help prevent cancer or its recurrence. And you get to help yourself or your loved one while sharing your passion for food and partaking in the warmth that preparing, cooking, and eating can bring to every person, every day.

Dr. Greer has the insight, knowledge, and common sense to bring a wonderful resource to a spectrum of individuals. For those seeking to prevent breast cancer or its recurrence, the information in this book is both scientifically sound and well displayed and presented. For food lovers who want the healthy benefits of Dr. Greer's impressive accomplishments and education, it is a valuable addition to your collection. For everyone, it is a thoughtful resource for the proactive and mindful pursuit of health.

Enjoy!

—Lanie Francis, MD
Assistant Clinical Professor of Medicine
University of Pittsburgh, Department of Medicine,
Division of Hematology and Oncology
UPMC Cancer Centers

Dedication

For Diane White

Acknowledgments

There is an Academy Awards list of people I should thank for supporting me on this endeavor. I would like to thank Dr. Loren Roth, for not letting me be a quitter when the going got tough, and Dr. Ron Glick, for introducing me to food and mindfulness as forms of healing. I am eternally thankful to my first mentor, Dr. Francesmary Modugno, for making me file IRB requests and do data entry so that I could more effectively understand how to conduct cancer research. I am exceptionally grateful to know two inspiring young women, Judi Holtzman Rosen and Gabrielle Lawrence Strand, who fought and beat breast cancer at a time in their lives when they should have been choosing preschools or packing healthy lunches. I am proud to call each of you my friend. Sincere gratitude goes to Gwyneth Catlin, for introducing me to beans, root vegetables, and tahini when I was in college and sharing many delightful meals and workouts. I extend great appreciation to Joe Negri, Angela Raso, Jeff Lazar, Sherrie Flick, Kurt Shaw, Eric Rotthoff, and Alex Ankeles for sharing their delicious recipes—and I apologize for not using all of them in this book. I also acknowledge Dr. Judy Balk and Dr. Lanie Francis, who built careers that focus not only on healing the sick but also on incorporating good nutrition into their treatment plans. Special thanks to the beautiful and brilliant Dr. Christine Mackey, for bragging to everyone about my great cooking, and to breast cancer survivor Dr. Jamie Stern, for taking care of herself while taking care of others. Finally, I could never have written this book without my mother, who served as active shopper, accountant, and newspaper clipper, and who has demonstrated that a diet of dark chocolate and nuts really can enhance longevity.

About the Author

Julia B. Greer, MD, MPH, is an assistant professor of medicine in the Division of Gastroenterology, Hepatology and Nutrition at the University of Pittsburgh School of Medicine. She was educated at Phillips Exeter Academy, Princeton University, Mount Sinai School of Medicine, and the Graduate School of Public Health at the University of Pittsburgh. She completed a National Cancer Institute–sponsored fellowship in cancer epidemiology and prevention, as well as a National Institutes of Health–funded research training fellowship in high-risk genetics. She holds a master's degree in cancer epidemiology. She has published numerous articles and book chapters on ovarian, breast, and pancreatic cancer, as well as on the effects of obesity, alcohol, and cigarette smoking on cancer and other types of diseases. She serves as a director for the required medical school course "Digestion and Nutrition" and for the elective course "Nutrition and Medicine" at the University of Pittsburgh School of Medicine. She is a lifelong foodie and exercise enthusiast who has given dozens of talks on nutrition and health. And she makes one mean banana bread.

CHAPTER 1

All About Breast Cancer

Much has been written about diet and cancer. In 1981 Richard Doll and Richard Peto published a comprehensive review discussing avoidable causes of cancer mortality in the United States and suggested that diet accounted for about 35 percent of cancer deaths; smoking accounted for a similar percentage. Since then, thousands of studies have assessed how various foods and nutrients relate to cancer risk. A constant stream of media on the subject has made people more aware than ever. We'll talk a lot about food and cancer in this book, but to have a full understanding of how dietary choices might impact breast cancer risk, it's valuable to know the basics about breast cancer. Being familiar with the various forms of breast cancer and their treatments will help you to see how healthy eating fits into the bigger picture of cancer prevention.

Incidence and Prevalence

Breast cancer is the most common type of cancer diagnosed in women in the United States and is second only to lung cancer as a leading cause of cancer death in females. The National Cancer Institute estimates that in 2011, 230,480 U.S. women were diagnosed with breast cancer and 39,520 women died from it. According to the American Cancer Society, rates of breast cancer increased between 1994 and 1999 and then decreased by about 2 percent each year for the years 1999–2006. The decreases in annual incidence were likely the consequence of the 2002 publication of results of the Women's Health Initiative study, which found that combined estrogen and progestin hormone replacement therapy (HRT) increased the risk of breast cancer, as well as heart disease, stroke, and blood clots, in older women. Many women stopped taking postmenopausal hormones after this study's results became widely known because doctors were more reluctant to prescribe them. As an aside, other studies have shown that estrogen-only HRT, which is prescribed for postmenopausal women who do not have a uterus, might be protective against breast cancer. There was also a drop in rates of mammography during these

Incidence Rates by Race and Ethnicity in the US	
Race/Ethnicity	**Incidence in Women** (per 100,000)
All races	124.0
White/Caucasian	127.3
Black/African-American	119.9
Asian/Pacific Islander	93.7
American Indian/Alaska Native	77.9
Hispanic	78.1

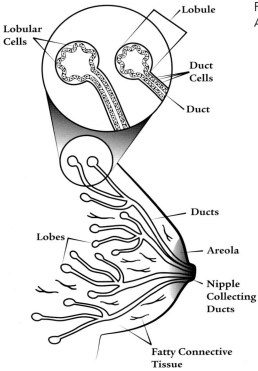

Figure 1.
Anatomy of the breast.

years, which may have delayed the diagnosis of breast cancer for some women, thereby lowering perceived incidence. Rates of breast cancer are higher in countries that have been industrialized for a long time and lower in more recently industrialized countries. For instance, in East Asia (China, Japan, North Korea, South Korea, and Taiwan) the incidence of breast cancer is about 21 cases per 100,000 compared with 85 per 100,000 in western Europe and 124 per 100,000 in the United States.

The most recent statistics for breast cancer prevalence in the United States are from January 1, 2008, when approximately 2.6 million women had a history of breast cancer. The figure includes anyone still living on January 1, 2008, who had been diagnosed with cancer of the breast at any point prior to January 1, 2008, and it encompasses individuals with active disease and those who were cured of the disease.

A Quick Review of Breast Anatomy

Breast tissue is primarily made up of lobules, ducts, fatty tissue, and connective tissue as shown in Figure 1. Lobules are the glands that make milk, while ducts are the long, thin tubes that carry the milk to the nipple. Each breast also contains blood vessels, which transfer nutrients, and lymphatic vessels, which carry the fluid known as lymph. Lymph helps the immune system fight infections and other types of diseases. Lymph vessels lead to very small, pea-shaped organs called lymph nodes. Lymph

1. Lateral auxilliary nodes
2. Pectoral nodes
3. Pectoral nodes
4. Subscrapular nodes
5. Central auxilliary nodes
6. Infraclavicular nodes
7. Parastemal nodes
8. Supraclavicular nodes

Figure 2.
Lymphatic drainage of the breast.

The Anti–Breast Cancer Cookbook

nodes are located all over the human body, and specific regions of lymph nodes associate with different bodily organs. Lymph nodes specific to the breast, as seen in Figure 2, are located around the chest, in the armpit (or axilla), and directly above the collarbone.

Types of Breast Cancer

There are two main types of breast cancer: invasive and noninvasive. An invasive cancer of the breast, known as a carcinoma, starts in the cells that line the ducts of the breasts or the breast milk glands and metastasizes, or spreads, into the surrounding breast tissue. When breast cancer metastasizes outside the breast, it is typically carried to some of the regional lymph nodes. This is why doctors often sample these nodes to see if they contain cancerous cells. Ductal carcinoma is more common than lobular carcinoma, but lobular carcinoma is more frequently bilateral, or diagnosed in both breasts. Of the 70 percent of all breast cancers that are invasive, approximately 55 percent are ductal carcinoma while about 15 percent are lobular carcinoma.

Noninvasive, or *in situ*, cancers are being more commonly diagnosed than ever before due to advancements in screening, although only 30 percent of all breast cancers fall into this category. In situ cancers are confined to the breast ducts or lobules. The majority of these, about 85 percent, are ductal carcinoma in situ, or DCIS. The remaining noninvasive cancers are lobular carcinoma in situ, or LCIS. Researchers believe that about 54,000 new cases of in situ breast cancer occurred among U.S. women in 2010.

Risk Factors for Breast Cancer

There are numerous risk factors for breast cancer that a person cannot control:

Gender
While it isn't discussed that much, men do get breast cancer. Women are about one hundred times more likely to get it, though. According to the American Cancer Society, the proportion of men diagnosed with breast cancer has remained quite stable over the past thirty years. This book focuses mainly on breast cancer in women.

Age
Older women are more likely to be diagnosed than younger women. The median age of diagnosis in the United States for 2005–2009 was sixty-one. Fewer than 12 percent of breast cancer cases were diagnosed in women under the age of forty-five during this time period.

Family History
Having one first-degree relative—a sister, mother, or daughter—diagnosed with breast cancer approximately doubles your risk. If two of your first-degree relatives have been diagnosed with breast cancer, your risk is about five times higher than average. Having a male relative with breast cancer also raises your risk.

Personal History of Breast Cancer
It seems unfair, but women who have had breast cancer in one breast are more likely to have a cancer recurrence in the remaining breast tissue of the same breast or in the other (contralateral) breast.

Race
White women are more likely to be diagnosed than black women, but black women have a higher fatality rate.

Dense Breast Tissue
On a mammogram, breast tissue is described by its density, meaning its ratio of breast and connective tissue to fat. It is difficult to detect cancer by mammogram when a woman's breast is very dense. Women whose breasts show significant density (greater than 75 percent breast and connective tissue compared to fat) have a four to five times increased risk of being diagnosed with breast cancer than those with minimal density (less than 10 percent).

A Diagnosis of Lobular Carcinoma in Situ
Laboratory research has shown that LCIS may behave as a precursor to more invasive forms of breast disease. A study presented at the 2010 yearly meeting of the American Society of Clinical Oncology found a 2 percent annual incidence of breast cancer among a large group of women who were undergoing surveillance due to a previous diagnosis of LCIS.

Age at Menarche and Menopause
Starting your period before age twelve (early menarche) or going through menopause after age fifty-five increases the risk of breast cancer. Having a greater number of periods increases your exposure to the hormones estrogen and progesterone, which seems to affect risk. Studies have shown that women who go through menopause after age fifty-five may have a 30 percent higher risk of breast cancer compared to women who experience menopause before age forty-five.

Mantle Field Radiation at a Young Age
The standard treatment for Hodgkin's disease is radiation to the neck, midchest, and armpits in the shape of a mantle (a type of cloak). Women who have undergone this type of radiation as children or young adults have an elevated risk of developing breast cancer fifteen to thirty years after receiving the treatment.

Some breast cancer risk factors are linked to behaviors or lifestyle choices:

Not Having Children
Women who have children at a young age or who have more than one child have reduced breast cancer risk compared to women who never give birth or those who have their first child after age thirty.

Recent Use of Birth Control Pills

Some studies have shown that women who take birth control pills have a greater risk than those who do not take "the pill," although the risk of breast cancer seems to return to normal once they have been off the pill for ten or more years. Many studies showing this relationship were conducted among women who used older versions of the pill, which contained higher levels of hormones than current ones.

Using Hormone Replacement Therapy after Menopause

HRT has been shown in some large-scale U.S. studies to increase the risk of postmenopausal breast cancer. HRT formulations that contain both progestin (a synthetic form of progesterone) and estrogen appear to elevate risk more than those that contain estrogen only. A British study called the Million Women Study, however, found a modestly increased risk of breast cancer among women who took estrogen-only formulations. We probably need to conduct more studies to better define risks associated with the different types of HRT.

Not Breastfeeding

Evidence suggests that breastfeeding lowers the risk of breast cancer, especially for women who breastfeed for one to two years. Regular breastfeeding of an infant causes ovulation to be suppressed about 90 percent of the time, serving as a natural form of contraception and also decreasing a woman's total lifetime number of menstrual cycles. In developed nations such as the United States, however, few women breastfeed for this duration.

Consuming Alcohol

Drinking one alcoholic beverage each day can raise a woman's lifetime risk of breast cancer slightly. According to some studies, women who drink two to five alcoholic beverages each day may have about one-and-a-half times the risk of developing breast cancer compared to women who do not drink alcohol.

Being Overweight or Obese

Carrying extra weight is especially associated with breast cancer in postmenopausal women. Central adiposity—having most of this weight concentrated around one's abdomen—translates to even greater breast cancer risk. Women who gain weight in adulthood appear to have higher risk than those who are heavy as children.

Lack of Exercise

Not exercising may increase breast cancer risk, while routine cardiovascular activity has been shown to reduce risk. There is no consensus on exactly how much activity is needed to reduce risk, but studies have found that exercise may decrease breast cancer risk from 20 to 80 percent and may also decrease the risk of having a recurrence of breast cancer following treatment.

Diet
Research shows that an unhealthful diet is related to cancer risk (see Chapter 2).

Early Onset Breast Cancer and BRCA1/BRCA2 Genetic Mutations

Breast cancer that occurs in a woman younger than forty years of age is considered to be "early onset." Although more than 200,000 women are diagnosed with breast cancer each year, fewer than 7 percent of cases occur in women under the age of forty. Women who have a strong family history of breast cancer tend to be diagnosed at younger ages than women in the general population. Their increased cancer risk may be linked to genetic mutations, which are heritable changes in the genetic sequence that can cause alterations in protein structure or function. In 1996 researchers identified two tumor suppressor genes, BRCA1 and BRCA2, that are responsible for the syndrome known as hereditary breast and ovarian cancer (HBOC). When tumor suppressor genes work properly, they keep cancers from occurring. When they've suffered a mutation, they are less capable of suppressing tumor formation. The BRCA genes are associated with an inability to repair double-stranded breaks in DNA, the genetic information that guides cell function, and are responsible for approximately 40 percent of cases of HBOC. In women who have a documented BRCA1 mutation, the average cumulative risk of developing cancer by the age of seventy ranges between 55 and 85 percent for breast cancer and between 16 and 60 percent for ovarian cancer. In BRCA2 mutation carriers, these same cumulative risks range between 37 and 85 percent for breast cancer and between 11 and 27 percent for ovarian cancer. Additionally, a family in which male breast cancer has occurred has a 60–76 percent chance of carrying a BRCA2 mutation.

Women who are diagnosed with breast or ovarian cancer and women who haven't been diagnosed but have multiple family members with breast or ovarian cancer—especially if they were diagnosed at a young age—may be advised to undergo BRCA1/2 genotyping (testing that evaluates genetic code) to determine if they carry one of these mutations. Individuals who test positive for one of these mutations should be followed by a high-risk breast cancer clinic and should have a treatment team consisting of a genetic counselor, different types of physicians, and often a psychologist and surgeon. The most reliable preventive treatment for women with BRCA1/2 mutations is prophylactic mastectomy and oophorectomy (surgical removal of the breasts and ovaries)—major life decisions that impact women's appearance, childbearing, and hormone production.

The following components of a woman's family history suggest that cancer might be caused by a mutation in the BRCA1 or BRCA2 gene:

- two or more first-degree (parent, sibling, or child) or second-degree (grandmother, granddaughter, aunt, niece, half sibling) relatives with breast or ovarian cancer
- breast cancer occurring before the age of fifty (premenopausal) in a close relative
- family history of both breast and ovarian cancer
- one or more relatives with two cancers (breast and ovarian cancer or two independent breast cancers)
- male relatives with breast cancer

Triple Negative Breast Cancer

Breast cancer can now be profiled to demonstrate whether it contains receptors for the female hormones estrogen and progesterone. Hormones bind to receptors and then activate breast cellular growth by a series of fairly complicated processes within the breast cells. Most breast cancers are hormone-receptor positive. About four out of every five breast cancers are estrogen-receptor positive. Of those tumors, 65 percent are also progesterone-receptor positive. If a cancer has receptors for either estrogen or progesterone, it is considered to be hormone-receptor positive. Breast cancer that is hormone-receptor positive is slightly slower growing and has a better chance of responding to hormone suppression treatments than cancer that is hormone-receptor negative.

Another gene used to profile breast tumors is HER-2. HER-2 is encoded by the ERBB2 gene, a known oncogene—or gene that can promote cancer—which has to be tightly regulated to prevent uncontrolled cell growth. Overexpression of the ERBB2 gene occurs in approximately 30 percent of breast cancers and is associated with a worse prognosis as well as a greater likelihood of breast cancer recurrence.

Breast tumors that lack estrogen and progesterone receptors and that are also HER-2 negative are called "triple negative." Overall, triple negative breast cancer is more challenging to treat and has a worse prognosis than other breast cancer profiles.

What You Can Do to Lower Your Risk

The lifetime risk of developing breast cancer is about one in eight, but you can take several steps to help lower your risk. For all women, proactive measures for decreasing breast cancer risk include maintaining a healthy weight as you get older, exercising regularly, avoiding alcohol, lowering your intake of saturated fat, and eating antioxidant-rich foods. Diet is probably the one factor over which we have the greatest control. Cooking nutritious food is a wonderful way to relax and socialize and can build healthy habits that last a lifetime.

Chapter 2 discusses how diet can specifically decrease your lifetime risk of developing breast cancer, diminish your risk of having a cancer recurrence, and help you to keep your immune system in great shape.

CHAPTER 2

The Role of Diet in Breast Cancer

Anyone can get cancer. There is no single diet, food, or nutrient that will keep you from getting cancer. However, in the same way that wearing a seat belt might keep you from being injured in a car accident, eating certain types of food may help protect you from many cancers, including breast cancer. Diet should be included as part of your cancer prevention plan, but it is not a cure for cancer and should always be combined with conventional medical treatments if necessary.

Weight and Breast Cancer

There has been considerable research on diet, weight, and the risk of breast cancer. Overall, gaining and carrying excess weight in the postmenopausal years seems to place women at greater risk of breast cancer than being heavy as an adolescent. The link seems to be with hormones and factors secreted by cells that may promote breast tumor growth.

High-Fat Diet

In the 1940s, scientists discovered that dietary fat could cause mammary tumors in mice and saw an ecological connection in humans. They noticed that women in developed countries had much higher rates of breast cancer than women in less industrialized countries. They also observed that when a woman moved from a low-risk area, such as Asia or Africa, to a high-risk area, such as the United States, her risk of getting breast cancer soon began to mirror that of women in her new country. The risk for her daughters also seemed to parallel their new country's average risk rather than that of their country of origin. The Western diet—characteristically high in fat, refined sugar, and processed foods—was blamed for the increased breast cancer risk noted in more developed countries.

The hypothesis was controversial. Researchers put it to the test, performing analysis after analysis, but they didn't detect greater breast cancer risk due to eating more dietary fat. In a 1996 study published in the *New England Journal of Medicine* that included 337,819 women, 4,980 of whom had been diagnosed with breast cancer, *no* appreciable difference in fat intake was observed between the women with breast cancer and the healthy women. What researchers eventually did find, however, was that breast cancer rates were higher in heavier women, especially heavy older women.

The theory about the connection between dietary fat and breast cancer has never fully been laid to rest. The question remains: If a woman eats a lot of high-fat foods and puts on extra pounds, couldn't her risk of disease be related to both what she eats and how much extra body fat she carries? While the relationship is still being defined, more recent research has in fact shown an association between dietary fat and primary breast cancer, as well as breast cancer recurrence. This connection makes sense because foods that are high in fat—such as red meat, full-fat dairy products, and fried foods—may influence a woman's body to produce more estrogen, which could spur the growth of breast tissue as well as other estrogen-sensitive cells. We also now know that eating a lot of saturated fat is simply not good for the human body. And man-made trans fats, unsaturated fats formed by hydrogenating oils to turn them into more shelf-stable solids, appear to cause even more chaos in the human body. Trans fats have been shown to raise LDL (bad cholesterol) and triglyceride levels and to lower levels of heart- and blood vessel–protective HDL (good cholesterol).

Additionally, eating a high-fat diet as a teenager may be associated with breast cancer risk as an adult. A study published in the *Journal of the National Cancer Institute* in 2003 showed that when girls ages eight to ten reduce the amount of fat that they ate—even by a small degree—their estrogen levels stayed significantly lower during the next several years. Compared to girls in this study who did not make changes to their diets, those who ate fewer animal-derived foods (mainly meat and dairy products) and ate more whole grains, legumes, fruits, and vegetables were shown to have a drop of 30 percent in levels of estradiol, one of the major forms of estrogen.

Weight and Diabetes

A key to good health also seems to be maintaining a height-appropriate weight as you age. Rates of obesity and overweight in the United States have leveled out in the past decade, with a frightening two-thirds of all U.S. adults being considerably above a healthy weight. Childhood overweight and obesity rates have increased threefold since 1985. Weight gain in adulthood is associated with increased risk of heart disease, diabetes, metabolic syndrome, and a variety of different types of cancer, including postmenopausal breast cancer. Some of these health issues, such as diabetes, are also associated with an elevated risk of developing breast cancer. In a study of 116,488 female nurses who were thirty to fifty-five years old and cancer-free at enrollment in 1976 and were followed through 1996, those with type II diabetes were at a 17 percent higher risk of developing postmenopausal breast cancer.

How do excess weight and diabetes relate to cancer? The risks of cancer associated with obesity have a lot to do with systemic inflammation and molecules that drive cell division and growth as well as the formation of blood vessels, which can provide a "food supply" to cancerous cells. Cancer risks linked to diabetes are likely the consequence of similar growth factors, such as insulin-like growth factors (IGFs), which cells secrete when you have diabetes or a prediabetic state called insulin resistance. So it's important to maintain a healthy weight.

What should you eat to maintain a healthy weight? A recently published article in the *New England Journal of Medicine* examined how certain everyday foods impacted weight gain in a study of more than 120,000 U.S. men and women. The men and women who participated in this study were not obese at the study start and were free from any chronic diseases. The calculated change in weight occurred over a four-year time span. The following table summarizes some of the results.

The results took into account a number of other factors that might have been associated with weight loss or gain, including body mass index (BMI) at the start of the study, duration of sleep, amount of time spent watching TV each day, alcohol

New England Journal of Medicine 2011 Study of 120,877 US Men and Women	
Food	Average weight gain per daily serving
French fried potatoes	+ 3.35
Potato chips	+ 1.69
Sugar-sweetened beverages	+ 1.00
Red meat	+ 0.93
Processed meat	+ 0.95
Trans fat	+ 0.65
Sweets and desserts	+ 0.41
Butter	+ 0.30
Food	Average weight loss per daily serving
Yogurt	- 0.82
Nuts	- 0.57
Fruit	- 0.49
Whole grains	- 0.37
Vegetables	- 0.22

consumption, and amount of physical activity. Regardless of what the study participants ate, weight gain was also associated with increased time spent watching TV, decreased physical activity, getting fewer than six hours of sleep per night, drinking a greater number of alcoholic beverages each day, and quitting smoking.

We know that weight gain can lead to obesity and diabetes, both of which are related to breast cancer in women. Not surprisingly, breast cancer risk in relation to food is similar to the risk of weight gain shown in the study described above.

Nutrition and Cancer Risk

Making connections between diet and cancer in the United States is not easy. There is no single diet in the country. Our choices range from traditional meat and potatoes, to locally grown produce, to fast food and microwavable meals. Figuring out exactly what people have eaten can be difficult for researchers. Nonetheless, a sizable body of research has been devoted to assessing the risks and protective effects of certain foods and nutrients in regard to breast cancer. I summarize this research below.

Saturated Fat and Red Meat
Saturated fat, found in high quantities in meat and other foods of animal origin, has been shown in some studies to be linked to breast cancer. Cancer researchers at the Ontario Cancer Institute published a meta-analysis of all the case-control and cohort studies published through July 2003 that examined breast cancer risk in relation to

dietary fat and fat-containing foods. Both the case-control and the cohort studies gave the same overall results, with higher total fat intake being associated with breast cancer. There was also a 17 percent higher relative risk of breast cancer due to high meat intake and a 19 percent greater risk of breast cancer due to a high intake of foods rich in saturated fat.

For more than half a century, researchers have recognized the link between red meat and poor health. In early 2012, the Harvard School of Public Health published a study that evaluated diet, health, and death data on 83,644 women and 37,698 men. The study followed the participants prospectively for more than twenty years. Study participants who ate one serving of unprocessed red meat per day had a 10 percent higher risk of dying from cancer compared with those who didn't, while those who ate a serving per day of processed red meat (such as cold cuts and hot dogs) had a 16 percent higher risk of dying from cancer compared with individuals who did not eat processed red meat. Death due to heart disease was even higher. Numerous studies have shown a link between meat and breast cancer.

In another study led by a group at Harvard, researchers prospectively evaluated 90,655 premenopausal women, ages twenty-six to forty-six, and found that eating animal

Major Types of Clinical Studies

Researchers perform three major types of studies to address nutrition and cancer risk in people. In general terms, studies are typically described as follows:

Case-Control Studies
Case-control studies compare cases (people with a diagnosis) to controls (people without the same diagnosis). When studying cancer and nutrition, the goal is to look back in time to determine whether there are differences between what people with cancer ate or drank compared to the control group.

Prospective Studies
Also known as cohort studies, prospective studies enroll (usually healthy) people at a certain point in time and follow them into the future, keeping track of changes in health or behavior, attempting to determine if what they are doing is related to the development of a certain condition. Randomized controlled trials are a particular type of prospective study in which some participants may be assigned to take a certain medication or engage in a health-related activity.

Meta-analyses
Meta is a Greek word that means "after," "beyond," "adjacent," or "self," and a meta-analysis is basically a "study of the studies." In cancer studies, a meta-analysis functions as a summary of previous case-control or prospective studies and clarifies the weighted, overall risk of cancer determined from all of these studies.

fat, especially from red meat and high-fat dairy products, was linked to an increased risk of developing breast cancer, while risks were not elevated by eating fat from vegetable sources. In this study, for women who were followed for an average of twelve years, the risk of estrogen/progesterone-receptor-positive breast cancer was almost doubled (97 percent higher) if they ate one-and-a-half servings of red meat per day compared with three or fewer servings per week.

Red meat may be linked to cancer because it is frequently cooked at high temperatures, such as when it's fried or grilled over an open flame. When muscle meat (beef, pork, poultry, fish, and seafood) is heated to very high temperatures, portions of the amino acids in the protein of the meat become a source of cancer- or mutation-causing (carcinogenic or mutagenic) substances known as heterocyclic amines, or HCAs. Research on HCAs has shown that they can move through the human body and become localized to breast tissue, where they can act metabolically, driving cancerous cell growth. Studies of other types of cancer, such as pancreatic cancer, have noticed as much as a 50 percent increased cancer risk when comparing study participants who ate the most grilled, fried, or otherwise well-done meat to participants who ate the least. You can decrease the amount of cancer-promoting substances you ingest by marinating meat before cooking it, as well as by heating it only until it's done but not charred. Limiting your intake of high-heat cooked meats is most protective.

Hormones in Meat and Milk

A study presented in 2010 at the annual meeting of the American Society of Clinical Oncology showed that U.S. beef and chicken had noticeable levels of estrogen, which was absent from Japanese beef and Brazilian chicken. This observation raised the idea that conventionally raised beef and poultry could potentially be associated with breast cancer if a person consumed a significant amount of this beef or chicken over a lifetime. How did the estrogen get in there? It appears that the soy feed (soy is high in estrogen) given to animals on many large-scale U.S. farms could be incorporated into the meat that makes it to our tables.

Some companies sell "hormone-free" milk, made from cows that are not fed growth hormone. But this type of milk seems to be more a marketing ploy than anything else. Cows and chickens make their own hormones and, in essence, can never be hormone free. Additionally, the hormones these companies tout as being dangerous—recombinant bovine growth hormone (rBGH) and recombinant bovine somatotropin (rBST)—are proteins that are destroyed by stomach acid and enzymes. They never make it into our bloodstream.

Organic milk, on the other hand, may be better for you than conventional milk. Milk from cows raised on organic farms has been shown to be higher in omega-3 fatty acids as well as conjugated linoleic acid, or CLA, a fatty acid that may help decrease body fat, lower blood sugar levels, and diminish the growth of breast tumors. A Swedish study published in 2011 sampled milk from eighteen organic and nineteen conventional dairy herds on three occasions during the indoor season from 2005 to 2006. The median (average midpoint) concentration of CLA was .63 percent in organic herds compared with .48 percent in conventional herds, and the content of total omega-3 fatty acids was 1.44 percent and 1.04 percent in organic and conventional milk, respectively. The researchers' statistical analysis demonstrated significantly higher concentrations of CLA and total omega-3 and omega-6 fatty acids in organic milk and a more desirable ratio of omega-6 to omega-3 fatty acids for the human consumer in organic milk.

Eating organic beef can have a small health advantage. Organic, grass-fed beef is leaner and contains higher levels of omega-3 fatty acids, vitamin E, beta-carotene, and other antioxidants than conventionally raised beef. While all cows graze on pasture for the first six months to a year, the majority finish their lives at a feedlot on a concentrated mix of soy, corn, grains, and various supplements, with added hormones and antibiotics. Cows raised on organic farms are not given antibiotics, and their feed does not contain man-made pesticides. Additionally, in theory the cattle are raised in humane settings, where they are able to roam freely rather than being kept in tight quarters and plumped up on corn and soy feed before going to slaughter. Organic beef does not contain the high levels of estrogen noted in conventionally raised beef.

Organically raised chickens may still be fed soy and corn, but their feed is often supplemented with oats, alfalfa, and fish oil, which could increase levels of vitamins and omega-3 fatty acids and which rarely contain harmful chemicals such as arsenic. By current U.S. law, all chicken available to consumers must be raised without added growth hormones.

Organic meat and milk may be a bit more expensive than nonorganic, but they're probably worth the splurge.

Antioxidants and Cancer: How to Protect Yourself from Breast Cancer

Antioxidants are substances that may protect cells from damage caused by the unstable molecules known as free radicals. Damaging free radicals can come from many sources: sunlight, carcinogens in cigarette smoke and charred meat, chemicals such as benzene, and the heme iron found in red meat. Free radical damage to cells may lead to DNA damage, which can contribute to cancer risk. Antioxidants interact with and stabilize free radicals, thereby preventing some of the damage free radicals might cause. Examples of antioxidants include beta-carotene, lycopene, resveratrol, quercetin, anthocyanidin, vitamins C and E, and many other substances. The chart on page 14 shows common food sources of various types of antioxidants.

Fruit and vegetables are especially rich in antioxidants. In a study of 1,551 women with a history of breast cancer, those with the highest plasma levels of carotenoids—a marker of vegetable intake—in their bloodstreams had a 43 percent lower risk of having a new breast cancer than those with the lowest carotenoid levels. Many of the foods in the table above have been specifically associated with a diminished risk of breast cancer.

Folate-Rich Foods
Dietary folate is found in leafy green vegetables such as spinach, collard greens, romaine and Bibb lettuce, arugula, watercress, chard, broccoli rabe, mustard greens, turnip greens, beet greens, endive, chicory, and mache. It is also found in asparagus, turnips, avocadoes, legumes, papayas, corn, broccoli, peas, and beef. Breads, cereals, and pasta are often enriched with folate.

Antioxidant	Common Food Sources
Selenium	Cereals (corn, wheat, oats, rice), nuts (brazil nuts, walnuts) legumes, animal products (beef, chicken, turkey, eggs, cheese), seafood (cod, tuna)
Vitamin E	Nuts/seeds and their oils, wheat germ oil, fortified cereals, green leafy vegetables, tomato products, pumpkin, sweet potatoes, blue crab, rockfish, mangoes, asparagus, broccoli, papaya
Carotenoids	Beta-carotene in dark orange, yellow, green vegetables; lutein in corn and egg yolks; lycopene in dark red fruits and vegetables (tomatoes, watermelon, papaya, pink/red grapefruit, guava)
Organosulfur Compounds	Broccoli, bok choy, Brussels sprouts, cauliflower, cabbage, spinach, watercress, onions, garlic, chives, collard/mustard greens, horse radish, kohlrabi, wasabi, arugula
Isoflavonoids (flavonoid)	Soy foods (tofu, tempeh, soybeans, soy nut butter, edamame, soy milk)
Flavonols (flavonoid)	Tomatoes, broccoli, leafy green vegetables (such as spinach), apricots, beans, fava beans, apples, chives, kale, leeks, pears, cranberries, onions, red grapes, blueberries, sweet cherries
Flavanols (flavonoid)	Tea, cacao beans (dark chocolate), wine
Flavones (flavonoid)	Basil, celery, artichokes, broccoli, parsley, rosemary, citrus fruit

Women have increased needs for folate when they are breastfeeding, and low folate intake in pregnant women has been associated with neural tube defects in their offspring. Folate is involved in the synthesis, repair, and function of DNA, so it is a necessary cofactor for tissues that have rapid turnover and divide often. DNA damage is the root cause of cancer. Therefore, it is not surprising that evidence suggests that a folate deficiency can damage DNA and cause cancer. Numerous studies have shown that diets low in folate are associated with increased risk of breast cancer as well as pancreatic and colon cancer. There is no risk to your health from eating a lot of folate-rich foods. If you have a varied diet that includes leafy greens as well as commonly fortified foods, it is virtually impossible to become folate deficient.

Legumes

Legumes are all types of beans and peas. Certain foods that aren't commonly thought of as being in the legume family include peanuts and pistachio nuts. Recipes you will find in this cookbook make use of legumes such as black beans, chickpeas, great northern beans, black-eyed peas, lentils, kidney beans, and edamame (soybeans).

Legumes are low in fat and are high in protein, fiber, potassium, iron, magnesium, folate, and vitamin C. Legumes make a nutritious and hearty meat substitute.

Replacing meat with legumes at least once a week lowers your overall consumption of saturated fat and may lower the risk of breast cancer.

The Nurses' Health Study II, the results of which were published in the *International Journal of Cancer,* was a large, prospective study of more than 90,000 premenopausal women between the ages of twenty-six and forty-six at the time of enrollment in 1991. The study evaluated dietary flavonols and flavonol-rich-food intake and found that women who ate beans or lentils two or more times per week had a 24 percent lower risk of developing breast cancer than women who ate beans or lentils less than once per month.

Green Tea

Green tea is rich in antioxidants such as tannins, catechins, and epigallocatechin gallate (EGCG), and lab studies have found that it can decrease the development or growth of stomach, prostate, lung, and liver tumors, as well as breast tumors. Some studies have shown that drinking green tea can lower the risk of breast cancer. Previous research in Asian populations noted that women who drank the most green tea had lower rates of primary breast cancer. A population-based case-control study conducted in Shanghai from 1996 to 2005 evaluated whether regular green tea consumption was associated with breast cancer risk among 3,454 incident cases and 3,474 controls ages twenty to seventy-four. Compared with nondrinkers of green tea, regular drinking of green tea was associated with a decreased risk (about 12 percent) for breast cancer. Among premenopausal women, both an increasing number of years of drinking green tea and an increasing quantity of green tea consumed were related to a reduction in breast cancer risk. A separate large study among U.S. women who had been diagnosed and treated for stage I or stage II breast cancer found that those who drank two to four cups of green tea each day lowered their risk of cancer recurrence by 44 percent when compared to women who never drank green tea.

Cruciferous Vegetables

Cruciferous vegetables include broccoli, cauliflower, bok choy, kale, Brussels sprouts, all colors of cabbage, rutabaga, turnips, and arugula. The name *crucifer* derives from the New Latin for "cross-bearing"; the four petals of the flowers of cruciferous plants resemble a cross. Crucifers are loaded with vitamins and minerals as well as fiber. In addition, lab studies have shown that compounds in cruciferous vegetables, such as isothiocyanates and indole-3-carbinol (I3C), are effective in keeping cancers from occurring as well as in slowing the growth of tumors that are already present. In breast cancer, cruciferous vegetables help trigger cell death and alter estrogen metabolism. I3C is a potent inducer of cytochrome P450 enzymes, a large class of enzymes in the human body that metabolize many substances and hormones, including estrogen. Additionally, diindolylmethane, a by-product of I3C metabolism, is a proposed cancer prevention agent because it protects the body from oxidative stress. Thus it is not entirely surprising that eating a large amount of cruciferous vegetables has been shown in some studies to decrease the risk of breast cancer. In a study of 3,035 women diagnosed with breast cancer who were identified through the Shanghai Cancer Registry and 3,037 closely matched healthy women from the general population, women who ate the most cruciferous vegetables and who also had a genetic variation in a detoxifying enzyme (the Val/Val genetic polymorphism in the GSTP1 gene) had a more than 50 percent reduction in breast cancer risk compared to women who ate fewer cruciferous vegetables and lacked this same genetic subtype.

Whole Grains

Typical whole grains include whole-wheat, bulgur, oats, barley, couscous, rye, buckwheat, popcorn, kasha, amaranth, spelt, millet, and brown rice.

Whole grains are cereal grains that contain the germ, endosperm, and bran, in contrast to refined grains, which retain only the endosperm. The tough, fibrous outer layer called bran protects the inside of the kernel. The interior contains mostly the starchy endosperm, whose job is to provide stored energy for the germ, the seed's reproductive kernel, which is nestled inside the endosperm. The germ contains vitamins, minerals, and unsaturated oils. Whole grains are also rich in fiber, plant enzymes, healthy types of fats, and hundreds of other valuable antioxidant phytochemicals.

The human body digests whole grains much more slowly than simple sugars, which keeps you from having spikes in insulin levels, potentially decreasing your risk of developing diabetes. Whole grains are also filling and contain insoluble fiber, which helps prevent constipation while nourishing the cells in your colon—thus decreasing your risk of developing colon cancer.

Refining grains began with the invention of industrialized roller mills in the late 1800s. Refining stripped the bran and germ from the grain to make it easier to chew. This process, still used today, also strips away from the whole grain more than half the B vitamins and 90 percent of the vitamin E, as well as virtually all the fiber. Refined grains are easier to chew but are also digested more rapidly, so they don't provide long-lasting energy or maintain consistent blood sugar levels the way whole grains do.

Do not confuse multigrain with whole grain. Multigrain means that a food contains more than one type of grain, although none of them may necessarily be whole grain. Only whole-grain foods contain all the nutritious grain elements.

When you are shopping for grains, you really can't tell just by looking at them whether the grains are whole. Be sure to read the labels. You can usually identify whole-grain foods by the ingredient list. If "whole-wheat" or "whole meal" is listed as the first ingredient, the item is a whole grain. Note that the label "de-germinated" means the germ has been removed, and "pearled" refers to a polishing process that removes either part or all of the bran and germ.

The Wheat Kernel

Husk

82% Endosperm

15% Bran

3% Germ

Nuts

Nuts and seeds such as almonds, walnuts, pecans, hazelnuts, cashews, macadamia nuts, sunflower kernels, pine nuts, and Brazil nuts contain polyphenol antioxidants such as caffeic and ellagic acid, magnesium, selenium, and protein. They are recognized by the FDA as being very low in saturated fat, as well as high in monounsaturated and polyunsaturated fats, and they may help lower LDL cholesterol.

In a study conducted by Dr. Elaine Hardman, published in 2011 in the journal *Nutrition and Cancer,* mice with mammary tumors were fed either a diet containing walnuts or one without walnuts. Compared to a diet without walnuts, consumption of walnuts significantly reduced tumor incidence (the fraction of mice with at least one tumor), multiplicity (the number of glands with a tumor in each mouse), and size. Gene expression analyses showed that eating the walnut diet altered the expression of multiple genes associated with the growth and differentiation of mammary cells.

Benign breast disease (BBD) encompasses fibrocystic changes, simple cysts, fibroadenomas, and other nonmalignant changes that may occur in the breast. BBD is a recognized marker of increased breast cancer risk and was recently studied in relationship to diet in young women. Among 29,480 women who completed a high school diet questionnaire in 1998, 682 BBD cases were confirmed between 1991 and 2001 and two major protective dietary findings were noted: (1) high school–aged females who ate two or more servings of nuts per week had a 36 percent lower risk of developing BBD than those who ate fewer than one serving per month; and (2) the girls with the greatest fiber intake in high school had a 25 percent lower risk of BBD as young women compared to those who ate very little fiber when they were in high school. This study suggests that dietary intake of fiber and nuts during adolescence may serve as a valuable means of reducing the chance of developing breast cancer in adulthood.

Omega-3 Fatty Acids

Omega-3 fatty acids (also called n-3 fatty acids or omega-3s) are polyunsaturated fatty acids essential for human health. They form cell membranes in our brains and neurons and also assist in the clotting of blood. Omega-3 fatty acids have recently been touted for possessing numerous health benefits, including lowering the risk of heart disease, stroke, autoimmune disorders, and inflammatory bowel disease and potentially decreasing the risk of developing cancer. Some of these beneficial effects come from their anti-inflammatory power and their ability to scavenge free radicals and reactive oxygen species.

Omega-3 fatty acids can generally be split into two major groups: those that come from plant sources and those that come from fatty fish. Alpha-linolenic acid (ALA) is the plant source of omega-3 and is found in walnuts, flaxseeds, chia seeds, legumes, various vegetable oils (such as canola oil), and, to a lesser extent, whole grains such as oats. ALA is also found in Brussels sprouts, certain green vegetables such as kale, and various leafy salad greens such as spinach. The types of omega-3 found in fatty fish are eicosapentaenoic acid (EPA) and docosahexaenoic acid (DHA). Fish that are rich in EPA and DHA are mainly deep-water fish such as salmon, herring, mackerel, anchovies, and sardines. Shark, swordfish, tuna, trout, sea bass, halibut, cod, and tilapia have EPA and DHA in lower concentrations.

Due to our higher consumption of meat and poultry compared to fish, the standard U.S. diet is lacking in sufficient omega-3 fatty acids. Our diets tend to contain more omega-6 fatty acids, which are found in corn, safflower, cottonseed, and soybean oils. Many vegetable oils that are rich in omega-3 fatty acids are also a good source of omega-6 fatty acids. There is a myth that omega-3s are good and that omega-6s are bad, which medical studies have not fully supported. Omega-6 fatty acids can also lower LDL cholesterol and protect against heart disease. But because the U.S. diet often consists of processed foods, which are rich in omega-6 fatty acids—especially soybean oil—we should seek to get more omega-3s. The desired ratio of omega-6 to omega-3 fatty acids for optimal health is about 3 to 1, but most Americans eat a diet with a ratio closer to 20 or 30 to 1.

Omega-3 fatty acids have been shown in various lab and animal studies to dampen the ability of cloned breast cancer cells to divide, which is how they might protect against both the development and progression of cancer. These fatty acids are also recognized as being capable of altering estrogen metabolism. One of the major omega-3 fatty acids I mentioned is EPA. PGE3, a by-product of EPA metabolism, can counterbalance the activity of aromatase—a cytochrome P450 enzyme that converts large carbon steroid molecules into estrogen. Therefore, dietary EPA can essentially decrease the level of active estrogen circulating in your body. Since estrogen stimulates breast cells to grow and divide, this omega-3 is protective against breast cancer.

A 2010 prospective study by researchers at the Fred Hutchinson Cancer Research Center in Seattle followed 35,016 postmenopausal women for six years and noted that regular use of fish oil supplements that contained EPA and DHA was linked with a 32 percent reduced risk of invasive ductal breast cancer, the most common form of breast cancer. Regular consumption of omega-3-rich foods has also been associated with a lower risk of colon and pancreatic cancer and may prevent the spread of breast cancer to bone.

To maximize your health, seek to get at least one source of omega-3—walnuts, homemade salad dressing containing an omega-3-rich oil, ground flaxseed meal, a tablespoon of healthy oil to cook your lunch or dinner, or fatty fish—in your diet every day. Because deep-water fish can be high in mercury, however, such fish probably should not be your only source of omega-3s. People who follow a vegetarian or vegan diet may need to take a DHA or EPA supplement. Vegetarian versions of these supplements are typically derived from marine algae. A number of antioxidants commonly found in vegetables, such as lycopene and beta-carotene, require the presence of fat to be absorbed. It makes sense to combine vegetables with healthy fats, especially omega-3 fats.

More on Flaxseed

Flaxseeds have been getting a lot of recent attention in regard to breast cancer, and here are the facts: Whole flaxseeds are indigestible and give you lots of fiber but few other benefits. Flaxseed oil contains ALA, the highly regarded omega-3 fatty acid, but no fiber. Flaxseed meal contains ALA and a bit of fiber but also contains phytoestrogens known as lignans. Neither the oil nor whole flaxseeds contain the lignan portion, although they are occasionally added to the oil.

In lab studies, lignans possess potent antioxidant properties, slow tumor growth, and might also act as an anti-estrogen, or weak estrogen. There is growing evidence that flaxseed meal may help decrease breast cancer risk in women. We know from previous studies in men with a history of prostate cancer that those who consumed 30 grams per day of ground flaxseed—about 3 tablespoons—had a 30–40 percent reduction in the rate of prostate cancer recurrence—a greater reduction than in men who ate a reduced-fat diet but didn't add ground flaxseed meal. However, because it contains a weak estrogen, flaxseed meal in large quantities may affect anti-estrogen treatment for hormone-receptor-positive breast cancer.

We have yet to clearly define these effects, so dieticians often place limits on ground flaxseed meal for women with a history of this type of breast cancer who are receiving anti-estrogen therapy. At our institution, we recommend that women in this category limit daily consumption of ground flaxseed meal to two tablespoons.

The Soy Conundrum

Soy foods include items such as tofu, tempeh, soybeans, soy nut butter, edamame, and soy milk. The question of whether soy is good for prevention of breast cancer is a complicated one.

Soy is a phytoestrogen, which means that it has estrogen-like properties. Breast cancer is known to be influenced by estrogen. As I mentioned in Chapter 1, estrogen acts as a growth factor for breast cancer by binding estrogen receptors on breast cells and inducing cell division and growth. (In scientific terms, estrogen is said to act as a mitogen.) The molecules found in soy foods that possess estrogen-like properties are called soy isoflavones.

Soy isoflavones have a flip side: While they bind to the estrogen receptor, they stimulate it much less powerfully than estrogen does. Complicating matters further, some isoflavones stimulate estrogen receptors at low concentrations but block them at high concentrations. So if a woman is young and has high estrogen levels, eating soy foods might actually be protective against breast cancer because the soy isoflavones will sit on this receptor and block the effects of estrogen.

Postmenopausal women no longer make estrogen from their ovaries, and their greatest source of estrogen comes from adipose tissue (body fat). Many medical professionals have been led to believe that we shouldn't recommend soy foods to postmenopausal women. With the lower bodily estrogen levels in postmenopausal women, it is plausible that soy could stimulate breast tissue growth and, by extension, breast cancer. Additionally, postmenopausal breast cancer tends to be estrogen- and progesterone-receptor-positive.

If you understand what I just wrote, then the evidence from medical studies will probably baffle you: Overall, research has shown that eating soy actually seems to protect older, rather than younger, women a bit more from getting breast cancer. Populations of women from places where soy is eaten frequently, such as Asia, also appear to be protected from breast cancer to a greater extent than women in nations where soy is eaten less frequently, such as the United States. Childhood exposure to soy may play a role.

Perhaps more importantly, breast cancer survivors do not appear to be at increased risk of having a recurrence of breast cancer if they eat soy. In fact, new evidence shows that eating soy may reduce the risk of breast cancer recurrence as well as overall mortality for breast cancer survivors. A study presented at the 102nd annual meeting of the American Association for Cancer Research used data from a multi-institution collaborative study, the After Breast Cancer Pooling Project, to investigate the association between eating soy foods and breast cancer outcomes among survivors. The study's lead researcher, Xiao-Ou Shu, MD, PhD, professor of medicine at Vanderbilt Epidemiology Center, noted, "There has been widespread concern about the safety of soy food for women with breast cancer. Soy foods contain large amounts of isoflavones that are known to bind to estrogen receptors and have both estrogen-like and anti-estrogenic effects. There are concerns that isoflavones may increase the risk of cancer recurrence among breast cancer patients because they have low estrogen levels due to cancer treatment. We're particularly concerned that isoflavones may compromise the effect of tamoxifen on breast cancer treatment because both tamoxifen and isoflavones bind to estrogen receptors."

The research study combined the resources of four National Cancer Institute–funded studies: the Shanghai Breast Cancer Survival Study; the Life After Cancer Epidemiology Study; the Women's Healthy Eating and Living Study; and the Nurses' Health Study. As a whole, these four studies included 18,312 women between the ages of twenty and eighty-three who had invasive primary breast cancer. The quantity of soy isoflavones eaten by 16,048 of these women after breast cancer diagnosis was measured. Researchers used food frequency questionnaires for a group of soy isoflavones in three of the four study groups and for tofu and soy milk consumption in one of the groups. Breast cancer outcomes were assessed an average of nine years after cancer diagnosis. Rates of recurrence and death among survivors who consumed the highest amounts of soy isoflavones (more than 23 mg per day) were compared with the outcomes of those whose intake was lowest (.48 mg per day or lower). The average daily soy isoflavone intake among U.S. women was 3.2 mg. In the Shanghai group, the amount was significantly higher at 45.9 mg. Women who ate the most soy isoflavones (more than 23 mg per day) had a 9 percent lower risk of mortality and a 15 percent lower risk for breast cancer recurrence than women in the lowest intake category. However, these results did not reach what scientists call statistical significance, which suggests that the findings could be due to chance or that more women needed to be included in the study to make solid conclusions.

The study's main author, Dr. Shu, therefore felt it might be beneficial for women, even those who have had breast cancer, to include soy food (not supplements) as part of their healthy diet. (She noted that soy supplements often vary from soy foods in both the type and amount of isoflavones in their formulation.) The takeaway here is that soy should be safe and helpful for the prevention of breast cancer as well as for decreasing the risk of breast cancer recurrence.

Dairy Products
Like soy foods, dairy products have received a lot of contradictory press in regard to breast cancer risk. The results of older studies of dairy products have varied considerably—showing them to be associated with increased risk or decreased risk or to have no association with breast cancer at all.

The most recent comprehensive studies, including one of the largest multicenter, prospective studies to date, which included 319,826 women from twenty-three major centers in ten European countries (Denmark, France, Germany, Greece, Italy, the Netherlands, Norway, Spain, Sweden, and the United Kingdom), as well as smaller single studies conducted in Norway, France, and China, show either no effect or a mildly protective effect of nonfat and low-fat dairy products and calcium intake on breast cancer risk. Nonfat and low-fat dairy foods, especially skim milk, were also associated with reduced risks of premenopausal breast cancer as well as colon cancer in separate, sizable U.S. studies.

High-fat dairy products may not be as protective. As mentioned earlier, organic dairy foods may have slightly greater health benefits for reducing breast cancer risk than conventionally produced dairy products. Nonetheless, studies of dairy have not adequately determined whether it is the food itself or the calcium and vitamin D in nonfat or low-fat dairy products that might help diminish breast cancer risk.

A large-scale study published in 2010 found that women under the age of fifty-three who had high blood levels of vitamin D had a significantly lower risk of developing breast cancer. Greater blood vitamin D levels have also been correlated to better survival among women who have been diagnosed with breast cancer. Nondairy foods that are rich in calcium include tahini, almonds, tofu, beans, salmon, sardines, oats (to a smaller degree), and fortified rice and soy beverages. Vitamin D is found naturally only in a few foods, including some fish (salmon, tuna, trout, herring, sardines), liver, and egg yolks but is added to milk, soy milk, and a few brands of orange juice. Just ten to twenty minutes of daily sun exposure on your uncovered skin can provide you with a good dose of vitamin D. People living in latitudes with cold temperatures and cloudy skies are often found to be low on vitamin D, as are dark-skinned individuals. Foods rich in calcium and vitamin D should be included as part of a healthy diet for women who are interested in lowering their breast cancer risk. Because many people don't get the recommended daily allowance of calcium or vitamin D, taking a supplement that combines the two is often a good idea.

Alcohol and Breast Cancer

Cancer experts are uncertain whether any level of alcohol consumption is safe for women. Alcohol promotes breast cancer by increasing circulating estrogen levels. A study published in the *Journal of the American Medical Association* in 2011 found that women who averaged three to six drinks a week were 1.15 times—or 15 percent—more likely to develop breast cancer than women who never consumed alcohol. In terms of cancer risk, this is not huge. However, we know that the current lifetime risk for a woman in the United States to develop breast cancer is a little over 12 percent and that one in eight U.S. women will be diagnosed with this cancer. Adding more risk on top of an already heightened risk may not be the wisest decision. Taking that into consideration, however, studies of red wine have shown that it inhibits breast tumors in the lab and may also modestly decrease breast cancer risk in women. Red wine contains polyphenol antioxidants such as resveratrol, which have health-protective and anti-inflammatory effects. So if you are going to have a drink, make it red wine and pair it with a meal that is rich in antioxidants and healthy protein and fats.

For women who have been treated for breast cancer, one clinician I know recommends capping weekly intake of alcohol at about 60 grams, which is equivalent to about four standard-size drinks. In the United States, a standard drink is described as containing about 14 grams of alcohol. This would translate to a 12-ounce beer (about 5 percent alcohol), an 8- to 9-ounce glass of malt liquor (7 percent alcohol), a 5-ounce glass of wine (12 percent alcohol), or 1.5 ounces of hard liquor (40 percent alcohol).

Onions, Garlic, Herbs and Spices

Numerous herbs and spices used in different cuisines have been shown to have potent antioxidant and anti-carcinogenic properties. Fenugreek and curcumin (found in turmeric) have very recently been shown to inhibit tumor growth in laboratory studies. A blend of other spices, including basil, black pepper, cinnamon, cloves, garlic powder, ginger, oregano, paprika, and rosemary, was recently shown to decrease insulin response as well as triglyceride levels in U.S. men who had just eaten a high-fat meal. These same spices contain numerous antioxidants that are known to be beneficial to your health and to have potential to decrease the initiation or growth of cancerous tumors.

Members of the allium family (such as onions, chives, shallots, and garlic) are also rich in antioxidants, including quercetin, and their consumption has been associated with decreased risks of many types of cancer, including lung and ovarian endometrial cancer. You can add spices to just about any dish to enhance flavor and promote good health instead of adding lots of extra fat and salt.

Takeaways

- Eat a varied diet that includes richly colored fruits and vegetables, nuts, legumes, leafy green and cruciferous vegetables, and lower-fat (preferably organic) versions of dairy products.
- Whole grains are rich in fiber and cancer-fighting nutrients and decrease the risk of developing diabetes. Go wheat, not white, for bread and pasta, and always choose whole grain.
- Grass-fed beef is more healthful than conventionally raised beef, and organic dairy products are a bit better for you than nonorganic varieties, although the high cost of these items might mean that you don't always buy them. Do your best to make wise but economical choices.
- Nut (walnut, hazelnut), avocado, olive, and cold-pressed canola oils are healthy forms of polyunsaturated and monounsaturated fat and are healthier than more saturated oils, such as palm and soybean oil.
- Fish, seafood, and lean poultry are wonderful protein sources.
- Drink alcoholic beverages in moderation (or not at all). Breast cancer experts say to limit your intake for both primary prevention of breast cancer as well as prevention of recurrence.
- Limit your intake of red meat, saturated fat, and muscle meat (beef, pork, poultry, and fish) cooked at high heat. Limit your intake of processed meat as well.
- Omega-3 fatty acids are important so, include ground nuts (walnuts, pecans, hazelnuts), flaxseed oil, flaxseed meal, and fatty fish such as salmon in your diet. Limits on ground flaxseed meal may be necessary for hormone-receptor-positive breast cancer survivors.
- Concentrate on eating fewer animal products and more plant-derived foods.
- Avoid trans fats, which are partially hydrogenated oils.
- Soy foods seem to be helpful for breast cancer prevention and to decrease rates of recurrence, although more studies in this area are needed. Aim for whole, unprocessed sources of soy.
- Maintain a healthy weight and exercise regularly (daily, if possible).
- Sleep is essential to keeping your immune system functioning properly; sleep deprivation is linked to numerous health issues including obesity, so get your rest!

CHAPTER 3

The Recipes

The recipes in this book represent a collection that I have accumulated over decades of interest in cooking and healthful eating. Many are my own; others have been given to me by friends, family members, and colleagues. Some were designed specifically for this book. They are made mainly of whole foods, whole grains, legumes, fruits, vegetables, lean protein sources, and healthy fats. I have included a small number of recipes that contain meat because most people in the United States do eat meat, but I made sure that these recipes include ingredients rich in antioxidants. Portion sizes are "normal" and designed to be combined to produce meals that provide energy and help to enhance your immune system.

Throughout the recipes, I take for granted that you will wash your fruits and vegetables and rinse your canned beans, even if I don't mention it. Make sure to wash mushrooms and scrub potatoes particularly well. If garlic is not supposed to be peeled, I add "unpeeled" after it in the ingredients list. Otherwise, assume you should peel it. Occasionally, you see butter on the ingredients list. A little butter or saturated fat in your diet is just fine. When a recipe calls for a lot of butter, however, I often choose a nonhydrogenated spread that is typically olive-oil based and lower in saturated fat content. Which brand you choose is up to you.

Each recipe is classified into one or more of the following categories based on ingredient options:

ᔕ Vegetarian—contains eggs or dairy products or both eggs and dairy products but does not contain meat, poultry, fish, or seafood

Ƴ Vegan—does not contain eggs, dairy products, meat, poultry, fish, seafood, or any food product that contains anything of animal origin

⊘ Gluten-free—does not contain wheat, rye, barley, spelt, Kamut (a brand of wheat), or triticale

If you are vegan, you probably know the drill about how to take recipes that contain animal products and make them into those that do not. Some of the fish and poultry recipes here can certainly be made using tofu or tempeh. You can buy vegan egg substitutes (or use flaxseed meal mixed with water) and dairy-free types of milk, yogurt, cream cheese, and sour cream. Additionally, many nonhydrogenated buttery spreads are made out of vegetable oils rather than butter.

Due to the increasing prevalence of gluten sensitivity and celiac disease in the United States, I mention which recipes can be made without gluten. However, you must be vigilant when purchasing recipe items such as broth or yogurt because some brands contain modified food starch or unnatural caramel color, either of which can be made from a wheat base. Some soy milks contain wheat extract. If a recipe is listed as "gluten-free," it means it is free of bread or flour products made from wheat, rye, or barley and can be easily prepared for a gluten-free diet. I do include oats as being gluten-free although I know there is some controversy about oats; if oats are a problem, use a brand guaranteed as gluten-free. You can substitute regular flour with soy or rice flour or a commercial gluten-free brand of flour (Bob's Red Mill is one of my favorites), use gluten-free bread crumbs instead of regular ones, use gluten-free pasta (such as a brown rice pasta) instead of regular pasta, and so on to adapt a recipe to a gluten-free diet.

Almost all the ingredients in these recipes can be found in basic grocery stores, although you might have to hunt a bit more for a few items, such as chipotle peppers in adobo sauce, miso (soy paste), or mirin (rice wine). If you need to make a substitution, type "substitution for . . ." into a search engine and you'll typically find lots of good substitutes.

When I mention that you should use a nonreactive bowl, I'm referring to material that won't react chemically with certain recipe ingredients, particularly those that are acidic. Nonreactive material includes ceramic, glass (Pyrex), and stainless steel. Almost all cookware these days is nonreactive, although metals such as copper, aluminum, and cast iron may be reactive.

The recipes are fairly simple, but I'd advise you to read through them first and make sure to give yourself enough time for preparation.

Cooking times can vary by the type of heat that you're using—whether gas or electric—and baking times often vary by the elevation in which you live.

Bon appétit!

MUFFINS, BREADS AND BREAKFAST FOODS

Vegetarian

Vegan

Gluten-Free

Almond-Pear Muffins ❧ 26
Apple-Cranberry Oatmeal Quick Bread ❧ 27
Banana-Blackberry Muffins ❧ 28
Banana-Oat Bran Pancakes ❧ 29
Blueberry-Banana Flax Pancakes with Sweet Strawberry Yogurt Topping ❧ 30
Blueberry-Bran Mini Muffins ❧ 31
Carrot-Apple Oat Muffins ❧ 32
Chicken, Spinach and Mushroom Quiche 33
Chocolate-Cashew Granola ❧ ✿ ⊘ 34
Chocolate-Pecan Pancakes ❧ 35
Cranberry-Pecan Oatmeal ❧ ⊘ 36
Cranberry-Walnut Pancakes ❧ 37
Crustless Salmon and Broccoli Quiche 38
Dark Chocolate Banana Bread with Pecans ❧ 39
Flax Buttermilk Pancakes with Peaches and Pecan Maple Syrup ❧ 40
Gingerbread Belgian Waffles ❧ 41
Gluten-Free Buttermilk Waffles ❧ ⊘ 42
Lemony Cream Cheese Pancakes with Blueberries ❧ ...43
Maple-Nut Granola ❧ ✿ ⊘ 44
Morning Glory Flax Muffins ❧ 45
Orange–Poppy Seed Muffins ❧ 46
Pineapple and Macadamia Nut Muffins ❧ 47
Strawberry-Hazelnut Breakfast Polenta ❧ ✿ ⊘ 48
Walnut, Date and Fennel Scones ❧ 49
Whole-Grain Irish Soda Bread ❧ ✿ 50
Whole-Wheat, Apple-Raspberry Muffins ❧ 51
Whole-Wheat Pumpkin Pancakes ❧ 52
Zucchini Nut Bread ❧ ✿ 53

The Anti–Breast Cancer Cookbook

Almond-Pear Muffins

Vegetarian

Ingredients:
Nonstick cooking spray
1 cup all-purpose unbleached white flour
1 cup whole-wheat pastry flour
3 tablespoons ground flaxseed meal
1/3 cup sugar
1 teaspoon baking powder
1 teaspoon baking soda
1 teaspoon ground cinnamon
1/4 teaspoon salt
1/4 teaspoon ground ginger
1/4 teaspoon ground cloves
2 large omega-3-enriched eggs
1/2 cup low-fat vanilla yogurt (preferably organic)
1/2 cup reduced-fat (2 percent) dairy milk or enriched soy milk
1/4 cup natural applesauce
2 tablespoons sunflower oil
1 teaspoon almond extract
1 cup fresh pear, peeled and chopped
1/2 cup almonds, chopped
1/4 cup wheat germ, divided

Preparation: Preheat oven to 400°F. Spray a 12-muffin pan with nonstick cooking spray or line with paper liners. In a large bowl, combine white flour, wheat flour, flaxseed meal, sugar, baking powder, baking soda, cinnamon, salt, ginger, and cloves. In another bowl, beat together eggs, yogurt, milk, applesauce, oil, and almond extract. Stir wet ingredients into dry ingredients just until moistened. Fold in pear, almonds, and 3 tablespoons wheat germ. Fill muffin cups 2/3 full and sprinkle remaining wheat germ on top. Bake 13–16 minutes or until a toothpick comes out clean. Cool for 5 minutes before removing from pans to wire racks to cool completely. Makes 12 medium muffins.

Nutritional information per muffin:
Calories: 245
Fat: 11 g
Saturated fat: 1 g
Carbohydrate: 29 g
Total sugars: 8 g
Protein: 8 g
Sodium: 190 mg
Cholesterol: 28 mg
Dietary fiber: 5 g

The Anti–Breast Cancer Cookbook

Apple-Cranberry Oatmeal Quick Bread

You can make this bread with cherries or strawberries instead of cranberries. Peel the apples if you feel you must, but they have more fiber with the peel on. Feel free to sprinkle chopped walnuts or pecans on top of the bread batter before you pop it in the oven.

Ingredients:
Nonstick cooking spray
1 cup low-fat vanilla yogurt
1 cup quick-cooking oats
1 large omega-3-enriched egg
1/4 cup natural applesauce
1/4 cup sunflower or cold-pressed canola oil
1/4 cup brown sugar, packed
2/3 cup all-purpose unbleached white flour
2/3 cup whole-wheat flour
2 tablespoons ground flaxseed meal
1 teaspoon baking soda
1 teaspoon ground cinnamon
1/4 teaspoon nutmeg
1/4 teaspoon salt
1 cup organic Fuji, Rome Beauty, or Granny Smith apples,
    unpeeled, diced
1/3 cup fresh cranberries, chopped

Preparation: Preheat oven to 350°F. Spray an 8 x 4 x 2½–inch loaf pan with nonstick cooking spray or coat very thinly with oil. In a small bowl, mix together yogurt and oats; set aside. In a large bowl, combine egg, applesauce, oil, and sugar. Stir in white flour, wheat flour, flaxseed meal, baking soda, cinnamon, nutmeg, and salt. Add yogurt mixture and stir. The batter should still be lumpy. Fold in apples and cranberries; pour into loaf pan. Bake 45–50 minutes until golden brown; a toothpick inserted in the middle of a muffin should come out clean. Remove from pan and let cool on a wire rack. Makes 12 medium-thick slices.

Nutritional information per serving:
Calories: 178
Fat: 5 g
Saturated fat: 1 g
Carbohydrate: 28 g
Total sugars: 13 g
Protein: 4 g
Sodium: 160 mg
Cholesterol: 15 mg
Dietary fiber: 3 g

Banana-Blackberry Muffins

Ingredients:
Nonstick cooking spray
1 cup all-purpose unbleached white flour
1/2 cup whole-wheat pastry flour
1/3 cup sugar
2 tablespoons ground flaxseed meal
2½ teaspoons baking powder
1 teaspoon cinnamon
1/4 teaspoon salt
3 tablespoons unsalted butter, melted
2 overripe bananas, mashed with a fork
6 ounces (about 2/3 cup) low-fat vanilla yogurt
3 tablespoons nonfat dairy milk
1 large omega-3-enriched egg, beaten
1/4 cup all-fruit blackberry preserves
1 cup fresh blackberries

Preparation: Preheat oven to 375°F. Spray a 12-muffin pan with nonstick cooking spray or line with paper liners. In a large bowl, combine white flour, wheat flour, sugar, flaxseed meal, baking powder, cinnamon, and salt. Stir until evenly distributed. In a separate bowl, combine butter, bananas, yogurt, milk, and egg; mix well. Add yogurt mixture to flour mixture and stir until just moistened. Spoon 1 heaping tablespoon batter into each muffin cup, add 1 teaspoon of blackberry preserves and a blackberry or two. Top with 1 tablespoon batter. Bake 15–17 minutes or until muffins are light brown and a toothpick comes out clean. Makes 12 medium muffins.

Nutritional information per muffin:
Calories: 174
Fat: 4 g
Saturated fat: 2 g
Carbohydrate: 30 g
Total sugars: 15 g
Protein: 3 g
Sodium: 69 mg
Cholesterol: 29 mg
Dietary fiber: 2 g

The Anti–Breast Cancer Cookbook

Banana-Oat Bran Pancakes

Ingredients:
3/4 cup oat bran
1/2 cup all-purpose unbleached white flour
1/4 cup whole-wheat flour
1 tablespoon baking powder
1/2 teaspoon cinnamon
1/4 teaspoon salt
1/4 cup Egg Beaters or equivalent pasteurized egg white product
1 cup reduced-fat (1 or 2 percent) dairy milk (preferably organic)
1 tablespoon pure maple syrup
2 teaspoons sunflower oil
Nonstick cooking spray
1 medium banana, thinly sliced
1 cup low-fat vanilla yogurt (preferably organic)
1 cup strawberries, chopped or thinly sliced

Preparation: In a large bowl, combine bran, white flour, wheat flour, baking powder, cinnamon, and salt. In a separate medium bowl, beat together Egg Beaters, milk, syrup, and oil. Add wet ingredients to dry ingredients and mix until just combined. Prepare a griddle or large frying pan by setting the heat to medium and spraying generously with cooking spray. (Spray again each time you cook a new batch of pancakes.) Spoon batter to make each pancake spread to about 4 inches. Add a few slices of banana to each pancake; make sure they lie flat. Cook until bubbles appear on top and edges start to look dry. Flip and cook other side to a golden brown. (It should take about 2 minutes to cook the first side and 1 minute to cook the second side.) Top each batch of three pancakes with a few tablespoons of yogurt and some strawberries. Makes about 4 servings of 3 medium pancakes each.

Nutritional information per serving:
Calories: 280
Fat: 4 g
Saturated fat: < 1 g
Carbohydrate: 48 g
Total sugars: 12 g
Protein: 12 g
Sodium: 450 mg
Cholesterol: 2 mg
Dietary fiber: 6 g

Blueberry-Banana Flax Pancakes with Sweet Strawberry Yogurt Topping

Ingredients:

Topping
2/3 cup low-fat plain yogurt (preferably organic)
1 tablespoon clover honey
1/4 teaspoon orange zest, finely grated
2 cups fresh strawberries, thinly sliced

Pancakes
2/3 cup buckwheat flour
1/2 cup whole-wheat or whole-wheat pastry flour
1/3 cup ground flaxseed meal
2 teaspoons baking powder
1 teaspoon baking soda
1/8 teaspoon salt
1/2 teaspoon orange zest
2 large omega-3-enriched eggs
2 tablespoons maple syrup
2 tablespoons sunflower or cold-pressed canola oil
1½ cups low-fat buttermilk (preferably organic)
Nonstick cooking spray
1 cup fresh or frozen blueberries
1/2 banana, thinly sliced

Preparation: To make topping, place yogurt in a small bowl. Add honey and orange zest; stir. Refrigerate until serving. To make pancakes, sift together buckwheat flour, wheat flour, flaxseed meal, baking powder, baking soda, and salt in a medium bowl; stir in orange zest. In a separate bowl, whisk together eggs, maple syrup, oil, and buttermilk. Pour wet mixture into dry ingredients and stir until just incorporated. Do not overmix. Heat a skillet over medium heat or preheat a nonstick grill to medium. Spray with nonstick cooking spray. Drop batter by about 1/4 cupfuls onto grill or skillet, leaving a few inches between pancakes. Put blueberries and a few slices of banana into each pancake. Cook until set around edges and bubbles stop forming, about 2–3 minutes. Flip and cook for another 1–2 minutes, until cooked through. Top each pancake with a dollop of sweet yogurt and a scoop of strawberries. Makes 4 servings of 3 medium pancakes each.

Nutritional information per serving:
Calories: 298
Fat: 9 g
Saturated fat: 2 g
Carbohydrate: 40 g
Total sugars: 22 g
Protein: 14 g
Sodium: 435 mg
Cholesterol: 80 mg

The Anti–Breast Cancer Cookbook

Blueberry-Bran Mini Muffins

These muffins are equally delicious if you choose to use cranberries, chopped strawberries, or a mixture of berries in place of the blueberries.

Ingredients:
Nonstick cooking spray
2 cups wheat bran
1/4 cup ground flaxseed meal
3/4 cup old-fashioned rolled oats
1/2 teaspoon ground cinnamon
1/4 teaspoon ground coriander
1 teaspoon orange zest
1 large omega-3-enriched egg plus 2 egg whites from large eggs
1/4 cup clover honey or maple syrup
1 cup nonfat dairy milk (preferably organic)
2 cups blueberries, fresh or thawed frozen
1/4 cup Grape-Nuts cereal (or equivalent generic brand)

Preparation: Preheat oven to 375°F. Spray 2 mini muffin pans with nonstick cooking spray or line with paper liners. In a large bowl, stir together bran, flaxseed meal, oats, cinnamon, coriander, and orange zest. In a separate smaller bowl, stir together egg and egg whites, honey or maple syrup, and skim milk. Pour egg mixture into dry ingredients and stir until just blended. Fold in blueberries and cereal. Pour into pan (about 2/3 full) and bake about 20 minutes, until a toothpick comes out clean. Fill any empty cups with water so they don't scorch. Makes 28–36 mini muffins, depending on how much you fill each cup.

Nutritional information per muffin:
Calories: 50
Fat: < 1 g
Saturated fat: 0 g
Carbohydrate: 8 g
Total sugars: 3 g
Protein: 2 g
Sodium: 20 mg
Cholesterol: 5 mg
Dietary fiber: 3 g

Carrot-Apple Oat Muffins

For variation, you can substitute dried cranberries, raisins, or dates for the dried cherries, and you can use any type of nut. Always fill any empty muffins cups with water to prevent scorching in the oven.

Ingredients:
Nonstick cooking spray
1⅓ cups all-purpose unbleached white flour
2/3 cup whole-wheat pastry flour
2 tablespoons ground flaxseed meal
1/4 cup oat bran
2 teaspoons baking powder
1/2 teaspoon baking soda
1/4 teaspoon salt
1 teaspoon ground cinnamon
1/4 teaspoon ground nutmeg
1/3 cup dark brown sugar, firmly packed
2 tablespoons natural applesauce
2 large omega-3-enriched eggs
1½ cups vanilla low-fat yogurt (preferably organic)
1/2 cup sunflower or cold-pressed canola oil
2 tablespoons water
1¼ cups Fuji, Braeburn, or Granny Smith apples, peeled and grated
1¼ cups carrots, peeled and finely grated
1/3 cup walnuts, chopped
1/3 cup dried tart cherries
2 tablespoons wheat germ

Nutritional information per muffin:
Calories: 175
Fat: 8 g
Saturated fat: 1 g
Carbohydrate: 22 g
Total sugars: 15 g
Protein: 3 g
Sodium: 125 mg
Cholesterol: 11 mg
Dietary fiber: 1 g

Preparation: Preheat oven to 400°F. Lightly spray 2 12-muffin pans with nonstick cooking spray or line with paper liners. In a large bowl, stir together white flour, wheat flour, bran, baking powder, baking soda, salt, cinnamon, and sugar; set aside. In a large bowl, whisk eggs until blended. Stir in yogurt, oil, and water. Pour wet ingredients over dry ingredients and stir with a rubber spatula just until half-moistened, about 8–10 strokes. Add apple, carrots, nuts, and cherries; stir until just combined. Do not overmix. Spoon batter into muffin cups, filling each cup about 3/4 full. Sprinkle the top of each with wheat germ. Bake until a toothpick inserted into the center of a muffin comes out clean, about 15–18 minutes. Let cool in the pan on a wire rack for 2 minutes, then turn onto rack to cool completely. Makes 18 medium muffins.

The Anti–Breast Cancer Cookbook

Chicken, Spinach and Mushroom Quiche

A study presented at the American Society of Clinical Oncology's 2010 annual meeting noted that meat from conventionally raised U.S. chickens might contain enough estrogen to impact breast cancer risk if eaten regularly. If you can afford it, use organically raised chicken, as well as organic milk and cheese, for this quiche.

Ingredients:
4 large omega-3-enriched eggs plus 2 egg whites from large eggs, beaten
1½ cups reduced-fat (2 percent) dairy milk
1/4 teaspoon ground nutmeg
1/2 teaspoon salt
1/2 teaspoon black pepper, freshly ground
2 cups fresh spinach, de-stemmed and chopped
2 cups fresh mushrooms, washed very well and sliced or chopped
1 cup cooked chicken breast, cubed
1/2 cup yellow onion, diced
1 cup shredded Swiss cheese, divided
1 cup reduced-fat shredded cheddar cheese, divided
1 (9-inch) whole-wheat deep-dish pie crust (see Apple-Strawberry Pie, page 188)

Preparation: Preheat oven to 400°F. Place beaten eggs and egg whites, milk, nutmeg, salt, and pepper in a large bowl and whisk together. Stir in spinach, mushrooms, chicken, onion, 3/4 cup Swiss cheese, and 3/4 cup cheddar cheese. Transfer to pie crust. Top with remaining Swiss cheese and cheddar cheese. Bake uncovered for about 35 minutes, or until cheese is bubbly and lightly browned. Makes 8 servings.

Nutritional information per serving:
Calories: 270
Fat: 16 g
Saturated fat: 8 g
Carbohydrate: 14 g
Total sugars: 3 g
Protein: 21 g
Sodium: 365 mg
Cholesterol: 122 mg
Dietary fiber: 2 g

Chocolate-Cashew Granola

Ingredients:
4½ cups old-fashioned rolled oats
1 cup sunflower seeds
3/4 cup white sesame seeds
3/4 cup natural (unsweetened) applesauce
1/4 cup unprocessed dark cocoa powder
2 teaspoons ground cinnamon
1 teaspoon ground ginger
1/3 cup clover honey or maple syrup
1/4 cup light brown sugar
2 cups raw cashew pieces
1 teaspoon kosher salt
2 tablespoons cold-pressed canola or sunflower oil

Preparation: Preheat oven to 310°F. Mix together all ingredients in a ceramic mixing bowl until evenly combined. Spread the mixture evenly on top of two heavy baking sheets and bake 50–60 minutes, turning halfway through baking. Let cool and store in an airtight container. Makes 36 servings of 1/4 cup each.

Nutritional information per serving:
Calories: 180
Fat: 10 g
Saturated fat: 2 g
Carbohydrate: 17 g
Total sugars: 5 g
Protein: 6 g
Sodium: 55 mg
Cholesterol: 0 mg
Dietary fiber: 3 g

Chocolate-Pecan Pancakes

If you do not have cold-pressed canola oil, use unsalted melted butter or a nonhydrogenated spread such as Smart Balance. Try these pancakes with some sliced bananas added to the batter after you've poured it onto the griddle. Mmmm!

Ingredients:
1½ cups reduced-fat (2 percent) dairy milk (preferably organic)
1/4 cup Egg Beaters (or 1 large omega-3-enriched egg plus 1 egg white from a large egg)
3 tablespoons cold-pressed canola oil
3/4 cup all-purpose unbleached white flour
3/4 cup buckwheat pancake flour
2/3 cup unsweetened cocoa powder
1/4 cup Splenda Brown Sugar Blend
1/3 cup pecans, chopped
3/4 teaspoon baking soda
1/2 teaspoon salt
1 cup fresh raspberries or sliced strawberries

Preparation: Combine milk, Egg Beaters, and oil in a small bowl and whisk until blended. In a separate bowl, combine white flour, buckwheat flour, cocoa powder, Brown Sugar Blend, baking soda, and salt; mix well. Add wet ingredients to dry ingredients and stir until just moistened (batter will be slightly lumpy). Heat griddle over medium heat until hot. (Test with drops of water, which should sizzle and then evaporate.) For each pancake, pour 1/4 cup batter onto griddle. Cook 1½–2 minutes or until batter is set around edges. Carefully turn over pancake; cook 1–2 minutes more or until cooked through. Repeat with remaining batter. Serve with berries on top. Makes about 16 pancakes, or 4 servings of 4 pancakes each.

Nutritional information per serving:
Calories: 420
Fat: 18 g
Saturated fat: 3 g
Carbohydrate: 54 g
Total sugars: 18 g
Protein: 11 g
Sodium: 510 mg
Cholesterol: 7 mg
Dietary fiber: 5 g

Cranberry-Pecan Oatmeal

This oatmeal is delicious with some chopped Fuji or Granny Smith apples or blueberries on top.

Ingredients:
2 cups old-fashioned rolled oats
1 cup apricot or mango nectar
2½ cups water
1 cup fresh cranberries, chopped
1 teaspoon ground cinnamon
Pinch of salt
1/4 cup pecans, chopped
1/2 cup low-fat vanilla or soy yogurt

Preparation: Place a dry skillet over medium-high heat and add oats. Toast oats, stirring regularly, until they are a bit darker in color and fragrant, about 2½–3 minutes. Remove from heat and place in a ceramic bowl. Place a deep, medium saucepan over medium heat; add nectar and water. Cook slowly until bubbles appear around the edges, but do not let liquid boil. Immediately stir in oats. Add cranberries, cinnamon, and salt; lower heat and cook, stirring occasionally, until oats are tender, about 6–7 minutes. Stir in pecans. Divide the oatmeal among 4 bowls. Top each bowl with 2 tablespoons yogurt. Serve immediately. Makes 4 servings.

Nutritional information per serving:
Calories: 345
Fat: 4 g
Saturated fat: < 1 g
Carbohydrate: 68 g
Total sugars: 12 g
Protein: 10 g
Sodium: 45 mg
Cholesterol: 125 mg
Dietary fiber: 8 g

The Anti–Breast Cancer Cookbook

Cranberry-Walnut Pancakes

Ingredients:

1⅓ cups all-purpose unbleached white flour
2/3 cup whole-wheat flour or whole-wheat pastry flour
1 tablespoon sugar
2 teaspoons baking powder
1 teaspoon baking soda
1/4 teaspoon cinnamon
2 large omega-3-enriched eggs plus 2 egg whites from large eggs,
   lightly beaten
2 cups low-fat buttermilk (preferably organic)
1/4 cup sunflower or cold-pressed canola oil
2/3 cup fresh cranberries, coarsely chopped
1/4 cup walnuts, chopped

Preparation: In a large bowl, combine white flour, wheat flour, sugar, baking powder, baking soda, and cinnamon; set aside. In a small bowl, combine eggs and egg whites, buttermilk, and oil; set aside. Preheat griddle to medium heat (400°F) or place large non-stick skillet over medium heat. Make a well in the middle of the dry ingredients and add the wet ingredients. Stir until just combined, then fold in cranberries and walnuts. Drop onto hot griddle or skillet by 1/4 cupfuls. Flip pancake when set around the edges, about 2–3 minutes. Cook for another 1–2 minutes, until light brown on the bottom. Makes about 18 medium pancakes, or 6 servings of 3 each.

Nutritional information per serving:
Calories: 305
Fat: 14 g
Saturated fat: 2 g
Carbohydrate: 32 g
Total sugars: 6 g
Protein: 10 g
Sodium: 470 mg
Cholesterol: 55 mg
Dietary fiber: 3 g

Crustless Salmon and Broccoli Quiche

Salmon provides a healthy dose of anti-inflammatory omega-3 fatty acids, and broccoli is loaded with powerful antioxidants.

Ingredients:
Nonstick cooking spray
3/4 cup cholesterol-free egg substitute (such as Egg Beaters)
1/4 cup green onion, chopped
1/4 cup plain nonfat yogurt
2 teaspoons all-purpose unbleached white flour
2 tablespoons fresh chives, chopped, or 1 teaspoon dried chives
1/8 teaspoon salt
1/8 teaspoon black pepper, freshly ground
3/4 cup fresh broccoli florets or frozen florets, thawed and drained
3 ounces (cooked weight) skinless wild salmon
2 tablespoons reduced-fat feta cheese, crumbled
2 small plum tomatoes, thinly sliced
1/4 cup fresh whole-wheat or whole-grain bread crumbs

Preparation: Preheat oven to 375°F. Spray a 6-cup rectangular casserole dish or 9-inch pie plate with nonstick cooking spray. Combine egg substitute, onions, yogurt, flour, chives, salt, and pepper in medium bowl; stir until well blended. Stir in broccoli, salmon, and cheese. Spread evenly in casserole or pie plate and top with tomato slices. Sprinkle bread crumbs over tomato slices. Bake uncovered 24–28 minutes, or until knife inserted into center comes out clean. Let stand at least 5 minutes. Cut in half before serving. Makes 2 servings of 1/2 quiche each.

Nutritional information per serving:
Calories: 215
Fat: 7 g
Saturated fat: 2 g
Carbohydrate: 19 g
Total sugars: 5 g
Protein: 19 g
Sodium: 465 mg
Cholesterol: 29 mg
Dietary fiber: 5 g

The Anti–Breast Cancer Cookbook

Dark Chocolate Banana Bread with Pecans

You can use walnuts, hazelnuts, or macadamia nuts in this bread instead of pecans. To get the greatest boost of antioxidants, use dark chocolate with 70 percent or greater cacao content.

Ingredients:
Nonstick cooking spray
4 very ripe bananas
2/3 cup sugar
2 large omega-3-enriched eggs
1/3 cup olive oil
1 teaspoon vanilla extract
1/3 cup oat flour
1⅔ cups whole-wheat flour
1 teaspoon baking soda
1/2 teaspoon salt
3 ounces dark chocolate, chopped
1/2 cup pecans, chopped

Preparation: Preheat oven to 350°F. Spray an 8½- or 9-inch loaf pan with nonstick cooking spray or rub lightly with oil. Combine bananas and sugar in a ceramic bowl; mix with a potato masher or a fork until smooth. Whisk together eggs, oil, and vanilla in a separate bowl; add banana/sugar mixture and stir until combined. Sift together oat flour, wheat flour, baking soda, and salt in a separate bowl; add to wet ingredients. Add chocolate and pecans; stir until just incorporated (batter should still be lumpy). Pour batter into pan. Bake for 50–60 minutes or until center is heated to 210°F and a toothpick inserted in the center comes out clean. Let cool in pan 15–20 minutes before transferring to a wire rack. Cool completely before slicing. Tightly wrapped bread will keep at room temperature for a few days and should last a week if refrigerated. Makes 12 servings.

Nutritional information per serving:
Calories: 270
Fat: 12 g
Saturated fat: 3 g
Carbohydrate: 36 g
Total sugars: 18 g
Protein: 5 g
Sodium: 180 mg
Cholesterol: 30 mg
Dietary fiber: 4 g

Flax Buttermilk Pancakes with Peaches and Pecan Maple Syrup

Ingredients:
1 cup whole-wheat pastry flour
1/4 cup ground flaxseed meal
2 teaspoons baking powder
1/2 teaspoon baking soda
1/4 teaspoon salt
1 cup low-fat buttermilk (preferably organic)
1 large omega-3-enriched egg
1 teaspoon clover honey or agave syrup
1 tablespoon cold-pressed canola oil
Nonstick cooking spray
1/2 cup pure maple syrup
1/3 cup pecans, toasted and coarsely chopped
2 fresh, ripe peaches, washed and sliced

Preparation: Combine flour, flaxseed meal, baking powder, baking soda, and salt in a large bowl. In a separate bowl, whisk together buttermilk, egg, honey or agave syrup, and oil. Add liquid ingredients to dry ones; gently stir until moistened but do not overmix. Batter should still be lumpy. Preheat griddle and spray with nonstick cooking spray. In the meantime, place maple syrup in a 1-quart saucepan over medium heat and warm. Add pecans, reduce heat to low, and keep warm. Pour about 1/4 cup batter onto griddle so that pancake spreads about 4–5 inches in diameter. Cook until bubbles appear, about 2 minutes, and flip. Cook other side until golden brown, about 1 minute more. Serve pancakes with peaches and pecan maple syrup. Makes 12 pancakes, or 4 servings of 3 pancakes each.

Nutritional information per serving:
Calories: 398
Fat: 14 g
Saturated fat: 1 g
Carbohydrate: 60 g
Total sugars: 28 g
Protein: 9 g
Sodium: 420 mg
Cholesterol: 46 mg
Dietary fiber: 8 g

The Anti–Breast Cancer Cookbook

Gingerbread Belgian Waffles

These waffles are delicious with some ripe, fresh strawberries sliced on top.

Ingredients:
1½ cups all-purpose unbleached white flour
1½ cups whole-wheat pastry flour
4 teaspoons baking powder
2 teaspoons ground cinnamon
2 teaspoons ground ginger
1/4 teaspoon nutmeg, freshly grated
1/4 teaspoon salt
4 large omega-3-enriched eggs
2/3 cup dark brown sugar, packed
1 cup canned 100 percent pure pumpkin
1¼ cups reduced-fat (2 percent) dairy milk (preferably organic)
1/2 cup dark molasses
1/2 cup nonhydrogenated buttery spread (such as Smart Balance), melted
Nonstick cooking spray

Preparation: Preheat waffle iron. In a large bowl, combine white flour, wheat flour, baking powder, cinnamon, ginger, nutmeg, and salt. In medium bowl, beat eggs and sugar until fluffy. One by one, beat in pumpkin, milk, molasses, and melted spread. Stir the wet ingredients into the dry ingredients until just moist. Do not over-mix (batter should be a bit lumpy). Spray waffle iron with nonstick cooking spray and cook 4 batches, 4 waffle sections each. Serve with toppings of choice. Makes 16 waffle sections, or 8 servings of 2 waffle sections each.

Nutritional information per serving:
Calories: 388
Fat: 8 g
Saturated fat: 3 g
Carbohydrate: 70 g
Total sugars: 31 g
Protein: 10 g
Sodium: 420 mg
Cholesterol: 95 mg
Dietary fiber: 5 g

Gluten-Free Buttermilk Waffles

Serve with your favorite toppings, such as mixed berries and bananas, or diced apples and cinnamon with vanilla yogurt.

Ingredients:
1½ cup rice flour
1/3 cup tapioca flour
1/3 cup cornstarch
3 teaspoons baking powder
1½ teaspoons sugar
1/8 teaspoon salt
2 extra-large omega-3-enriched eggs plus 1 egg white from a large
   egg, lightly beaten
1¾ cups low-fat buttermilk (preferably organic)
1/4 cup sunflower or cold-pressed canola oil
1 teaspoon vanilla extract
Nonstick cooking spray (or extra oil)

Preparation: Preheat waffle iron. In a large bowl, stir together rice flour, tapioca flour, cornstarch, baking powder, sugar, and salt. Add eggs, buttermilk, oil, and vanilla; mix well. Spray waffle iron with nonstick cooking spray (or per iron's instructions) and cook 3 batches of 4 waffle sections each. Cook until browned. Makes about 12 waffle sections, or 4 servings of 3 waffle sections each.

Nutritional information per serving:
Calories: 386
Fat: 14 g
Saturated fat: 3 g
Carbohydrate: 55 g
Total sugars: 7 g
Protein: 10 g
Sodium: 520 mg
Cholesterol: 10 mg
Dietary fiber: 1 g

The Anti–Breast Cancer Cookbook

Lemony Cream Cheese Pancakes with Blueberries

You can make these pancakes with any type of flour, including all-purpose unbleached white flour, whole-wheat flour, or gluten-free pancake flour, such as Bob's Red Mill brand. These pancakes make the perfect brunch before or after a morning of intense physical activity, such as biking or skiing.

Ingredients:
1½ cups any combination of baking flour (such as 3/4 cup whole-wheat pastry flour and 3/4 cup buckwheat flour)
1 tablespoon sugar
1 tablespoon baking powder
1/2 teaspoon baking soda
Pinch of salt
2 large omega-3-enriched eggs, separated into yolks and whites
1 cup low-fat buttermilk (preferably organic)
6 ounces reduced-fat cream cheese, cut into small pieces
1 tablespoon unsalted butter, melted
1 teaspoon vanilla extract
2 tablespoons lemon juice
3½ teaspoons lemon zest
Nonstick cooking spray
1½ cups fresh blueberries

Preparation: Stir together flour, sugar, baking powder, baking soda, and salt in a medium bowl. In a separate bowl, whisk together egg yolks and buttermilk. Add cream cheese and mix until cream cheese has separated into uniformly small lumps, about the size of large cottage cheese curds. Stir in melted butter, vanilla, lemon juice, and lemon zest. Add dry ingredients to wet ingredients and stir to combine. Whisk together egg whites until stiff but not dry and fold gently into batter. Heat a griddle or cast-iron pan over medium-high heat, until a drop of water sizzles. Lower heat to medium and spray with nonstick cooking spray. Drop batter into pan by 1/4 to 1/3 cupfuls. Once it has spread, drop a small handful of blueberries on top. Cook until the bubbles have burst, about 3 minutes, and flip. Cook on second side until light brown and puffy, about 2–3 minutes. Serve with fresh, sliced strawberries or your favorite healthy topping. Makes 4 servings of 3 pancakes each.

Nutritional information per serving:
Calories: 385
Fat: 14 g
Saturated fat: 9 g
Carbohydrate: 52 g
Total sugars: 14 g
Protein: 13 g
Sodium: 750 mg
Cholesterol: 125 mg
Dietary fiber: 5 g

Maple-Nut Granola

Ingredients:
Nonstick cooking spray
4 cups old-fashioned rolled oats
1/2 cup raw cashews, chopped or broken into pieces
1/2 cup raw almonds, chopped
1/2 cup sunflower seeds
1/2 cup millet
1/2 cup maple syrup
1/4 teaspoon salt
1/2 teaspoon cinnamon
1/3 cup raisins or chopped dates (or a combination of both)

Preparation: Preheat oven to 350°F. Spray a large baking sheet with nonstick cooking spray or use a nonstick baking sheet. In a large bowl, combine all ingredients. Stir until mixture is moist and of even consistency. Spread mixture onto baking sheet. Bake until golden brown, stirring occasionally, about 30–35 minutes. Transfer sheet to a cooling rack and let cool completely. Store in the refrigerator in an airtight container. Makes about 24 servings of 1/4 cup each.

Nutritional information per serving:
Calories: 140
Fat: 5 g
Saturated fat: < 1 g
Carbohydrate: 20 g
Total sugars: 6 g
Protein: 4 g
Sodium: 18 mg
Cholesterol: 0 mg
Dietary fiber: 3 g

Morning Glory Flax Muffins

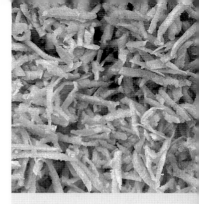

Ingredients:
1 cup all-purpose unbleached white flour
1/2 cup whole-wheat pastry flour
3/4 cup ground flaxseed meal
3/4 cup oat bran
1/3 cup Splenda Brown Sugar Blend or 1/2 cup brown sugar, packed
3 tablespoons whole flaxseeds
2 teaspoons baking soda
1 teaspoon baking powder
1/4 teaspoon salt
2 teaspoons cinnamon
1 cup shredded carrots
1/2 cup walnuts, chopped
1/4 cup raisins
3/4 cup reduced-fat (2 percent) dairy milk or enriched soy milk
2 extra-large omega-3-enriched eggs, lightly beaten
1 teaspoon vanilla extract

Preparation: Preheat oven to 350°F. Combine white flour, wheat flour, flax meal, oat bran, sugar, flaxseeds, baking soda, baking powder, salt, and cinnamon in a large bowl. One at a time, stir in carrots, walnuts, raisins, milk, eggs, and vanilla, until the mixture is evenly moist. Spray 2 muffin pans with nonstick cooking spray or line with paper liners. Pour or spoon batter into 18 of the muffin cups about 3/4 full. Fill remaining cups with water to avoid scorching. Bake for 16–20 minutes, or until a toothpick comes out clean. Makes 18 medium muffins.

Nutritional information per muffin:
Calories: 175
Fat: 7 g
Saturated fat: 0 g
Carbohydrate: 20 g
Total sugars: 5 g
Protein: 6 g
Sodium: 195 mg
Cholesterol: 20 mg
Dietary fiber: 5 g

Orange–Poppy Seed Muffins

Ingredients:
Nonstick cooking spray
1 cup whole-wheat pastry flour
1 cup all-purpose unbleached white flour
2 teaspoons baking powder
3 tablespoons poppy seeds
2 large omega-3-enriched eggs
1 teaspoon vanilla extract
1/4 cup light brown sugar
2/3 cup vanilla nonfat yogurt
1/4 cup sunflower or cold-pressed canola oil
1 tablespoon plus 1 teaspoon orange zest, finely grated
1/4 cup frozen orange juice concentrate, thawed to room temperature

Preparation: Preheat oven to 350° F. Spray a 12-muffin pan with nonstick cooking spray or line with paper liners. In a large bowl, sift together wheat flour, white flour, baking powder, and poppy seeds. In another mixing bowl, whisk together eggs, vanilla extract, sugar, yogurt, sunflower or canola oil, orange zest, and orange juice concentrate. Fold wet ingredients into dry ingredients with a rubber spatula until just combined and very thick. Divide batter among muffin cups, filling each 2/3 full. Bake 25–30 minutes until lightly browned and a toothpick inserted into muffin center comes out clean. Cool on a wire rack. Makes 12 medium muffins.

Nutritional information per muffin:
Calories: 168
Fat: 6 g
Saturated fat: < 1 g
Carbohydrate: 22 g
Total sugars: 6 g
Protein: 4 g
Sodium: 20 mg
Cholesterol: 31 mg
Dietary fiber: 2 g

Pineapple and Macadamia Nut Muffins

Ingredients:

Topping:
1/4 cup unsweetened shredded coconut
3/4 cup plus 2 tablespoons all-purpose unbleached white flour, divided
1/4 cup plus 1 tablespoon Splenda Brown Sugar Blend, divided
5 tablespoons chopped macadamia nuts, divided
2 tablespoons coconut or sunflower oil, divided

Muffins:
Nonstick cooking spray
1 cup whole-wheat flour
1 teaspoon baking powder
1/4 teaspoon baking soda
1/8 teaspoon salt
1/2 teaspoon ground cinnamon
1 large omega-3-enriched egg plus 1 egg white from a large egg
3/4 cup vanilla Greek yogurt
2 teaspoons unsalted butter, at room temperature
1/2 teaspoon vanilla extract
1½ cups pineapple (preferably fresh), finely diced

Preparation: Preheat oven to 400°F. To make topping, combine coconut, 2 tablespoons white flour, 1 tablespoon Splenda Brown Sugar Blend, and 2 tablespoons nuts in a small bowl. Drizzle with 1 tablespoon oil; stir to combine; set aside. Spray a 12-muffin pan with nonstick cooking spray or line with paper liners. To make muffins, sift together remaining 3/4 cup white flour, whole-wheat flour, baking powder, baking soda, salt, and cinnamon in a medium bowl. In a separate bowl, combine remaining 1/4 cup Splenda Brown Sugar Blend, remaining 1 tablespoon oil, egg, egg white, yogurt, butter, and vanilla; beat until well blended. Make a well in the center of dry ingredients and add wet ingredients; stir until just combined. Fold in pineapple and remaining 3 tablespoons nuts. Divide batter among the muffin cups. Sprinkle with topping and gently press into batter. Bake muffins until golden brown and a toothpick inserted in the center comes out clean, 20–22 minutes. Let cool in the pan for 10 minutes, then remove from pan and let cool on a wire rack at least 5 minutes more before serving. Makes 12 medium muffins.

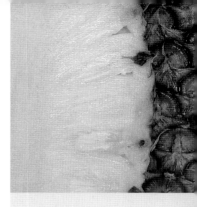

Nutritional information per muffin:
Calories: 215
Fat: 10 g
Saturated fat: 4 g
Carbohydrate: 25 g
Total sugars: 9 g
Protein: 6 g
Sodium: 105 mg
Cholesterol: 15 mg
Dietary fiber: 3 g

Strawberry-Hazelnut Breakfast Polenta

This polenta can be made with almonds or cashews and topped with any type of berry, as well as ripe, fresh peaches. It is a delicious breakfast or late-night dish that is rich in protein, vitamins, and minerals.

Ingredients:

1/2 cup plus 2 tablespoons hazelnuts (enough to make 1/2 cup hazelnut meal)
4 cups reduced-fat (2 percent) dairy milk (preferably organic) or soy, rice, or almond milk
3/4 cup quick-cooking polenta
3 tablespoons nonhydrogenated spread (such as Smart Balance or Fleischmann's Olive Oil Spread)
1/3 cup pure maple syrup or clover honey
1 cup fresh strawberries, hulled and chopped, divided
1/2 teaspoon vanilla extract
Pinch cinnamon (or to taste)
1/2 cup low-fat vanilla yogurt or vanilla soy yogurt

Preparation: Place hazelnuts in a food processor or coffee grinder and process into meal. Bring milk to a boil in a medium sauce-pan over medium-high heat. Reduce heat to low and add polenta, whisking constantly until smooth. Add hazelnut meal and continue whisking until the polenta thickens and becomes creamy. Add nonhydrogenated spread and whisk until it melts completely. Turn off heat and whisk in maple syrup or honey, vanilla, cinnamon, and most of the strawberries. Serve with a dollop of yogurt and a few of the remaining strawberries. Makes 6 servings.

Nutritional information per serving:

Calories: 355
Fat: 9 g
Saturated fat: 2 g
Carbohydrate: 58 g
Total sugars: 24 g
Protein: 12 g
Sodium: 165 mg
Cholesterol: 15 mg
Dietary fiber: 3 g

Walnut, Date and Fennel Scones

Fennel seeds are rich in antioxidants known to decrease inflammation. Combined with crunchy, omega-3-rich walnuts, these scones are amazingly flavorful and good for you.

Ingredients:

Scones
Nonstick cooking spray
1 cup all-purpose unbleached white flour
1 cup whole-wheat pastry flour
1/3 cup white sugar
1 tablespoon light brown sugar
2 teaspoons baking powder
1/2 teaspoon salt
5 tablespoons unsalted butter, chilled, cut into 1/2-inch cubes
2 egg yolks from large omega-3-enriched eggs
1/2 cup low-fat organic buttermilk
1/2 cup dates, chopped
1/3 cup walnuts, toasted and chopped
1 tablespoon fennel seeds

Glaze
1 large omega-3-enriched egg, beaten
1 tablespoon water

Preparation: Preheat oven to 400°F. Spray a large baking sheet with nonstick cooking spray or oil lightly. To make scones, whisk together white flour, wheat flour, white sugar, brown sugar, baking powder, and salt in a large bowl until combined. Add butter. Using fingertips, blend mixture until coarse meal forms. Whisk egg yolks and buttermilk in a small bowl until blended. Slowly fold egg mixture into flour mixture. Gently stir in dates, walnuts, and fennel seeds. Turn dough onto a lightly floured work surface and knead gently, just until smooth, about 4 turns. Divide dough in half; pat each half into a 6-inch round. Cut each round into 6 wedges to make individual scones. Transfer scones to baking sheet. To make glaze, combine egg and water. Brush scones with glaze. Bake until scones are light brown, about 17–19 minutes. Serve warm or at room temperature. Makes 12 scones.

Nutritional information per scone:
Calories: 215
Fat: 9 g
Saturated fat: 3 g
Carbohydrate: 30 g
Total sugars: 13 g
Protein: 4 g
Sodium: 150 mg
Cholesterol: 65 mg
Dietary fiber: 3 g

Whole-Grain Irish Soda Bread

This bread is rich in fiber and complex carbohydrates. It tastes amazing toasted with a small dab of orange marmalade and makes a unique sandwich bread.

Ingredients:
1/2 cup soy milk
2 teaspoons apple-cider vinegar
2 cups all-purpose unbleached white flour
2 cups whole-wheat flour
2 teaspoons salt
3/4 teaspoon baking powder
1 teaspoon baking soda
1 cup sunflower seeds
Nonstick cooking spray

Preparation: Preheat oven to 375° F. In a small bowl, stir together milk and vinegar; set aside. In a large bowl, combine white flour, wheat flour, salt, baking powder, and baking soda. Stir in sunflower seeds; add soy milk and vinegar mixture; stir. Knead into smooth, pliable dough. Lightly spray a cookie sheet or pizza pan with non-stick cooking spray or use a nonstick sheet or pan. Shape dough into a round loaf about 3 or 4 inches high. Bake 35–40 minutes. Cool on a cooling rack. This bread is absolutely delicious if eaten when still warm but is also great on the second or third day. Makes 16 servings of 1 slice each.

Nutritional information per slice:
Calories: 144
Fat: < 1 g
Saturated fat: 0 g
Carbohydrate: 30 g
Total sugars: 5 g
Protein: 4 g
Sodium: 294 mg
Cholesterol: 0 mg
Dietary fiber: 3 g

The Anti–Breast Cancer Cookbook

Whole-Wheat, Apple-Raspberry Muffins

Ingredients:
Nonstick cooking spray
2 cups whole-wheat or wheat bran flakes cereal
1 cup low-fat buttermilk (preferably organic)
3/4 cup plus 1 tablespoon whole-wheat flour (or whole-wheat
    pastry flour)
3 tablespoons ground flaxseed meal
1/2 cup Fuji, Rome Beauty, or Granny Smith apple, finely chopped
1/3 cup fresh raspberries
1/4 cup unsweetened apple juice
3 tablespoons brown sugar
1 large omega-3-enriched egg
3/4 teaspoon baking soda
1/2 teaspoon ground cinnamon
1/4 teaspoon salt

Preparation: Preheat oven to 400°F. Spray a 12-muffin pan with
nonstick cooking spray or line with paper liners. Place cereal in
large bowl and pour buttermilk on top. Let sit until cereal is soft,
about 8 to 10 minutes. Add flour, flaxseed meal, apple, raspberries,
apple juice, sugar, egg, baking soda, cinnamon, and salt; stir until
evenly distributed and batter is just moistened. Pour into muffin
cups; fill 2/3 full. Bake about 20–22 minutes, or until toothpick
comes out clean. Remove from pan immediately and let cool on
wire rack. Refrigerate after two days to ensure freshness; muffins
can be frozen and reheated. Makes 12 medium muffins.

**Nutritional information
per muffin:**
Calories: 102
Fat: 2 g
Saturated fat: < 1 g
Carbohydrate: 17 g
Total sugars: 5 g
Protein: 4 g
Sodium: 120 mg
Cholesterol: 15 mg
Dietary fiber: 3 g

Whole-Wheat Pumpkin Pancakes

Vegetarian

These pancakes are delicious with pure maple syrup and diced bananas, berries, or sweet-tart apples.

Ingredients:
1½ cups whole-wheat pastry flour
2 tablespoons ground flaxseed meal
1 teaspoon baking soda
2 teaspoons baking powder
1/8 teaspoon salt
1½ teaspoons ground cinnamon
1/4 teaspoon ground ginger
1/4 teaspoon ground nutmeg
1 cup canned 100 percent pure pumpkin, mashed with a fork
1⅓ cups low-fat buttermilk (preferably organic)
2 large omega-3-enriched eggs
1/2 cup reduced-fat sour cream
2 teaspoons vanilla extract
1½ tablespoons brown sugar
Nonstick cooking spray

Preparation: In a large bowl, combine flour, flaxseed meal, baking soda, baking powder, salt, cinnamon, ginger, and nutmeg. Stir until evenly distributed; set aside. In a separate bowl, whisk together pumpkin, buttermilk, eggs, sour cream, vanilla, and sugar. Add wet mixture to dry ingredients; stir gently, just until a batter forms. (It's okay if the batter is lumpy.) Preheat griddle or skillet and spray with nonstick cooking spray. Ladle batter onto warm griddle or skillet in 3- to 4-tablespoon portions. Cook for 2–3 minutes, until bubbles form and burst. Flip and heat on other side until set, fragrant, and lightly brown around the edges, about 1–2 minutes more. Makes 16 medium pancakes, or 4 servings of 4 pancakes each.

Nutritional information per serving:
Calories: 325
Fat: 8 g
Saturated fat: 2 g
Carbohydrate: 50 g
Total sugars: 11 g
Protein: 13 g
Sodium: 680 mg
Cholesterol: 550 mg
Dietary fiber: 10 g

The Anti–Breast Cancer Cookbook

Zucchini Nut Bread

This delicious bread is rich in fiber, folate, and vitamin E. If you want to make this bread vegan, replace the egg and egg white with a vegan egg replacer or 1½ tablespoons ground flaxseed meal mixed with 1/4 cup water. If the batter seems dry, add 1 tablespoon unsweetened applesauce.

Ingredients:
Nonstick cooking spray
1½ cups whole-wheat pastry flour
1/2 cup brown sugar or 1/3 cup Splenda Brown Sugar Blend
1 teaspoon baking powder
1/2 teaspoon baking soda
1/4 teaspoon ground cinnamon
1/4 teaspoon ground nutmeg
1/4 teaspoon ground cloves
1/4 teaspoon salt
1 large omega-3-enriched egg plus 1 egg white from a large egg
3 tablespoons sunflower or olive oil
1¼ cups zucchini, grated and tightly packed
1 tablespoon vanilla extract
3/4 cup canned crushed pineapple, drained of liquid
2 tablespoons pecans, chopped

Preparation: Preheat oven to 350°F. Spray an 8½- or 9-inch loaf pan with nonstick cooking spray. In a large bowl, sift together flour, brown sugar or Splenda Brown Sugar Blend, baking powder, baking soda, cinnamon, nutmeg, cloves, and salt. Set aside. In another large bowl, combine egg, egg white, oil, zucchini, vanilla, and pineapple; mix well. Add flour mixture to egg mixture and stir gently until just combined. Do not overmix. Pour batter into loaf pan and sprinkle with chopped pecans. Bake until bread is golden brown and set in the center (an inserted toothpick comes out clean), about 55–60 minutes. Makes 12 slices.

Nutritional information per slice:
Calories: 164
Fat: 4 g
Saturated fat: < 1 g
Carbohydrate: 29 g
Total sugars: 20 g
Protein: 3 g
Sodium: 70 mg
Cholesterol: 18 mg
Dietary fiber: 3 g

DIPS AND SAUCES

Vegetarian   **Vegan**   **Gluten-Free**

Almond-Hazelnut Dip 55
Asian Ginger Dressing 56
Avocado-Tomatillo Salsa 56
Coffee Barbecue Sauce 57
Corn, Bean and Avocado Salsa 58
Cranberry-Apple-Pecan Conserve 59
Creamy Avocado Dressing 60
Feta and Roasted Red Pepper Dip 61
Ginger-Tomato Dipping Sauce 62
Grape Salsa 62
Green Chile Poblano Pesto 63
Herbed Flaxseed and Olive Oil Dressing 64
Lemon-Herb Marinade (for Fish) 65
Low-Fat Creamy Ranch Dressing 65
Miso-Tahini Sauce 66
Pomegranate Vinaigrette 67
Raspberry Vinaigrette 67
Roasted Pepper Dressing 68
Salsa Verde—Italian Style 69
Sesame Dressing 70
Shallot Dressing 70
Tangerine Balsamic Sauce 71
Toasted Pumpkin-Seed Pesto 71
Tricolored Pepper Salsa 72
Walnut Vinaigrette 72

Almond-Hazelnut Dip

This spicy dip is delicious on raw vegetables or apple slices. It's also a great bread spread.

Ingredients:
2/3 cup hazelnuts, boiled and skins removed
2/3 cup raw almonds
1 large, vine-ripened tomato, chopped
1/4 cup fresh parsley leaves
2 tablespoons red wine vinegar
3 garlic cloves, pressed
1 teaspoon clover honey
1 teaspoon smoked paprika
1/2 teaspoon sea salt, ground
1/8 teaspoon cayenne pepper
1/8 teaspoon turmeric
2 tablespoons extra-virgin olive oil
2 tablespoons walnut or flaxseed oil

Preparation: Place hazelnuts, almonds, tomato, parsley, vinegar, garlic, honey, paprika, salt, cayenne pepper, and turmeric in a food processor; pulse until combined. With the motor running, slowly add olive oil and walnut or flaxseed oil until a thick mixture has formed. Add a small amount of water to thin as necessary. Refrigerate for at least 20 minutes before serving. Makes about 18 servings of 2 tablespoons each.

Nutritional information per serving:
Calories: 94
Fat: 8 g
Saturated fat: < 1 g
Carbohydrate: 3 g
Total sugars: < 1 g
Protein: 2 g
Sodium: 46 mg
Cholesterol: 0 mg
Dietary fiber: 2 g

Asian Ginger Dressing

Ingredients:
1/4 cup wheat-free tamari or reduced-sodium soy sauce
Juice of 1 lemon or 2 teaspoons refrigerated lemon juice
4 small garlic cloves, minced
3 tablespoons fresh ginger root, minced
1 teaspoon Dijon mustard
2 teaspoons clover honey
2 teaspoons sesame seeds
Sea salt, ground, to taste
Black pepper to taste, freshly ground
1/2 cup toasted sesame oil
1/2 cup extra-virgin olive oil

Preparation: In a small bowl, whisk together tamari or soy sauce, lemon juice, garlic, ginger, mustard, honey, sesame seeds, salt, and pepper. Once thoroughly combined, add sesame oil and then olive oil in a steady stream, whisking constantly. Pour into a glass jar and chill until served. Makes 12 servings of 2 tablespoons each.

Nutritional information per serving:
Calories: 150
Fat: 16 g
Saturated fat: 2 g
Carbohydrate: 1 g
Total sugars: < 1 g
Protein: < 1 g
Sodium: 95 mg
Cholesterol: 0 mg
Dietary fiber: < 1 g

Avocado-Tomatillo Salsa

Ingredients:
2 cups tomatillos, husked, rinsed, and coarsely chopped
1 medium serrano chile with seeds, minced (remove seeds if you like less heat)
3 tablespoons fresh lime juice
2 large avocados, halved, peeled, pitted, and diced
2/3 cup white onion, chopped
1/2 cup cilantro, chopped
1/2 teaspoon fine sea salt
1/2 teaspoon black pepper, freshly ground

Preparation: Place tomatillos and chiles in a food processor. Pulse on and off, processing until a coarse puree forms. Pour into a medium ceramic bowl. Add lime juice, avocados, onion, cilantro, salt, and pepper. Serve or cover and chill. Makes about 3½–4 cups, roughly 20 servings.

Nutritional information per serving:
Calories: 30
Fat: 2 g
Saturated fat: < 1 g
Carbohydrate: 3 g
Total sugars: < 1 g
Protein: < 1 g
Sodium: 42 mg
Cholesterol: 0 mg
Dietary fiber: 1 g

The Anti–Breast Cancer Cookbook

Coffee Barbecue Sauce

This tangy barbecue sauce is perfect with any vegetarian, poultry, fish, or lean meat dish. If you like more heat, substitute hotter peppers for the jalapeños.

Ingredients:
1/2 cup brewed espresso or strong, dark coffee
1 cup ketchup (I use a reduced-sugar brand)
1/2 cup cider vinegar
1/2 cup light brown sugar, packed
1 cup yellow onion, finely chopped
2 garlic cloves, crushed
2 fresh jalapeño peppers, seeded and minced
2 tablespoons hot, dry mustard mixed with 1 tablespoon warm
    water
2 tablespoons Worcestershire sauce (Lea & Perrins and others make
    gluten-free sauce)
2 tablespoons ground cumin
2 tablespoons chili powder

Preparation: Place all ingredients in a small saucepan or stock pot and stir to combine. Bring to a simmer over medium-high heat. Lower heat until mixture is just simmering; let simmer about 20 minutes. Remove pot from heat and allow mixture to cool. Once cooled completely, puree in a blender or food processor fitted with a steel blade. Use immediately or store for up to 2 weeks in a resealable container. Makes about 3 cups, or 12 servings of 1/4 cup each.

Nutritional information per serving:
Calories: 82
Fat: 4 g
Saturated fat: 0 g
Carbohydrate: 17 g
Total sugars: 13 g
Protein: 1 g
Sodium: 275 mg
Cholesterol: 0 mg
Dietary fiber: 1 g

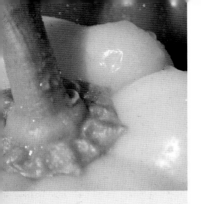

Corn, Bean and Avocado Salsa

This salsa contains omega-3 fatty acids, fiber, and beta-carotene. It's delicious with whole-grain flax or corn chips as well as on tacos, burritos, or enchiladas. I had a little on my veggie omelet, and it was simply delicious.

Ingredients:
1 ripe avocado, peeled, pitted, and cut into chunks
1½ cups fresh (or thawed frozen) corn kernels
1/2 cup red bell pepper, diced
1/2 cup orange bell pepper, diced
3 tablespoons red onion, minced
1¾ cups cooked black beans (rinsed and drained, if using canned beans)
1/2 small jalapeño pepper, minced
1/2 teaspoon sea salt
1/2 teaspoon chili powder
1/2 teaspoon ground coriander
1/2 teaspoon ground cumin
1/4 cup flat-leaf parsley, minced
2 tablespoons flaxseed oil
1 tablespoon extra-virgin olive oil
1 tablespoon balsamic vinegar
2 teaspoons fresh lime juice

Preparation: Place all ingredients in a large ceramic bowl and stir until combined. Chill or serve immediately. Makes about 20 servings of 1/4 cup each.

Nutritional information per serving:
Calories: 62
Fat: 3 g
Saturated fat: < 1 g
Carbohydrate: 8 g
Total sugars: 1 g
Protein: 2 g
Sodium: 121 mg
Cholesterol: 0 mg
Dietary fiber: 2 g

The Anti–Breast Cancer Cookbook

Cranberry-Apple-Pecan Conserve

Ingredients:
3/4 cup water
1⅔ cups turbinado sugar (raw sugar)
3/4 teaspoon ground cinnamon or 1 cinnamon stick
1/4 teaspoon allspice
1/4 teaspoon nutmeg
2 bags (12 ounces each) fresh cranberries, divided
2 medium apples (Braeburn, Jonagold, Gala, Empire, Honey Crisp,
    or Fuji work well), peeled and chopped
1½ cups walnut pieces, toasted
2 tablespoons orange marmalade
1 tablespoon brandy (optional)

Preparation: Place water in a large, heavy pot over medium heat. Add sugar, cinnamon or cinnamon stick, allspice, nutmeg, and about half of the cranberries; bring to a simmer. Continue to simmer, stirring occasionally, about 5 minutes, until cranberries start to pop. Add half of remaining cranberries and cook an additional 5 minutes. Add apples, walnut pieces, remaining cranberries, and orange marmalade; simmer for 5–7 more minutes. Add brandy and simmer 1 more minute. Discard cinnamon stick. Makes about 32 servings of 2 tablespoons each.

Nutritional information per serving:
Calories: 82
Fat: 4 g
Saturated fat: 0 g
Carbohydrate: 17 g
Total sugars: 13 g
Protein: 1 g
Sodium: 275 mg
Cholesterol: 0 mg
Dietary fiber: 1 g

Creamy Avocado Dressing

Ingredients:
1/2 cup unsweetened, unflavored soy milk or reduced-fat
(2 percent) dairy milk
6 ounces silken tofu (half of a typical block)
1/4 cup reduced-fat sour cream
1/4 cup olive oil mayonnaise
1/4 cup fresh lemon juice
1/4 cup fresh parsley leaves
3 green onions, chopped (green section only)
15–18 large basil leaves, chopped
2 small garlic cloves, minced
2 teaspoons Dijon mustard
1 ripe avocado, peeled, pitted, and sliced
1/2 teaspoon paprika
1/2 teaspoon fine sea salt
1/2 teaspoon black pepper, freshly ground

Preparation: Place all items into a food processor or blender and process until smooth. Adjust seasonings if desired. Refrigerate until serving. Makes about 8 servings of 2 tablespoons each.

Nutritional information per serving:
Calories: 104
Fat: 8 g
Saturated fat: 1 g
Carbohydrate: 5 g
Total sugars: 0 g
Protein: 4 g
Sodium: 200 mg
Cholesterol: 4 mg
Dietary fiber: 2 g

The Anti–Breast Cancer Cookbook

Feta and Roasted Red Pepper Dip

Flaxseed oil contains omega-3 fatty acids and also has a light, nutty flavor. If you can't find flaxseed oil, you can make this dip using all olive oil.

Ingredients:
4 medium red bell peppers
2 small garlic cloves, peeled and minced
1/2 teaspoon fine sea salt, divided
1/4 teaspoon black pepper, freshly ground
1/2 cup feta cheese, crumbled
2 tablespoons lemon juice (preferably freshly squeezed)
2½ tablespoons fine, whole-grain bread crumbs or gluten-free
    bread crumbs
1½ tablespoons extra-virgin olive oil
1 tablespoon flaxseed oil
3 tablespoons fresh basil leaves, chopped

Preparation: Place an oven rack about 6 inches from the broiler element and set broiler to high heat. Place whole peppers on rimmed, heavy-duty, baking sheet. Broil peppers for about 20 minutes, turning every 5 minutes or so with tongs, until the skin chars on all sides and peppers soften. Remove from oven and place in large ceramic bowl. Cover bowl with foil or plastic wrap until peppers are cool enough to handle, then peel skin and remove stems and seeds. Mash garlic with 1/4 teaspoon salt to form a paste. Place peppers, remaining salt, black pepper, cheese, lemon juice, bread crumbs, and oil in a food processor (or blender) and process until mixture is smooth. Transfer to a nonreactive bowl and stir in garlic paste and basil. Serve immediately or refrigerate and serve at room temperature. Makes about 2½ cups, or about 10 servings of 1/4 cup each.

Nutritional information per serving:
Calories: 72
Fat: 5 g
Saturated fat: 1 g
Carbohydrate: 1 g
Total sugars: 6 g
Protein: 2 g
Sodium: 163 mg
Cholesterol: 5 mg
Dietary fiber: 2 g

Ginger-Tomato Dipping Sauce

Ingredients:
1/2 can (14½ ounces) diced tomatoes, undrained
2 garlic cloves, peeled
2 tablespoons onion, chopped
1 tablespoon jalapeño chile, seeded and chopped
1 tablespoon fresh ginger root, chopped
1/4 teaspoon salt
1 teaspoon olive oil

Preparation: Process tomatoes, onion, chile, ginger root, and salt in a food processor or blender until smooth. In a small skillet, place sauce and oil; sauté until thickened, about 5 minutes. Makes about 3/4 cup, or 12 servings of 1 tablespoon each.

Nutritional information per serving:
Calories: 25
Fat: 1 g
Saturated fat: 0 g
Carbohydrate: 3 g
Total sugars: 1 g
Protein: 0 g
Sodium: 175 mg
Cholesterol: 0 mg
Dietary fiber: 0 g

Grape Salsa

This recipe comes from my friend Jeff Lazar's sister, Vicki Uhrinek. It is great on whole-grain flax or corn tortilla chips. I recently tried it on top of grilled tilapia—delicious!

Ingredients:
3/4 cup red grapes, chopped or quartered
3/4 cup green grapes, chopped or quartered
1/2 cup red bell pepper, diced
1/4 cup yellow onion, finely diced
2 tablespoons fresh basil, minced
1 tablespoon extra-virgin olive oil
1 tablespoon lime juice
1/2 teaspoon salt
1/4 teaspoon hot sauce

Preparation: Combine all ingredients in a bowl. Stir and serve. Makes about 20 servings of 2 tablespoons each.

Nutritional information per serving:
Calories: 20
Fat: < 1 g
Saturated fat: 0 g
Carbohydrate: 4 g
Total sugars: 3 g
Protein: < 1 g
Sodium: 55 mg
Cholesterol: 0 mg
Dietary fiber: 0 g

Green Chile Poblano Pesto

This pesto is delicious on chicken or fish, or over whole-grain pasta with broccoli, tomatoes, and any other mixture of cruciferous vegetables and leafy greens.

Ingredients:
2 poblano peppers, seeded and chopped
1/2 cup cilantro leaves
1/3 cup Parmesan cheese, freshly grated
2½ tablespoons walnuts
2 garlic cloves
1/8 teaspoon red pepper flakes, crushed (or to taste)
1/8 teaspoon salt
1/8 teaspoon black pepper, freshly ground
1/3 cup extra-virgin olive oil

Preparation: In a food processor, combine poblano peppers, cilantro, cheese, walnuts, garlic, red pepper flakes, salt, and black pepper. Process until finely chopped. With the motor running, add oil in a steady stream. Process until smooth. Makes about 1½ cups, or 12 servings of 2 tablespoons each.

Nutritional information per serving:
Calories: 92
Fat: 8 g
Saturated fat: 1 g
Carbohydrate: 1 g
Total sugars: 0 g
Protein: 1 g
Sodium: 10 mg
Cholesterol: 3 mg
Dietary fiber: < 1 g

Herbed Flaxseed and Olive Oil Dressing

Ingredients:
1/3 cup fresh lemon juice
2 teaspoons grainy brown mustard
2 tablespoons fresh chives, chopped
2 tablespoons parsley, chopped
1 teaspoon dried basil
1 teaspoon dried oregano leaves
1 garlic clove, roughly chopped
2 tablespoons flaxseed oil
1/4 cup extra-virgin olive oil
1/8 teaspoon fine sea salt
1/8 teaspoon black pepper, freshly ground

Preparation: In a food processor or blender, combine lemon juice, mustard, chives, parsley, basil, oregano, and garlic; blend until smooth. Slowly add oil in a fine stream and blend until slightly creamy. Season with salt and pepper. Makes 1 cup, or 8 servings.

Nutritional information per serving:
Calories: 95
Fat: 10 g
Saturated fat: 1 g
Carbohydrate: 2 g
Total sugars: < 1 g
Protein: 1 g
Sodium: 25 mg
Cholesterol: 0 mg
Dietary fiber: < 1 g

The Anti–Breast Cancer Cookbook

Lemon-Herb Marinade (for Fish)

Ingredients:
1/3 cup fresh lemon juice
1 teaspoon lemon zest
2 teaspoons horseradish
1 garlic clove, peeled and halved
3/4 teaspoon dried oregano leaves
1/4 teaspoon dried basil
1/4 teaspoon salt
1/4 teaspoon black pepper, freshly ground
1/3 cup high-quality olive oil

Preparation: Combine lemon juice, lemon zest, horseradish, garlic, oregano, basil, salt, and pepper in a blender or food processor. Blend together and gradually add oil in a steady stream. Pour over fish fillets (4–6 ounces) of choice, turning once to coat. Cover and refrigerate 8 hours to overnight. Cook fish on grill or broiler. Makes enough marinade for 8 servings of fish.

Nutritional information per serving:
Calories: 80
Fat: 9 g
Saturated fat: 1 g
Carbohydrate: 1 g
Total sugars: < 1 g
Protein: < 1 g
Sodium: 50 mg
Cholesterol: 0 mg
Dietary fiber: < 1 g

Low-Fat Creamy Ranch Dressing

Many times I have seen a nutritious salad destroyed by 300–400 calories— mainly fat calories—of ranch dressing poured on top of it. This dressing is much lower in calories than your typical ranch and contains very little fat, but it is still full of flavor.

Ingredients:
1/4 cup plain low-fat yogurt
1/4 cup olive oil mayonnaise
1 tablespoon white vinegar
2 teaspoons Dijon mustard
1/4 teaspoon dried thyme leaves
1/4 teaspoon black pepper, freshly ground
1 green onion, minced

Preparation: Place all ingredients in a small bowl. Mix with a fork until well blended. Cover and refrigerate. Stir dressing before each use to achieve a uniform, best consistency. Makes about 1 cup, or 8 servings of 2 tablespoons each.

Nutritional information per serving:
Calories: 29
Fat: 2 g
Saturated fat: < 1g
Carbohydrate: 2 g
Total sugars: < 1 g
Protein: 1 g
Sodium: 80 mg
Cholesterol: 3 mg
Dietary fiber: 0 g

Miso-Tahini Sauce

This dressing is wonderful on salads and sandwiches (especially falafel and other pita bread sandwiches) and is great on top of warm brown rice sprinkled with sunflower seeds.

Ingredients:
1/2 cup water, more as needed to thin
2 tablespoons mellow (light) miso
2/3 cup tahini
1 garlic clove, peeled and minced
1 teaspoon orange zest
2 teaspoons lemon juice
1/2 teaspoon paprika
1/2 teaspoon ground cumin
2 tablespoons fresh parsley, finely chopped

Preparation: In a medium bowl, whisk together all ingredients. For a thinner sauce, add more water. Makes 10 servings of 2 tablespoons each.

Nutritional information per serving:
Calories: 95
Fat: 8 g
Saturated fat: 1 g
Carbohydrate: 2 g
Total sugars: < 1 g
Protein: 4 g
Sodium: 180 mg
Cholesterol: 0 mg
Dietary fiber: < 1 g

The Anti–Breast Cancer Cookbook

Pomegranate Vinaigrette

Ingredients:
2 cups 100 percent pomegranate juice
1 teaspoon sugar
1/2 teaspoon salt
2½ teaspoons balsamic vinegar
2 teaspoons extra-virgin olive oil

Preparation: Over medium-high heat in a medium, stainless-steel or nonreactive saucepan, bring the pomegranate juice to a boil. Reduce heat slightly but keep juice boiling, until reduced to less than 1 cup, approximately 10–15 minutes. Remove from heat. Stir in sugar, salt, vinegar, and oil; set aside to cool. Use immediately or place in a resealable glass or plastic container and chill. Keeps for up to 1 week in the refrigerator but best if used within a few days. Makes 2 cups, or 16 servings of 2 tablespoons each.

Nutritional information per serving:
Calories: 28
Fat: < 1 g
Saturated fat: 0 g
Carbohydrate: 6 g
Total sugars: 4 g
Protein: 0 g
Sodium: 120 mg
Cholesterol: 0 mg
Dietary fiber: 0 g

Raspberry Vinaigrette

Ingredients:
1/4 cup balsamic vinegar
1/4 cup raspberry all-fruit preserves
3/4 teaspoon black pepper, freshly ground
1/2 teaspoon salt
3/4 cup extra-virgin olive oil

Preparation: Place vinegar, preserves, pepper, and salt in a blender or food processor and puree until evenly combined. Add oil in a steady stream and process until mixture is blended and smooth. Cover dressing tightly and store up to 2 weeks. Shake well before using. Dressing is most flavorful if brought to room temperature before serving. Makes 2 cups, or 16 servings of 2 tablespoons each.

Nutritional information per serving:
Calories: 115
Fat: 10 g
Saturated fat: 1 g
Carbohydrate: 3 g
Total sugars: 2 g
Protein: 0 g
Sodium: 73 mg
Cholesterol: 0 mg
Dietary fiber: 0 g

Roasted Pepper Dressing

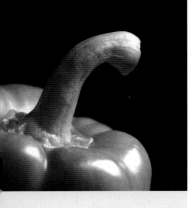

Turmeric is rich in the antioxidant curcumin, which has been shown to have potent cancer-fighting properties. It also gives turmeric its rich yellow color.

Ingredients:
1 large red bell pepper
1/2 cup rice vinegar (balsamic or red wine vinegar will work in a pinch)
6 garlic cloves, peeled
1 tablespoon Thai red curry paste (more to taste)
1/8 teaspoon turmeric
3/4 teaspoon salt
1/2 cup extra-virgin olive oil
1/2 cup flaxseed oil

Preparation: Preheat broiler. Cut bell pepper into quarters and remove seeds and membranes with a sharp knife. Place pepper pieces on a foil-lined baking sheet, skin-side up; broil until blackened, about 7–10 minutes. Meanwhile, set out a ceramic bowl filled with very cold water. Remove peppers from oven and immerse in cold water. Slide peels off and drain peppers on a towel. Place pepper pieces in a blender or food processor. Add vinegar, garlic, curry paste, turmeric, and salt. Process on high, until mixture becomes thick and is well emulsified. With motor running, slowly add olive oil and flaxseed oil. Serve immediately or store in refrigerator in an airtight container. Makes 20 servings of 2 tablespoons each.

Nutritional information per serving:
Calories: 76
Fat: 8 g
Saturated fat: 1 g
Carbohydrate: 1 g
Total sugars: < 1 g
Protein: < 1 g
Sodium: 105 mg
Cholesterol: 0 mg
Dietary fiber: < 1 g

The Anti–Breast Cancer Cookbook

Salsa Verde—Italian Style

This salsa is perfect with chicken or fish, or just spread it on toasted bread. It contains lutein-rich leafy greens, as well as magnesium and monounsaturated fat from the almonds and olive oil.

Ingredients:
1/4 cup raw almonds
1 cup fresh flat-leaf parsley leaves, packed
1/2 cup fresh basil, packed
1/2 cup cilantro leaves, packed
2 large garlic cloves, chopped
1/8 teaspoon red chili flakes
1/2 teaspoon salt
Pepper, freshly ground
2/3 cup extra-virgin olive oil
1 tablespoon white wine vinegar

Preparation: Preheat oven to 400°F. Spread almonds in a pie pan or baking sheet and toast until lightly golden, about 7–8 minutes. Transfer to a plate to cool. Place a large pot of water over medium heat and bring to a boil. Sprinkle with salt. Add parsley and basil and blanch for 1 minute. Drain leaves and transfer immediately to a colander; run under cold water or soak in an ice bath. When leaves have cooled, squeeze dry. Place almonds, parsley, basil, cilantro, garlic, chili flakes, salt, and 3 or 4 grinds of pepper into a blender or food processor. Turn on and gradually pour in oil, until mixture becomes a thick puree. Pour into a resealable container and refrigerate overnight. Before serving, allow to return to room temperature. Stir in vinegar just prior to serving to prevent discoloration. Makes about 20 servings of 2 tablespoons each.

Nutritional information per serving:
Calories: 68
Fat: 6 g
Saturated fat: 1 g
Carbohydrate: 1 g
Total sugars: < 1 g
Protein: < 1 g
Sodium: 75 mg
Cholesterol: 0 mg
Dietary fiber: < 1 g

Sesame Dressing

Nutritional information per serving:
Calories: 85
Fat: 9 g
Saturated fat: 1 g
Carbohydrate: < 1 g
Total sugars: 0 g
Protein: 0 g
Sodium: 45 mg
Cholesterol: 0 mg
Dietary fiber: 0 g

Ingredients:
2 tablespoons rice vinegar
2 teaspoons Dijon mustard
3/4 teaspoon fresh ginger root, minced
1/8 teaspoon fine sea salt
1/8 teaspoon black pepper, freshly ground
1/2 cup toasted sesame oil

Preparation: Whisk together all ingredients in a small bowl or blend in a food processor. Makes 12 servings of about 1 tablespoon each.

Shallot Dressing

This dressing is delicious over brown or red rice with some chopped parsley and English cucumbers. It's also wonderful on a mixed-green salad with roasted peppers, chopped nuts, and goat cheese.

Nutritional information per serving:
Calories: 100
Fat: 9 g
Saturated fat: 1 g
Carbohydrate: 2 g
Total sugars: 1 g
Protein: 1 g
Sodium: 20 mg
Cholesterol: 0 mg
Dietary fiber: 0 g

Ingredients:
2 tablespoons high-quality olive oil
3 large shallots, minced
2 medium garlic cloves, minced
2 tablespoons grape-seed oil
1½ teaspoons granulated white sugar
2 tablespoons wheat-free tamari or reduced-sodium soy sauce
1 teaspoon toasted sesame oil
1/8 teaspoon fine sea salt
1 tablespoon rice vinegar
1½ tablespoons lemon juice
Black pepper, freshly ground, to taste

Preparation: Place a small saucepan over medium-low heat. Add oil and heat about 1 minute. Add shallots and garlic; heat until fragrant and light brown. Remove from heat; add grape-seed oil, sugar, tamari or soy sauce, sesame oil, salt, vinegar, lemon juice, and black pepper. Stir until sugar dissolves and all ingredients are well mixed. Serve immediately over salad or a heated grain. Cover and refrigerate for up to 3 days. Makes about 6 servings of 1½–2 tablespoons each.

Tangerine Balsamic Sauce

This vitamin C–rich sauce is perfect to drizzle over fish or poultry. I like to brush it on scallops prior to broiling and then serve the scallops with a bit more sauce for added flavor.

Ingredients:
1½ cups fresh tangerine juice
1/3 cup balsamic vinegar
1½ teaspoons sugar
1½ teaspoons orange zest, grated

Preparation: In a medium saucepan, combine tangerine juice, vinegar, and sugar. Cover and cook over medium-high heat about 8–9 minutes, until thickened. Remove saucepan from heat and stir in orange zest. Serve immediately. Makes 6 servings of 1/4 cup each.

Nutritional information per serving:
Calories: 40
Fat: 0 g
Saturated fat: 0 g
Carbohydrate: 10 g
Total sugars: 9 g
Protein: < 1 g
Sodium: < 1 mg
Cholesterol: 0 mg
Dietary fiber: < 1 g

Toasted Pumpkin-Seed Pesto

Ingredients:
1 bunch fresh basil
1 large garlic clove, peeled
1/2 cup extra-virgin olive oil
1/3 cup pumpkin seeds, shelled and toasted
1/4 teaspoon salt
1/4 teaspoon white pepper
3 tablespoons Parmigiano-Reggiano cheese, freshly grated
1/8 teaspoon nutmeg

Preparation: Wash basil thoroughly in cold water. Remove stems. Place in food processor with garlic; pulse to chop. With machine running, gradually add oil in a slow stream. Stop machine and add pumpkin seeds, salt, pepper, cheese, and nutmeg. Pulse a few times to coarsely chop pumpkin seeds. Makes 8 servings of about 2 tablespoons each.

Nutritional information per serving:
Calories: 86
Fat: 9 g
Saturated fat: 1 g
Carbohydrate: < 1 g
Total sugars: 0 g
Protein: 2 g
Sodium: 30 mg
Cholesterol: < 1 mg
Dietary fiber: 0 g

Tricolored Pepper Salsa

This beta-carotene-rich salsa is fantastic with broiled or grilled fish or chicken or any other dish that could use some extra tang.

Ingredients:
1 red bell pepper, finely chopped
1 yellow bell pepper, finely chopped
1 orange bell pepper, finely chopped
1 large red onion, finely chopped
1 teaspoon garlic, crushed
1 tablespoon cilantro, finely chopped
½–1 jalapeño pepper, seeded and minced
1/2 teaspoon Tabasco sauce
Salt and pepper to taste

Preparation: Mix all ingredients together in a large bowl and stir until well blended. Chill approximately 1 hour before serving. Drain off excess liquid before topping entrée. Makes about 2 cups, or 6 servings of 1/3 cup each.

Nutritional information per serving:
Calories: 36
Fat: 0 g
Saturated fat: 0 g
Carbohydrate: 8 g
Total sugars: 2 g
Protein: 1 g
Sodium: < 1 mg
Cholesterol: 0 mg
Dietary fiber: 2 g

Walnut Vinaigrette

Ingredients:
1/4 cup champagne vinegar (or other high-quality white wine vinegar)
2 teaspoons Dijon mustard
1/2 shallot, finely chopped
2 teaspoons fresh thyme leaves, finely chopped
3/4 cup walnut oil
3/4 extra-virgin olive oil
1/2 teaspoon fine sea salt
1/4 teaspoon black pepper, freshly ground
3 tablespoons walnuts, chopped

Preparation: Place vinegar, mustard, shallot, and thyme in a food processor; cover and process until smooth. With the machine running, add walnut oil and olive oil slowly, about 1 tablespoon at a time, until emulsified. (If the mixture gets too thick, add about 1 tablespoon ice water.) Season with salt and pepper; stir in walnuts. Makes about 2 cups, or 16 servings of 2 tablespoons each.

Nutritional information per serving:
Calories: 100
Fat: 11 g
Saturated fat: 1 g
Carbohydrate: < 1 g
Total sugars: < 1 g
Protein: < 1 g
Sodium: 30 mg
Cholesterol: 0 mg
Dietary fiber: < 1 g

The Anti–Breast Cancer Cookbook

SIDE DISHES

 Vegetarian   Vegan   Gluten-Free

Aromatic Basmati Rice ❧ ⊘ 74
Bean Salad with Creamy Herb Dressing ❧ ⊘ 75
Black-Eyed Peas with Kale ❧ ϒ ⊘ 76
Buckwheat with Broccoli and Red Bean Sauce ❧ ϒ ⊘ ...77
Butternut Squash and Shiitake Mushroom Risotto ❧ ⊘ ...78
Cabbage and Carrot Slaw ❧ ⊘ 79
Cauliflower-Potato-Pepper Bake ❧ ⊘ 80
Eggplant Sauté with Italian Herbs and Shallots ❧ ⊘ 81
Haricots Verts with Toasted Walnut-Cranberry Vinaigrette ❧ ϒ ⊘ ...82
Herb-Roasted Brussels Sprouts and Purple Potatoes ❧ ϒ ⊘ ...83
Italian Pasta Salad ❧ ϒ ⊘ 84
Kale and Potato Vegetable Hash ❧ ⊘ 85
Maple-Roasted Acorn Squash ❧ ϒ ⊘ 86
Mashed Rosemary Yams and Potatoes ❧ ⊘ 87
Moroccan Potato Casserole ❧ ϒ ⊘ 88
Pecan-Apple Sweet Potatoes ❧ ϒ ⊘ 89
Quinoa with Black Beans ❧ ϒ ⊘ 90
Quinoa with Edamame ❧ ⊘ 91
Roasted Carrots and Parsnips ❧ ϒ ⊘ 92
Ron's Quinoa Tabbouleh ❧ ϒ ⊘ 93
Rosemary Polenta and Roasted Vegetables ❧ ⊘ 94
Squash Risotto with Arugula ❧ ⊘ 95
Wild Rice Casserole ❧ ϒ ⊘ 96
Yellow Split-Pea Puree ❧ ⊘ 97

Aromatic Basmati Rice

Most people know about white basmati rice, but brown basmati has more valuable whole-grain antioxidants and it is loaded with flavor. This recipe is rich in lycopene, vitamin A, and magnesium.

Ingredients:
1 tablespoon olive oil or unsalted butter
1/2 cup red bell pepper, finely diced
1/2 cup yellow bell pepper, finely diced
1/2 cup medium yellow onion, chopped
1 garlic clove, crushed
1/2 teaspoon ground turmeric
1½ cups brown basmati rice, well rinsed
3 cups reduced-sodium chicken or vegetable broth
3 tablespoons dark raisins
3 tablespoons dried currants or chopped dates
1 cinnamon stick
1/2 teaspoon salt
3 tablespoons slivered almonds
4 whole sprigs cilantro

Preparation: In a large skillet over low heat, warm oil or melt butter. Add red pepper, yellow pepper, onion, garlic, and turmeric. Cook, stirring frequently, about 9–10 minutes, until onion is tender. Stir in rice, broth, raisins, currants or dates, cinnamon stick, and salt. bring to a boil and reduce heat to low. Cover and cook about 15 minutes, or until liquid is absorbed. Remove skillet from heat and let cool for about 5 minutes. Remove and discard cinnamon stick. Fluff rice with a fork. Transfer rice to a platter; top with almonds and cilantro and serve. Makes 6 servings.

Nutritional information per serving:
Calories: 180
Fat: 4 g
Saturated fat: 1 g
Carbohydrate: 30 g
Total sugars: 16 g
Protein: 5 g
Sodium: 212 mg
Cholesterol: 5 mg
Dietary fiber: 2 g

The Anti–Breast Cancer Cookbook

Bean Salad with Creamy Herb Dressing

Fiber-rich beans are slowly digested, so they don't spike blood sugar levels and may help prevent diabetes. Plus, they are full of antioxidants such as saponins and phytic acid, which have been shown to slow the growth of cancerous cells in lab studies.

Ingredients:

1 cup cooked chickpeas (rinsed and drained if using canned)
1 cup cooked cannellini beans (rinsed and drained if using canned)
1 cup cooked black beans (rinsed and drained if using canned)
2 scallions, thinly sliced (green part only)
1 cup orange or red bell pepper, diced (about 1 medium pepper)
2 tablespoons low-fat Greek yogurt
1½ tablespoons low-fat sour cream
1 tablespoon grainy brown mustard
1 teaspoon fresh lemon juice
2 teaspoons fresh rosemary or 1/2 teaspoon dried rosemary
1/4 teaspoon fine sea salt
1/4 teaspoon black pepper, freshly ground
1/4 teaspoon turmeric
2 teaspoons extra-virgin olive oil
1/4 cup fresh parsley or cilantro leaves, chopped

Preparation: Place chickpeas, cannellini beans, black beans, scallions, and bell pepper in a large mixing bowl. To make dressing, place yogurt, sour cream, mustard, lemon juice, rosemary, salt, black pepper, and turmeric in a small food processor and whirl to combine. With the motor running, drizzle in oil. (Alternatively, all dressing ingredients can be whisked together in a small bowl.) Add dressing to bean mixture and stir to combine. If serving immediately, top with chopped parsley or cilantro. (Alternatively, cover and refrigerate for up to 8 hours, adding the herbs just before serving.) Makes 4 servings.

Nutritional information per serving:
Calories: 226
Fat: 5 g
Saturated fat: < 1 g
Carbohydrate: 35 g
Total sugars: 8 g
Protein: 11 g
Sodium: 380 mg
Cholesterol: 3 mg
Dietary fiber: 11 g

Black-Eyed Peas with Kale

This recipe also works well with other dried beans, such as adzuki beans, black beans, or lentils. If you use green or brown lentils, trim the cooking time from 1 hour to about 45 minutes.

Ingredients:
1½ cups dried black-eyed peas
8 cups water
1 cup yellow onion, chopped (about 1 medium onion)
4 garlic cloves, peeled
1 bay leaf
1 teaspoon dried sage
1/2 teaspoon sea salt
4 cups kale (lacinato is better than curly), de-stemmed, coarsely chopped, packed
1/4 cup toasted sesame or olive oil
3 tablespoons fresh lemon juice
1/4 teaspoon sweet smoked paprika
Pinch crushed red pepper flakes (to taste, optional)
Black pepper, freshly ground, to taste

Preparation: Soak peas overnight in a large soup pot of water. (Alternatively, place peas in a large soup pot with enough cold water to cover by 3 inches. Bring to a boil and continue to boil about 1 minute. Remove from heat. Cover and let stand 1 hour.) Drain peas; return to pot. Add water, onion, garlic, bay leaf, and sage; bring to a boil. Reduce heat, cover, and simmer until peas are tender, at least 1 hour. Stir in salt and kale; cook about 4 minutes. Drain and place in a large, nonreactive bowl. (You can reuse the drained liquid as a broth to make vegetable soup—just cover and chill.) Add oil, lemon juice, paprika, and pepper flakes; toss. Season with black pepper. Makes 8 servings.

Nutritional information per serving:
Calories: 125
Fat: 9 g
Saturated fat: 1 g
Carbohydrate: 13 g
Total sugars: 1 g
Protein: 3 g
Sodium: 125 mg
Cholesterol: 0 mg
Dietary fiber: 3 g

Buckwheat with Broccoli and Red Bean Sauce

A friend passed this recipe along to me, noting that you can make the sauce with just about any type of bean as well as other varieties of nut butter or tahini.

Ingredients:
4 cups reduced-sodium vegetable broth
1 large bunch broccoli
2 cups buckwheat groats
1/4 teaspoon salt (preferably sea salt or kosher salt)
1 can (15½ ounces) kidney beans, rinsed and drained
1 large roasted red pepper in water (about half the contents of a
    typical jar)
1 shallot, sliced
2 tablespoons fresh lemon juice
2 tablespoons almond butter, stirred to smooth consistency (so oil
    is integrated)
1/2 teaspoon chili powder
1/4 teaspoon ground cumin
1/4 teaspoon smoked sweet paprika
1/4 teaspoon ground coriander
1/8 teaspoon cayenne pepper (optional)
1/4 cup fresh parsley, chopped

Preparation: Place broth in a large saucepan and bring to a boil. Peel broccoli stems with a sharp knife and slice into 1/2-inch-thick rounds; set aside. Break or cut broccoli tops into bite-size florets. Add groats and salt to boiling broth. Cover and simmer 10–12 minutes, or until liquid has been absorbed. In the meantime, place beans, red pepper, shallot, lemon juice, almond butter, chili powder, cumin, paprika, coriander, cayenne pepper, and parsley in a food processor or blender and puree. Boil some water in a medium soup pot and place broccoli stems and florets in a steamer basket. Steam about 5 minutes, or until bright green and slightly tender. Place groats on a serving platter or 8 separate dinner plates. Top with steamed broccoli and bean sauce and serve. Makes 8 servings of about 1 cup each.

Nutritional information per serving:
Calories: 186
Fat: 3 g
Saturated fat: < 1 g
Carbohydrate: 32 g
Total sugars: 3 g
Protein: 9 g
Sodium: 325 mg
Cholesterol: 0 mg
Dietary fiber: 9 g

Butternut Squash and Shiitake Mushroom Risotto

This dish could easily serve as a main course. Pair it with lentil soup and nine-grain bread for a wholesome meal. You can substitute vegetable broth for a vegetarian version.

Ingredients:
1 small butternut squash (about 1 pound)
4 cups reduced-sodium chicken broth, divided
2 teaspoons high-quality olive oil
1/3 cup yellow onion, diced
Fine sea salt to taste
Black pepper, freshly ground, to taste
1¼ cups shiitake mushrooms, washed very well and sliced
2 small garlic cloves, minced
1 shallot, minced
3 tablespoons fresh basil, finely chopped
1 teaspoon fresh thyme, minced
1 cup Arborio rice
1/4 cup Parmesan cheese, freshly shaved, divided

Preparation: Preheat oven to 350°F. Cut squash in half and remove seeds. Place squash, cut-side up, in a ceramic baking dish. Cook for 45–55 minutes, until tender. (Alternatively, you can microwave the squash on high power until tender, about 13–15 minutes, in stages of 2–3 minutes.) Cool slightly, scoop out flesh in tablespoon-size pieces, and reserve. Discard skin. Meanwhile, heat broth in a saucepan on medium-high heat until boiling; lower heat to simmer. Place a separate, medium pot over medium heat and add oil. Add onion and cook until translucent, about 5–6 minutes. Season with salt and pepper. Add mushrooms and cook until tender, about 7–8 minutes. Add garlic, shallot, basil, and thyme; cook about 2 minutes, until fragrant. Add rice to the onion mixture; stir and reduce heat to low. Add about 1 cup broth to the rice mixture. Stir occasionally until broth is absorbed. Continue to add broth about 1/2 to 1 cup at a time, stirring at regular intervals. Cook 20–25 minutes, until creamy but al dente. Stir in 2 tablespoons cheese and squash. Remove from heat and season with additional salt and pepper if desired. (If the risotto is too thick, add a little more broth until it becomes creamy.) Divide among 4 serving dishes (soup plates work well) and sprinkle with remaining cheese. Serve immediately. Makes 4 servings of about 1/2 cup each.

Nutritional information per serving:
Calories: 265
Fat: 5 g
Saturated fat: 2 g
Carbohydrate: 45 g
Total sugars: 18 g
Protein: 10 g
Sodium: 180 mg
Cholesterol: 6 mg
Dietary fiber: 4 g

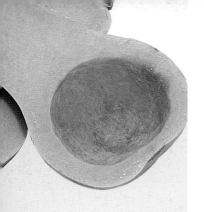

Cabbage and Carrot Slaw

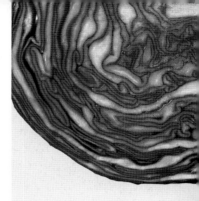

Cabbage contains organosulfur compounds known to inhibit the growth of cancer. Red cabbage also contains antioxidant anthocyanins, the same health-promoting compounds found in berries and red or purple grapes. Try this dish with Grilled Chicken Wraps (see page 137) or Spicy Turkey Relleno Burgers (see page 144).

Ingredients:
2 cups carrots, peeled and coarsely shredded
1 cup red cabbage, coarsely shredded
1 cup green or white cabbage, coarsely shredded
1 cup red bell pepper, diced (about 1 medium red bell pepper)
3 scallions, minced
2 tablespoons rice vinegar
1½ tablespoons sesame oil
2 teaspoons lime juice
2 teaspoons clover honey
2 teaspoons reduced-sodium, wheat-free tamari
2 tablespoons feta or goat cheese, crumbled

Preparation: Combine carrots, red cabbage, green cabbage, pepper, and scallions in a large serving bowl. To make dressing, whisk together vinegar, oil, lime juice, honey, and tamari in a small bowl. Pour dressing over vegetables and mix until evenly combined. Let stand 15–20 minutes; add cheese and serve. Makes 8 servings.

Nutritional information per serving:
Calories: 55
Fat: 3 g
Saturated fat: 1 g
Carbohydrate: 5 g
Total sugars: 3 g
Protein: 1 g
Sodium: 95 mg
Cholesterol: 0 mg
Dietary fiber: 2 g

Cauliflower-Potato-Pepper Bake

This recipe is high in antioxidant beta-carotene, anthocyanins, and isothiocyanates. The isothiocyanates in the cauliflower change estrogen metabolism, creating a by-product that is less likely than the original estrogen metabolite to promote the growth of breast cells, which may lower your risk of developing cancer.

Ingredients:
Nonstick cooking spray
1 medium purple potato, peeled and cut into bite-size pieces
1 medium red bell pepper, seeded and coarsely chopped
2½ cups cauliflower florets, cut into bite-size pieces
1 tablespoon olive oil
1/2 teaspoon garlic powder
1/4 teaspoon onion powder
Salt to taste
Black pepper, freshly ground, to taste
2 tablespoons reduced-fat (2 percent) dairy milk
1/4 cup reduced-fat feta cheese, crumbled or flaked
2 tablespoons fresh flat-leaf parsley, minced

Preparation: Preheat oven to 400°F. Spray a 9-inch baking dish with nonstick cooking spray and set aside. In a medium bowl, toss potato, red pepper, and cauliflower with oil, garlic powder, and onion powder. Season with salt and pepper as desired. Transfer vegetables to baking dish. Drizzle milk evenly over top. Sprinkle with cheese. Cover tightly with foil and bake 35–40 minutes, or until vegetables are tender. If desired, finish by placing dish under broiler for about 30 seconds, watching carefully, until cheese browns but does not burn. Garnish with parsley and serve hot. Makes 6 servings.

Nutritional information per serving:
Calories: 92
Fat: 3 g
Saturated fat: 1 g
Carbohydrate: 12 g
Total sugars: 2 g
Protein: 4 g
Sodium: 40 mg
Cholesterol: 4 mg
Dietary fiber: 2 g

The Anti–Breast Cancer Cookbook

Eggplant Sauté with Italian Herbs and Shallots

I found this recipe online many years ago and gradually made changes until it suited my tastes. Feel free to add more garlic or shallots or experiment with other Italian cheeses.

Ingredients:
2 teaspoons high-quality olive oil
2 medium garlic cloves, crushed
2 shallots, diced
5½ cups eggplant, cut into 1-inch cubes (1 medium eggplant, about 1½ pounds)
1/4 teaspoon fine sea salt
1/8 teaspoon black pepper, freshly ground
1½ tablespoons fresh basil, chopped (or 1½ teaspoons dried basil)
1½ tablespoons fresh oregano, chopped (or 1½ teaspoons dried oregano)
3 tablespoons grated provolone cheese

Preparation: Place a medium skillet over medium heat. Add oil and heat about 1 minute. Add garlic and shallot; heat 1–2 minutes. Add eggplant, salt, pepper, oregano, and basil; sauté until eggplant is tender and lightly browned on both sides, 6–7 minutes. Remove from heat and place on a serving platter. Sprinkle with cheese and serve. Makes 4 servings.

Nutritional information per serving:
Calories: 75
Fat: 3 g
Saturated fat: 1 g
Carbohydrate: 9 g
Total sugars: 2 g
Protein: 3 g
Sodium: 155 mg
Cholesterol: 4 mg
Dietary fiber: 4 g

Haricots Verts with Toasted Walnut-Cranberry Vinaigrette

The walnuts and walnut oil in this recipe contain omega-3 fatty acids, which have anti-inflammatory properties and may reduce the risk of developing cancer. You can substitute dried tart cherries for the dried cranberries.

Ingredients:
1/3 cup walnut oil
2 shallots, minced
3 tablespoons plus 2 teaspoons sherry or other red wine vinegar, divided
2 tablespoons fresh mint, chopped
1/2 teaspoon coarse kosher salt
1 teaspoon sugar
1/2 teaspoon plus additional black pepper, freshly ground
1/3 cup dried cranberries
1½ pounds haricots verts, trimmed
1/2 cup walnuts, chopped

Preparation: To make vinaigrette, whisk together oil, shallots, sherry, mint, salt, sugar, and pepper in a small bowl. Mix in cranberries; set aside. Place a large soup pot full of salted water on high heat and bring to a boil. Meanwhile, fill a large bowl with water and ice; set aside. Add haricots verts to boiling water and cook until tender but crisp, about 3–4 minutes. Drain haricots verts and transfer to bowl with ice water to cool. Drain. Toss haricots verts, walnuts, and vinaigrette together in a large bowl. Transfer to platter and serve. Makes 6 servings.

Nutritional information per serving:
Calories: 210
Fat: 14 g
Saturated fat: 1 g
Carbohydrate: 18 g
Total sugars: 5 g
Protein: 3 g
Sodium: 110 mg
Cholesterol: 0 mg
Dietary fiber: 4 g

Herb-Roasted Brussels Sprouts and Purple Potatoes

Ingredients:
3/4 pound Brussels sprouts (preferably large)
1 cup yellow onions, thinly sliced
1 tablespoon cold-pressed canola or olive oil, divided
3/4 teaspoon dried rosemary
1/2 teaspoon fine sea salt, divided
3/4 pound small (1–2 inches in diameter) purple potatoes
Salt to taste
Black pepper to taste

Preparation: If your oven holds 2 baking sheets side by side, place rack in the center. If not, arrange racks in top and bottom thirds of oven. Preheat oven to 400°F. Remove tough outer leaves from Brussels sprouts and cut crosswise into 3–4 rounds, about 1/2 inch thick. In a medium bowl, combine Brussels sprouts and onions. Add 2 teaspoons oil, rosemary, and 1/4 teaspoon salt; mix to coat. Spread vegetables in thick layer on a foil-covered baking sheet. Place potatoes in same bowl and drizzle with remaining 1 teaspoon oil. Add remaining salt and mix to coat. Place potatoes on second foil-covered baking sheet; set aside. Place both baking sheets in oven. Bake Brussels sprouts with onions for 15 minutes. Stir, mixing in any browned bits, and rearrange in a thick layer. Roast until Brussels sprouts are almost tender, about another 12–15 minutes, then return Brussels sprout mixture to mixing bowl. Bake potatoes for 30 minutes, or until a knife pierces the largest ones easily. Transfer potatoes to cutting board and cut crosswise into 1/2-inch slices. Add potatoes to Brussels sprout mixture. Season to taste with salt and pepper and serve. Makes 4 servings.

Nutritional information per serving:
Calories: 140
Fat: 3 g
Saturated fat: < 1 g
Carbohydrate: 24 g
Total sugars: 7 g
Protein: 4 g
Sodium: 100 mg
Cholesterol: 0 mg
Dietary fiber: 5 g

Italian Pasta Salad

This recipe is perfect for parties, luncheons, or cookouts. If you need to serve a larger crowd, the recipe doubles or triples easily.

Ingredients:

Vinaigrette
2 tablespoons extra-virgin olive oil
2 tablespoons white wine vinegar
1/2 teaspoon dried basil
1/2 teaspoon dried oregano leaves
1/2 teaspoon black pepper, freshly ground

Salad
8 ounces whole-wheat fusilli pasta or gluten-free, brown-rice
   fusilli pasta
1 cup frozen edamame, shelled
1 cup broccoli florets
1 small zucchini, sliced in thin quarter rounds
1/2 red bell pepper, diced
1/2 cup carrot, shredded
1/4 medium red onion, very thinly sliced
1 cup grape tomatoes, halved
1/8 teaspoon fine sea salt

Preparation: To prepare vinaigrette, place oil, vinegar, basil, oregano, and pepper in a small bowl and stir until combined; set aside. To prepare salad, bring a large pot of water to a boil; add pasta. Cook according to package instructions, but about 4–5 minutes before pasta is done cooking, add edamame. Cook until pasta is al dente. Add broccoli florets but heat only 20–25 seconds. Drain water from pot and transfer pasta mixture to a large serving bowl. Toss in zucchini, pepper, carrot, and onion. Pour vinaigrette over vegetables and stir until combined. Cover and refrigerate until ready to serve. Just before serving, mix in tomatoes and sprinkle with salt. Makes 8 servings of about 1 cup each.

Nutritional information per serving:
Calories: 165
Fat: 5 g
Saturated fat: 1 g
Carbohydrate: 25 g
Total sugars: 11 g
Protein: 6 g
Sodium: 145 mg
Cholesterol: 0 mg
Dietary fiber: 9 g

Kale and Potato Vegetable Hash

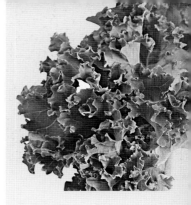

This veggie hash is great with dinner or with a breakfast of sunny-side-up omega-3-enriched eggs. If you can find and afford organic potatoes and kale, use them in this recipe.

Ingredients:
2 tablespoons olive oil
2 tablespoons nonhydrogenated spread (such as Smart Balance or Fleischmann's Olive Oil Spread)
1 garlic clove, peeled and thinly sliced
1/2 pound Yukon Gold potatoes, diced
1/2 pound purple potatoes, diced
1/2 pound fresh shiitake mushrooms, washed very well and diced
1 medium red bell pepper, seeded and diced
1 small acorn squash, diced
1 shallot, finely chopped
1/2 teaspoon fine sea salt
1/2 teaspoon black pepper, freshly ground
1 cup kale, chopped
4 sprigs fresh sage

Preparation: Place oil in a large skillet over medium heat and tilt so that skillet bottom is well coated. Add spread and heat until warm and melted. Add garlic, potatoes, mushrooms, pepper, squash, and shallot; season with salt and pepper. Cook for 25 minutes, stirring occasionally, until potatoes are tender. Add kale and sage to skillet; continue heating until kale has wilted, about 5–6 minutes, and serve. Makes 6 servings.

Nutritional information per serving:
Calories: 170
Fat: 6 g
Saturated fat: 1 g
Carbohydrate: 25 g
Total sugars: 2 g
Protein: 4 g
Sodium: 170 mg
Cholesterol: 0 mg
Dietary fiber: 4 g

Maple-Roasted Acorn Squash

Ingredients:
Nonstick cooking spray
6 small acorn squash (about 1 pound each), halved lengthwise and seeded
1½ tablespoons cold-pressed canola or olive oil, divided
1/2 teaspoon salt
1/2 teaspoon black pepper, freshly ground, divided
1½ cups yellow onion (about 1 large or 2 medium onions), diced
2 large (preferably organic), Fuji, Braeburn, or Rome Beauty apples (unpeeled), cored and diced
1/3 cup roasted pistachio nuts, shelled and coarsely chopped
2 tablespoons fresh sage, chopped
1 tablespoon fresh thyme, chopped
1/3 cup pure maple syrup, divided
Thyme sprigs (optional)

Preparation: Preheat oven to 350°F. Spray a roasting pan with nonstick cooking spray. Brush about 1 teaspoon oil on cut sides of squash halves. In a small bowl, mix together salt and pepper. Season squash halves with half of the salt/pepper mixture. Arrange squash, cut-side down, in pan. Cover pan tightly with foil; bake 30 minutes. Uncover pan; turn squash cut-side up. Bake 30 more minutes and remove from oven. Meanwhile, warm remaining oil in a skillet over medium-high heat. Add onion and sauté 5 minutes. Add apples, nuts, sage, thyme, and remaining salt/pepper mixture; sauté 3 minutes. Divide apple mixture equally among squash halves, mounding it into each cavity. Drizzle each with about 1/2 tablespoon maple syrup. Bake, uncovered, an additional 20 minutes (25–30 minutes if prepared ahead of time and refrigerated). Serve hot, garnished with thyme sprigs. Makes 12 servings of 1/2 squash each.

Nutritional information per serving:
Calories: 178
Fat: 2 g
Saturated fat: < 1 g
Carbohydrate: 36 g
Total sugars: 11 g
Protein: 3 g
Sodium: 55 mg
Cholesterol: 1 mg
Dietary fiber: 5 g

Mashed Rosemary Yams and Potatoes

To add some fiber you can leave the peel on or partially peel the potatoes in this recipe. Using organic, unpeeled potatoes is an even better option because the skin is typically less dense and is free of synthetic pesticide residue.

Ingredients:
5 garlic cloves
3 tablespoons olive oil
1 pound potatoes, peeled and cubed
1 pound sweet potatoes, peeled and cubed
1/3 cup reduced-fat (2 percent) dairy milk
2 tablespoons unsalted butter
1/2 teaspoon dried rosemary
4 tablespoons Parmesan cheese, freshly grated, divided
1/2 teaspoon salt
1/2 teaspoon black pepper, freshly ground
Nonstick cooking spray

Preparation: Preheat oven to 350°F. Place garlic in a small oven-proof bowl and drizzle with oil; roast for 30 minutes, until very soft. Cool, peel, and reserve oil. Cover potatoes and yams in a large pot of salted water and boil until tender, about 25–30 minutes. Drain, reserving about 1 cup of liquid. Place potatoes in a mixing bowl. Add milk, butter, rosemary, garlic, and reserved oil; mash until smooth, adding reserved cooking liquid as needed to attain desired consistency. Mix in 3 tablespoons cheese, salt, and pepper. Spray an 8 x 8 x 2–inch baking dish with nonstick cooking spray and add potato mixture. Sprinkle with remaining 1 tablespoon cheese. Bake for about 45 minutes, until heated through and golden brown on top. Makes 6 servings.

Nutritional information per serving:
Calories: 190
Fat: 9 g
Saturated fat: 3 g
Carbohydrate: 23 g
Total sugars: 3 g
Protein: 4 g
Sodium: 189 mg
Cholesterol: 12 mg
Dietary fiber: 3 g

Moroccan Potato Casserole

Ingredients:
Nonstick cooking spray
4 medium garlic cloves
3/4 teaspoon salt, divided
1 teaspoon sweet smoked paprika
1/2 teaspoon chili powder
1/2 teaspoon ground cumin
1/4 teaspoon ground cayenne pepper
3/4 cup fresh parsley, chopped
1/2 cup fresh cilantro, chopped
1 tablespoon fresh lemon juice
3 tablespoons red wine vinegar
3 tablespoons olive oil, divided
1/4 teaspoon black pepper, freshly ground
1½ pounds organic baby Red Bliss potatoes, quartered or cut into
    1/2-inch-thick cubes
1 red bell pepper, diced
1 yellow bell pepper, diced
1 green bell pepper, diced
4 celery stalks, cut into 2-inch pieces
1 pound vine-ripe tomatoes, each cut into 6–8 wedges
1 cup cooked chickpeas (rinsed and drained if canned)

Preparation: Preheat oven to 350°F. To make herb sauce, spray a large shallow baking dish with nonstick cooking spray. Combine garlic, 1/2 teaspoon salt, paprika, chili powder, cumin, and cayenne pepper in a food processor. Process until mixture forms a paste. Add parsley and cilantro; pulse a few times to blend. Add lemon juice, vinegar, and 2 tablespoons oil; blend. Season with remaining 1/4 teaspoon salt and black pepper. In a large bowl, combine potatoes, yellow pepper, green pepper, and celery. Add herb sauce and toss to coat. Transfer to baking dish. Scatter tomatoes over potato mixture. Drizzle remaining 1 tablespoon oil on top and cover with foil; bake for 35 minutes. Remove foil, add chickpeas, and continue baking until vegetables are tender, about 1 hour longer. Serve warm. Makes 8 servings.

Nutritional information per serving:
Calories: 175
Fat: 6 g
Saturated fat: < 1 g
Carbohydrate: 26 g
Total sugars: 4 g
Protein: 5 g
Sodium: 265 mg
Cholesterol: 0 mg
Dietary fiber: 5 g

The Anti–Breast Cancer Cookbook

Pecan-Apple Sweet Potatoes

This dish is wonderful in the fall, when apples are at their peak of ripeness. Most nonhydrogenated spreads are dairy-free, which would make the dish vegan. You can also use unsalted butter instead of spread, which will make the dish vegetarian but will slightly change the nutritional information.

Ingredients:
3 pounds (about 6 or 7) sweet potatoes
Nonstick cooking spray
5 apples (any combination of Fuji, Braeburn, Empire, or Rome Beauty will work well), peeled, cored, and sliced into large, thin pieces
1/3 cup sugar
1 cup water
3 tablespoons nonhydrogenated buttery spread (such as Smart Balance or Fleischmann's Olive Oil Spread)
1½ tablespoons cornstarch
1/2 teaspoon salt
1/2 teaspoon ground cinnamon
1/4 teaspoon nutmeg
1/4 teaspoon ground ginger
1/3 cup pecans, chopped

Preparation: Preheat oven to 350°F. Place potatoes in a large pot and cover by 2 inches with water. Bring to a boil, reduce heat, and simmer until potatoes are tender, about 20–25 minutes (test tenderness by cutting into a large piece with a knife). Remove from heat, drain water, and let dry on a towel or paper towels. Let potatoes cool until they can be touched and peeled. Spray a large casserole dish with nonstick cooking spray. Cut potatoes into 1/2-inch-thick slices and alternate with apple slices in the casserole. In a saucepan, place sugar, water, nonhdrogenated spread, cornstarch, and salt; bring to a boil. Lower heat and simmer until thickened. Pour mixture over potatoes and apples. Sprinkle with cinnamon, nutmeg, and ginger. Top with pecans. Bake until lightly browned and fragrant, about 1 hour. Let cool or serve immediately. This dish is delicious, warm or cold, the second day. Makes 10 servings.

Nutritional information per serving:
Calories: 190
Fat: 4 g
Saturated fat: < 1 g
Carbohydrate: 37 g
Total sugars: 18 g
Protein: 2 g
Sodium: 150 mg
Cholesterol: 0 mg
Dietary fiber: 4 g

Quinoa with Black Beans

Quinoa is an edible grain-like seed related to beets and spinach. It is rich in fiber, iron, calcium, and protein and contains the essential amino acid lysine. Quinoa takes on the flavor of other ingredients in recipes, so cooks often add extra onions and spices to quinoa-containing dishes.

Ingredients:
1 teaspoon olive oil
1 cup yellow onion, chopped
1/2 cup red bell pepper, finely diced
3 garlic cloves, peeled and chopped
3/4 cup quinoa
1½ cups reduced-sodium vegetable broth
1 teaspoon ground cumin
1/4 teaspoon turmeric
1/4 teaspoon salt
1/4 teaspoon black pepper
Pinch cayenne pepper
1 cup frozen corn kernels
2 each (15½ ounces each) black beans, rinsed and drained
1/2 cup fresh cilantro, chopped

Preparation: Place a medium saucepan over medium heat and add oil. Tilt saucepan to coat bottom with oil. Stir in onion, bell pepper, and garlic; sauté until lightly browned. Mix quinoa into the saucepan and cover with vegetable broth. Season with cumin, turmeric, salt, black pepper, and cayenne pepper. Bring mixture to a boil. Cover, reduce heat, and simmer about 20 minutes. Fluff with a fork. Add corn and stir. Simmer 5–7 minutes until heated through, stirring occasionally. Mix in beans and cilantro; cook an additional 2–3 minutes, until warm throughout, and serve. Makes 6 servings.

Nutritional information per serving:
Calories: 159
Fat: 3 g
Saturated fat: 0 g
Carbohydrate: 26 g
Total sugars: 3 g
Protein: 7 g
Sodium: 350 mg
Cholesterol: 0 mg
Dietary fiber: 6 g

The Anti–Breast Cancer Cookbook

Quinoa with Edamame

Ingredients:
1 cup quinoa
2 cups reduced-sodium vegetable broth
2 cups (about 10 ounces) edamame, frozen, shelled, and thawed
1/2 cup red bell pepper, chopped
1/2 cup yellow bell pepper, chopped
2 teaspoons lime zest
1½ tablespoons lime juice
1½ tablespoons sesame oil
1 teaspoon dried tarragon
1/2 teaspoon dried oregano leaves
1/2 teaspoon fine sea salt
1/2 teaspoon black pepper, freshly ground
3 tablespoons raw cashew pieces
3 tablespoons goat cheese, crumbled

Preparation: Place quinoa in a dry skillet over medium heat. Toast, stirring frequently, for about 5 minutes. Transfer to a fine sieve and rinse thoroughly. Meanwhile, bring broth to a boil in a medium saucepan over high heat. Add quinoa and return to a boil. Cover, reduce heat to low, and simmer gently for 8–10 minutes. Remove lid and, without stirring the quinoa, add edamame. Cover and continue to cook until edamame is tender and quinoa has softened a bit, about 7–9 minutes. Drain any remaining water and place in a large ceramic mixing bowl. Add red pepper and yellow pepper to quinoa mixture and toss to combine. To make dressing, whisk together lime zest, lime juice, sesame oil, tarragon, oregano, salt, and pepper in a large bowl. Pour dressing over quinoa and stir until uniformly distributed. Transfer to a serving platter or separate bowls or plates. Top with cashews and cheese and serve. Makes 6 servings.

Nutritional information per serving:
Calories: 220
Fat: 11 g
Saturated fat: 2 g
Carbohydrate: 28 g
Total sugars: 2 g
Protein: 12 g
Sodium: 280 mg
Cholesterol: 6 mg
Dietary fiber: 6 g

Roasted Carrots and Parsnips

Parsnips are a creamy-white root vegetable from the same family as carrots, fennel, celeriac, and parsley root. They are low in calories and sugar content and rich in fiber, vitamin C, vitamin K, copper, and folate.

Ingredients:
1 pound fresh carrots, peeled
1 pound fresh parsnips, peeled
3 tablespoons high-quality olive oil
1/2 teaspoon salt
1/2 teaspoon black pepper, freshly ground
1½ teaspoons fresh rosemary, chopped
1 teaspoon fresh sage, chopped
1/4 cup water

Preparation: Preheat oven to 350°F and place rack in lower third of oven. Cut carrots on the diagonal into approximately 3/4-inch-thick pieces. Halve parsnips crosswise in the narrow section. Diagonally cut the narrow portions into 3/4-inch-thick slices. Quarter the wider portions lengthwise and core. Then diagonally cut the flesh into 3/4-inch-thick slices. Toss parsnips and carrots with oil, salt, pepper, rosemary, and sage in a large bowl. Spread in a large shallow baking pan (1 inch deep) and pour water on top. Roast vegetables until tender, about 50–55 minutes. Makes 8 servings.

Nutritional information per serving:
Calories: 110
Fat: 5 g
Saturated fat: < 1 g
Carbohydrate: 15 g
Total sugars: 5 g
Protein: 1 g
Sodium: 145 mg
Cholesterol: 0 mg
Dietary fiber: 5 g

The Anti–Breast Cancer Cookbook

Ron's Quinoa Tabbouleh

This highly nutritious tabbouleh comes from Dr. Ron Glick, medical director of the Center for Integrative Medicine at the University of Pittsburgh Medical Center. He says it is great with tofu or feta on top and can be served with a healthy protein, such as fish or chicken, as well as in vegetarian dishes. It's made with quinoa rather than bulgur wheat, so it's gluten-free.

Ingredients:
1⅓ cups water
2/3 cup quinoa, soaked in a bowl of water for 5–10 minutes, then strained into a separate bowl
1/2 bunch green onions, diced
1/2 cup red bell pepper (about 1/2 pepper), diced
2 bunches flat-leaf parsley, de-stemmed and chopped
1/3 cup baby carrots, diced
2/3 cup walnuts, chopped
1/3 cucumber (optional), diced
1 cup (more if you like) cherry or grape tomatoes, sliced in half or quartered (depending on size)
1/2 cup dried cranberries (Craisins by Ocean Spray are Ron's choice, although they are sugary)
1/2 cup fresh or bottled lemon juice
1/2 cup extra-virgin olive oil
Black pepper, freshly ground, to taste

Preparation: Place water in a medium soup pot and bring to a boil. Add quinoa and return to a boil. Reduce heat and simmer for 10 minutes, covered. Remove from burner and set aside but leave covered and let cool. Meanwhile, place onions, bell pepper, parsley, carrots, walnuts, cucumber, tomatoes, and cranberries in a very large nonreactive bowl. Add cooled quinoa and stir. Add lemon juice, oil, and black pepper. Serve or refrigerate in a sealed container for up to 1 week. Makes 12 servings.

Nutritional information per serving:
Calories: 195
Fat: 12 g
Saturated fat: 1 g
Carbohydrate: 18 g
Total sugars: 6 g
Protein: 3 g
Sodium: 15 mg
Cholesterol: 0 mg
Dietary fiber: 3 g

Rosemary Polenta and Roasted Vegetables

Ingredients:

Roasted Vegetables
1 medium zucchini, diced
1 red bell pepper, cored and diced into 1½-inch-square pieces
1 green bell pepper, cored and diced into 1½-inch-square pieces
1 large tomato, cored and cut into eighths
2 celery ribs, sliced diagonally into 1/2-inch-thick pieces
8 garlic cloves, peeled
1 teaspoon dried thyme
Black pepper, freshly ground
3 tablespoons olive oil, divided
2 medium onions, cut into slices ½ inch thick
Salt to taste

Polenta
4½–5 cups water
1/2 teaspoon salt
1¼ cups yellow or white cornmeal
1 tablespoon unsalted butter, cut into tiny pieces
2 tablespoons rosemary, freshly snipped (or 2 teaspoons dried rosemary)
1/4 cup Parmesan cheese, freshly grated

Preparation: Preheat oven to 425°F. To prepare vegetables, place zucchini, red pepper, green pepper, tomato, celery, and garlic in a large bowl. Sprinkle with thyme, black pepper, and 2 tablespoons oil; toss to coat. Spread vegetables on a large baking sheet in a single layer; set aside. Pour remaining 1 tablespoon olive oil into a pie plate or 9- or 10-inch shallow pan and spread evenly to coat. Carefully place onions in the dish, keeping them intact. Rub the bottom of the onions in the oil to coat; turn each slice over. Place vegetables and onions in oven and cook 25–30 minutes, removing midway (at about 15 minutes) to turn with tongs or a spatula. When the vegetables are lightly brown and tender, remove from oven and season with salt. Let cool. To prepare polenta, place water in a large saucepan or stock pot. Heat at medium-high and add salt; bring to a boil. Reduce heat to medium and whisk in cornmeal. Whisk until polenta is thick and begins to pull away from sides of pan, about 16–18 minutes. Stir in butter and cheese. Serve polenta topped with roasted vegetables. Makes 8 servings.

Nutritional information per serving:
Calories: 190
Fat: 8 g
Saturated fat: 2 g
Carbohydrate: 25 g
Total sugars: 34 g
Protein: 4 g
Sodium: 160 mg
Cholesterol: 7 mg
Dietary fiber: 3 g

Squash Risotto with Arugula

When choosing a butternut squash, look for one that is all one color, preferably solid beige. Choose a heavy one, so it is rich in beta-carotene and vitamin C.

Ingredients:
1 butternut squash (about 3½–4 pounds)
1¾ cups water
2 cups reduced-sodium vegetable broth
Nonstick cooking spray
2 cups baby arugula
1/4 teaspoon black pepper, freshly ground, divided
1½ teaspoons olive oil
1/2 cup yellow onion, finely diced
1 cup Arborio or other short-grain rice
1/4 cup dry white wine
2 tablespoons reduced-fat (2 percent) dairy milk
1/4 cup Parmesan cheese, freshly grated

Preparation: Preheat oven to 375°F. Cut squash in half lengthwise; discard seeds and membrane. Place squash halves, cut-sides down, on a baking sheet. Bake for 50 minutes or until squash is tender. Cool. Peel squash; mash pulp. Set aside 1 cup pulp, reserving remaining pulp, if desired, for another recipe such as soup or puree. Bring water and broth to a simmer in a large saucepan. Keep warm over low heat. Place a Dutch oven coated with cooking spray over medium-high heat; add arugula and sauté 2 minutes or until wilted. Place arugula in a bowl; sprinkle with 1/8 teaspoon black pepper. Set aside. Place oil in Dutch oven. Add onion; sauté about 3 minutes or until lightly browned. Add rice and sauté about 1–2 minutes, stirring. Stir in wine and 1/2 cup broth mixture from saucepan. Stirring constantly, cook 3–4 minutes or until liquid is nearly absorbed. Add 2 cups broth mixture, 1/2 cup at a time, stirring constantly. Wait until each portion of liquid is absorbed before adding the next. Stir in the 1 cup squash pulp. Repeat procedure with remaining 1¼ cups broth mixture. Stir in arugula mixture and milk. Remove from heat; stir in cheese. Sprinkle with remaining 1/8 teaspoon black pepper. Makes 6 servings of about 3/4 cup each.

Nutritional information per serving:
Calories: 279
Fat: 3 g
Saturated fat: 1 g
Carbohydrate: 57 g
Total sugars: 7 g
Protein: 7 g
Sodium: 125 mg
Cholesterol: 4 mg
Dietary fiber: 7 g

Wild Rice Casserole

This casserole combines brown rice and wild rice, but you can substitute wehani or basmati rice for a portion of the brown rice and red or black rice for the wild rice. This is a great holiday recipe that is rich in fiber and deliciously seasoned.

Ingredients:
4 cups water
1/2 teaspoon salt, divided
3/4 cup long-grain brown rice
3/4 cup wild rice blend
1 tablespoon olive oil
1 small yellow onion, chopped
1 pound fresh mushrooms, washed very well and sliced (I use a
    combination of shiitake and cremini mushrooms)
1/2 cup parsley, finely chopped
1 cup celery, diced
1/4 teaspoon crumbled sage
1/4 teaspoon dried rosemary
1/8 teaspoon black pepper
1/8 teaspoon dried marjoram
1/8 teaspoon dried thyme
1/2 cup walnuts, chopped or in pieces

Preparation: Bring water to a boil; add 1/4 teaspoon salt, brown rice, and wild rice. Lower to a simmer, then cover and cook until rice is tender but still firm, about 35–40 minutes. Remove from heat and set aside. Preheat oven to 350°F and place a large oven-proof skillet or ceramic flame-top roaster over medium heat. Add oil and heat about 30–45 seconds. Add onion and mushrooms; sauté about 4–6 minutes, until onion becomes transparent and mushrooms have softened. Add parsley, celery, and rice; stir to combine. Add sage, rosemary, pepper, marjoram, thyme, remaining 1/4 teaspoon salt, and walnuts; stir again. Cover and place in oven; bake for 15 minutes and serve. Makes 8 servings.

Nutritional information per serving:
Calories: 198
Fat: 7 g
Saturated fat: < 1 g
Carbohydrate: 30 g
Total sugars: 2 g
Protein: 6 g
Sodium: 129 mg
Cholesterol: 0 mg
Dietary fiber: 3 g

The Anti–Breast Cancer Cookbook

Yellow Split-Pea Puree

Ingredients:
8 ounces dried yellow split peas
2 cups water
2 medium yellow onions, thinly sliced separately, divided
1 medium carrot, peeled and sliced
1 small leek, washed very well and chopped
2 small celery ribs, sliced
1/4 teaspoon dried thyme
1/4 teaspoon dried marjoram
2 teaspoons fresh lemon juice
1/4 teaspoon salt
1/4 teaspoon black pepper, freshly ground
Nonstick cooking spray
1 tablespoon unsalted butter

Preparation: Place peas in a large bowl and cover with some water by 1 inch. Let them sit for at least 1 hour and as much as overnight. Drain and rinse with some water a few times. Add peas and some water to a large saucepan. Add 1 onion, leek, celery, thyme, and dried marjoram; simmer over low to low-medium heat for about 30 minutes, until the peas have softened and the vegetables are tender. Pour off any unabsorbed liquid and place vegetable mixture in a food processor or blender; pulse or process until smooth. Transfer to a shallow heat- or ovenproof dish and season with lemon juice, salt, and pepper. Stir until well combined. Preheat oven broiler. Spray a skillet with nonstick cooking spray and place over medium heat. Add butter and remaining 1 onion; heat until onion is caramelized, about 6–7 minutes, turning as necessary. Pour onion and butter on top of vegetable mixture. Place baking dish in oven and heat about 5–7 minutes, until onion and top of puree are lightly browned. (Mixture can also be finished by baking in a regular oven for about 8 minutes at 350°F.) Makes 8 servings.

Nutritional information per serving:
Calories: 135
Fat: 2 g
Saturated fat: 1 g
Carbohydrate: 21 g
Total sugars: 4 g
Protein: 8 g
Sodium: 65 mg
Cholesterol: 4 mg
Dietary fiber: 8 g

SOUPS AND SALADS

Vegetarian

Vegan

Gluten-Free

Soups

Acorn Squash and Apple Soup 99
Almond and Celery Soup 100
Angela's Aromatic Chicken Stew 101
Beef Stew with Sun-Dried Tomatoes 102
Black Bean and Pumpkin Soup 103
Broccoli and Leek Soup 104
Cauliflower and Jarlsberg Soup 105
Chipotle Turkey and Bean Chili 106
Cocoa-Scented Black Bean Chili 107
Creamy Carrot Soup 108
Curried Red Lentil Soup 109
Lentil and Chickpea Stew 110
Mahi Mahi Fisherman's Stew 111
Miso Soup with Udon Noodles 112
Spiced Pumpkin Soup 113
Turkey and Winter Vegetable Stew 114
Vegetarian Vegetable Soup 115
White-Bean and Poblano Chili 116

Salads

Arugula and White-Bean Salad 117
Asian Sesame Salad with Soba Noodles 118
Chicken and Navy Bean Salad 119
Grilled Corn and Shrimp Salad 120
Grilled Salmon Salad 121
Japanese Miso Cabbage Salad 122
Jicama, Green Bean and Pomegranate-Pecan Salad 123
Mango-Ginger-Carrot Salad 124
Mixed Greens and Papaya Salad with Cumin-Lime Vinaigrette 125
Mushroom Barley Salad 126
Nutty Pea Salad 127
Panzanella Bread Salad 128
Roasted Beets, Greens and Walnut Salad 129
Sesame Beef, Spinach and Watercress Salad 130
Vegetarian Cobb Salad with Citrus-Miso Dressing 131

Acorn Squash and Apple Soup

Ingredients:
1 medium acorn squash (about 1 pound)
1 tablespoon olive oil
1 medium yellow onion, chopped
1 leek (white part only), rinsed well and chopped
1 sweet-tart apple (such as Braeburn, Fuji, or Granny Smith),
    peeled, cored, and chopped
3 cups reduced-sodium chicken or vegetable broth
1/3 cup low-fat sour cream
1/4 teaspoon sea salt
1/4 teaspoon black pepper, freshly ground
2 tablespoons pumpkin seeds
Additional broth to thin soup (optional)

Preparation: Preheat oven to 375°F. Cut acorn squash in half lengthwise; remove seeds and pulp. Set on a rimmed baking sheet. Bake until flesh is tender when pierced, 55–70 minutes (depending on size). Remove squash from oven and let cool. Meanwhile, place a large, heavy pan over medium-high heat and add oil; warm oil about 1 minute. Add onion and leek to oil and sauté for about 4 minutes, until onion is translucent. Add apple and cook over medium heat for about 1 minute. Scrape out squash pulp and combine with apple mixture. Reduce heat to medium-low, cover, and cook about 5 minutes, stirring often. Add broth and sour cream to the pan, cover, and bring to a boil over high heat. Reduce heat to low, season with salt and pepper, and simmer about 30 minutes. Remove pan from heat and let soup cool for a few minutes. In a blender or food processor, puree soup in batches until smooth. Return soup to pan and reheat just before serving. Add more broth to thin soup as desired. Garnish each serving with 1/2 tablespoon pumpkin seeds. Makes 4 servings.

Nutritional information per serving:
Calories: 120
Fat: 4 g
Saturated fat: < 1 g
Carbohydrate: 18 g
Total sugars: 6 g
Protein: 3 g
Sodium: 330 mg
Cholesterol: 5 mg
Dietary fiber: 3 g

Almond and Celery Soup

Ingredients:
1 medium yellow onion, finely chopped (about 1 cup)
6 celery stalks, finely chopped
1½ tablespoons parsley, coarsely chopped
1 teaspoon dried dill weed
1/2 teaspoon fine sea salt
1/2 cup (about 2 ounces) raw or blanched almonds
2 cups reduced-sodium chicken or vegetable broth
2 cups organic reduced-fat (1 or 2 percent) dairy milk or
    unflavored, fortified soy milk
1 large omega-3-enriched egg yolk, lightly beaten
1/4 cup plain, nonfat Greek yogurt
1 tablespoon fresh chives, chopped

Preparation: Place a large saucepan over medium heat. Add onion, celery, parsley, dill, salt, almonds, broth, and milk; bring to a boil. Reduce heat and simmer gently for 12–14 minutes, until vegetables are tender. Remove from heat and let cool for 4–5 minutes. Pour soup into blender or food processor and process until smooth. Return to a clean saucepan (or wipe other saucepan clean). Stir egg yolk into the yogurt. Add yogurt mixture to soup and stir until blended. Reheat soup over low heat, until warm but not boiling. Ladle into small bowls and sprinkle with chives. Makes 6 servings.

Nutritional information per serving:
Made with 1 percent dairy milk
Calories: 125
Fat: 6 g
Saturated fat: 1 g
Carbohydrate: 11 g
Total sugars: 3 g
Protein: 7 g
Sodium: 260 mg
Cholesterol: 38 mg
Dietary fiber: 3 g

The Anti–Breast Cancer Cookbook

Angela's Aromatic Chicken Stew

This recipe comes from Angela Raso, an amazing cook and close friend of the family. She recommends adding the frozen peas just as you finish preparing the stew so they maintain their crunch. Celery and basil contain the antioxidant phytochemical luteolin, a bioflavonoid known to have potent cancer-fighting properties. If desired, serve over a bed of steamed brown rice or other whole grain.

Ingredients:
2 tablespoons olive oil
6 boneless, skinless chicken breasts, cubed (preferably free-range chicken)
1 cup celery, diced
1 cup yellow onion (about 1 medium onion), diced
3 tablespoons parsley, chopped
3 tablespoons fresh basil, chopped
1 teaspoon fine sea salt
1 teaspoon black pepper, freshly ground
3/4 teaspoon poultry seasoning
4 cups reduced-sodium, 99 percent gluten-free and fat-free chicken stock or broth
2 cups whole baby carrots
3 tablespoons cornstarch
1 cup cold water
1 bag (1 pound) frozen peas

Preparation: Set an 8-quart soup pot over medium heat and coat with oil, tilting the pot a few times until oil is evenly distributed. Add chicken, celery, onion, parsley, basil, salt, pepper, and poultry seasoning. Let cook, stirring occasionally, about 20 minutes, until chicken and vegetables are evenly heated and chicken is lightly browned. Add stock and carrots and reduce heat to medium-low; let simmer about 40 minutes, until carrots are tender. In a small bowl, dissolve cornstarch in water and add to pot. Heat until thickened, stirring occasionally. Add peas and stir. Makes 10 servings.

Nutritional information per serving:
Calories: 185
Fat: 5 g
Saturated fat: < 1 g
Carbohydrate: 13 g
Total sugars: 4 g
Protein: 20 g
Sodium: 375 mg
Cholesterol: 44 mg
Dietary fiber: 3 g

Beef Stew with Sun-Dried Tomatoes

This hearty, protein- and antioxidant-rich stew requires a whole day to cook but is thoroughly worth the wait. Frying, grilling, or blackening red meat can create additional carcinogens, but stewing it keeps the temperature low, letting you avoid those cancer-causing molecules.

Ingredients:
1 cup sun-dried tomatoes (not packed in oil)
1½ pounds lean beef stew meat (preferably grass-fed)
12 small purple potatoes (about 1½ pounds)
1 medium yellow onion, cut into 8 wedges
8 ounces baby-cut carrots (about 30)
2¼ cups water, divided
1 teaspoon salt
1/2 teaspoon dried oregano leaves
1/2 teaspoon dried basil
1 bay leaf
2 tablespoons all-purpose unbleached white flour

Preparation: Rehydrate tomatoes by covering and soaking in 2 cups water for 1 to 2 hours; drain and coarsely chop. Mix tomatoes, meat, potatoes, onion, carrots, 2 cups water, salt, oregano, basil, and bay leaf in a 3½- to 4-quart crock pot. Cover and cook on low heat 8–9 hours or until vegetables and beef are tender. In a small bowl, mix together remaining 1/4 cup water and flour; gradually stir into beef mixture. Cover and cook on high heat 10–15 minutes or until slightly thickened. Remove bay leaf. Makes 6 servings.

Nutritional information per serving:
Calories: 350
Fat: 15 g
Saturated fat: 6 g
Carbohydrate: 25 g
Total sugars: 6 g
Protein: 28 g
Sodium: 455 mg
Cholesterol: 80 mg
Dietary fiber: 4 g

The Anti–Breast Cancer Cookbook

Black Bean and Pumpkin Soup

Ingredients:
1 tablespoon olive oil
1 medium onion, finely chopped
3 cups gluten-free, low-sodium vegetable stock or broth
2 cups ripe tomatoes, chopped (about 3 medium beefsteak or 6–7 Roma tomatoes)
1 can (15½ ounces) black beans, rinsed and drained
2 cans (15 ounces each) 100 percent pure pumpkin
1 cup evaporated skim milk or organic half-and-half
1½ teaspoons curry powder
1½ teaspoons ground cumin
1/4 teaspoon cayenne pepper
1/4 teaspoon salt
1/4 teaspoon black pepper, freshly ground
2 tablespoons fresh chives, chopped

Preparation: Place a soup pot over medium heat. Add oil and warm for about 1 minute. Add onion; sauté about 5–6 minutes, until soft and translucent. Add broth, tomatoes, beans, and pumpkin. Stir to combine and bring to a boil. Reduce heat to medium-low and stir in milk or half-and-half, curry, cumin, cayenne pepper, salt, and black pepper. Simmer 5 minutes and serve garnished with chives. Makes 6 servings.

Nutritional information per serving:
Made with evaporated skim milk
Calories: 200
Fat: 3 g
Saturated fat: 0 g
Carbohydrate: 34 g
Total sugars: 12 g
Protein: 9 g
Sodium: 290 mg
Cholesterol: 0 mg
Dietary fiber: 10 g

Broccoli and Leek Soup

Ingredients:
1½ tablespoons olive oil
3 leeks, rinsed and finely chopped (white and green portions)
3 small garlic cloves, minced
2 pounds fresh broccoli, trimmed, with florets and stalks cut into
    1-inch pieces
5 cups reduced-sodium vegetable stock
1 cup water
1/4 teaspoon sweet smoked paprika
1/4 teaspoon turmeric
1/4 teaspoon sea salt
1/4 teaspoon black pepper, freshly ground
2/3 cup reduced-fat sour cream or vegan sour cream (such as
    Tofutti brand), divided
2 tablespoons fresh chives, finely chopped
2 tablespoons walnuts, chopped

Preparation: Place a large soup pot over medium heat. Add oil and heat about 1 minute. Add leeks and garlic; sauté until softened, about 4–5 minutes. Add broccoli and sauté, stirring frequently, until slightly softened, about 2–4 additional minutes. Add stock and water. Season with paprika, turmeric, salt, and pepper; bring to a boil. Reduce heat and simmer, partially covered, until vegetables are tender, about 18–20 minutes. Remove from heat and let stand for about 3–4 minutes. Stir in 1/2 cup sour cream. Use a blender or food processor to puree the soup in batches until smooth. Return soup to pot and reheat for a few minutes over low-medium heat. Ladle the soup into warmed bowls and garnish with remaining sour cream, chives, and chopped walnuts. Serve immediately. Makes 6 servings.

**Nutritional information
per serving:**
Calories: 190
Fat: 6 g
Saturated fat: < 1 g
Carbohydrate: 24 g
Total sugars: 6 g
Protein: 6 g
Sodium: 280 mg
Cholesterol: 2 mg
Dietary fiber: 6 g

The Anti–Breast Cancer Cookbook

Cauliflower and Jarlsberg Soup

Cauliflower is a high-fiber vegetable loaded with vitamin C and folate. It also contains isothiocyanates, whose intake has been associated with a reduced risk of breast cancer.

Ingredients:
1 large cauliflower
5 cups reduced-sodium vegetable stock
6 ounces farfalle pasta (preferably whole-wheat or mixed whole-grain)
2/3 cup whole milk (preferably organic, DHA-enriched)
1/2 teaspoon nutmeg, freshly grated
Pinch of cayenne pepper
1/4 cup reduced-fat Jarlsberg Swiss cheese, cut into 1/2-inch pieces
Salt and black pepper, freshly ground, to taste
1/4 cup watercress, de-stemmed and chopped

Preparation: Cut central stalk and leaves from cauliflower and discard. Divide cauliflower into similarly sized florets. In a large pot, bring stock to a boil and add cauliflower. Simmer 10–12 minutes, until tender. Remove cauliflower with a slotted spoon and place in a blender or food processor. Add pasta to stock and simmer 10 minutes, until tender. Drain stock into a container, reserving pasta, and pour stock over cauliflower in a blender or food processor. Add milk, nutmeg, and cayenne pepper; blend until smooth. Press through a strainer into the empty pot and stir in pasta. Reheat soup, adding cheese after soup has warmed. Season with salt and pepper as desired. Add watercress and serve. Makes 6 servings.

Nutritional information per serving (extra salt not included):
Calories: 185
Fat: 2 g
Saturated fat: 1 g
Carbohydrate: 32 g
Total sugars: 6 g
Protein: 10 g
Sodium: 210 mg
Cholesterol: 6 mg
Dietary fiber: 5 g

Chipotle Turkey and Bean Chili

You can also make this chili using lean ground chicken, ground beef (grass-fed), or a vegetarian ground meat substitute. This chili is great on the second or third day, and it can be frozen in small containers for future use.

Ingredients:
1 tablespoon high-quality olive oil
1 medium yellow onion, diced
1/2 cup red bell pepper, diced
1/2 cup orange or yellow bell pepper, diced
2 carrots, peeled and diced
1 celery rib, diced
1 teaspoon chili powder
1 teaspoon ground cumin
1 pound lean ground turkey
2 cans (15 ounces each) diced fire-roasted tomatoes, undrained
3 chipotle chiles in adobo sauce, minced
2 tablespoons adobo sauce from chipotle chiles in adobo
1/2 teaspoon dried oregano
1/2 teaspoon dried basil
1/4 teaspoon cayenne pepper
1 can (15½ ounces) kidney beans, undrained
1 can (15½ ounces) black beans, undrained
1 can (15½ ounces) black-eyed peas, undrained
1/2 teaspoon sea salt, ground
1/2 teaspoon black pepper, freshly ground

Preparation: Place a large soup pot over medium heat and add oil; warm oil about 1 minute. Add onion, red bell pepper, orange bell pepper, carrots, and celery. Sauté until soft, about 10–12 minutes. Stir in chili powder and cumin until combined. Add ground turkey. Increase heat to high and cook until meat is browned through. Add tomatoes, chipotle chiles, adobo sauce, oregano, basil, and cayenne pepper; reduce heat to medium and heat for 30 minutes, stirring occasionally. Stir in kidney beans, black beans, and peas; cook for an additional 20–30 minutes, until liquid has dissolved. Season with salt and black pepper. Makes 8 servings.

Nutritional information per serving:
Calories: 250
Fat: 3 g
Saturated fat: < 1 g
Carbohydrate: 32 g
Total sugars: 5 g
Protein: 12 g
Sodium: 415 mg
Cholesterol: 35 mg
Dietary fiber: 10 g

The Anti–Breast Cancer Cookbook

Cocoa-Scented Black Bean Chili

Ingredients:
1 tablespoon olive oil
1 cup yellow onion, diced
1/2 teaspoon sea salt
3 celery stalks, diced
2 carrots, peeled and diced
2 chipotle chiles in adobo sauce, minced
1 medium red or orange bell pepper, seeded and diced
1/2 medium green bell pepper, seeded and diced
2 medium, ripe tomatoes, pureed in a blender or food processor
4 cups gluten-free, reduced-sodium vegetable broth
1 can (15½ ounces) black beans, rinsed and drained
1 can (15½ ounces) kidney beans, rinsed and drained
2 tablespoons unprocessed, unsweetened cocoa powder
1/2 teaspoon black pepper, freshly ground
1/2 teaspoon cumin
1/4 teaspoon smoked paprika
1/4 cup fresh cilantro, coarsely chopped

Preparation: Place a large pot or 5-quart Dutch oven over medium heat and add olive oil. Warm oil about 1 minute, and then add onion and salt. Cook, stirring occasionally, until onions are soft and translucent, about 5–6 minutes. Add celery, carrots, chiles in adobo sauce, red or orange pepper, and green pepper; continue cooking, stirring occasionally, until vegetables have softened, about 7–8 minutes. Add tomatoes and broth; bring to a boil. Reduce heat; simmer about 18–20 minutes or until vegetables are very tender. Stir in black beans, kidney beans, cocoa powder, black pepper, cumin, and paprika; return to a simmer for about 5 minutes. Stir in cilantro and serve. Makes 4 large servings.

Nutritional information per serving:
Calories: 216
Fat: 4 g
Saturated fat: < 1 g
Carbohydrate: 35 g
Total sugars: 8 g
Protein: 9 g
Sodium: 450 mg
Cholesterol: 0 mg
Dietary fiber: 12 g

Creamy Carrot Soup

This simple soup is not only easy to make, but it is very low in fat and calories and high in antioxidants, such as quercetin and beta-carotene. Substitute the unbleached white or whole-wheat pastry flour with rice flour to make this soup gluten-free.

Ingredients:
2 tablespoons olive oil
2 garlic cloves, chopped
3/4 cup yellow onion, diced
1 tablespoon ginger, peeled and chopped
3 cups carrots, peeled and chopped
4 cups gluten-free, reduced-sodium vegetable broth or stock
3 tablespoons brown rice, short- or medium-grain
1/2 teaspoon cumin
1/2 teaspoon sweet paprika
Pinch cayenne pepper
1/8 teaspoon salt
1/8 teaspoon black pepper
1 cup low-fat plain yogurt (preferably organic)
2½ tablespoons all-purpose unbleached white or whole-wheat
     pastry flour

Preparation: In a small stock pot, heat oil over a medium-high flame. Once oil is warm, add garlic, onions, and ginger; sauté until onions begin to soften and turn translucent, about 5–7 minutes. Add carrots, broth, and rice; season with cumin, paprika, cayenne, salt, and pepper. Simmer for 30 minutes or until carrots break apart easily. Using a blender or food processor, puree the soup until smooth. Return soup to the pot over medium heat. In a small bowl, combine yogurt and flour; blend until well mixed. Stir this mixture into the soup, being careful not to bring soup back to a boil. Makes 6 servings.

Nutritional information per serving:
Calories: 160
Fat: 6 g
Saturated fat: 1 g
Carbohydrate: 22 g
Total sugars: 7 g
Protein: 4 g
Sodium: 195 mg
Cholesterol: 5 mg
Dietary fiber: 4 g

The Anti–Breast Cancer Cookbook

Curried Red Lentil Soup

You can add other vegetables to this soup, such as chopped celery and carrots, to make it more of a stew. It is spicy and delicious. If you use brown or French green lentils, you will need to cook them for about 20 minutes longer than red lentils.

Ingredients:
4 cups water, more if necessary
2 cups red lentils
1 tablespoon olive oil
1 large sweet yellow onion, diced
2 cups baby spinach
2 tablespoons curry paste
1 tablespoon curry powder
1 teaspoon ground turmeric
1 teaspoon ground cumin
1 teaspoon chili powder
1/2 teaspoon salt
2 small garlic cloves, minced
1 teaspoon ginger root, minced
1 can (14½ ounces) tomato puree (with no salt added)

Preparation: Wash lentils in some cold water until water runs clear. Place a large soup pot containing water over high heat and bring to a boil. Reduce heat to low and add lentils. Simmer, covered, until lentils are tender, about 25 minutes. Add more water if necessary. While lentils cook, place a large skillet or saucepan over medium heat and add oil. Heat about 30 seconds or until oil is warm, then add onions and spinach. Cook about 10–12 minutes, until onions caramelize and spinach is wilted, stirring or shaking occasionally to prevent burning. Meanwhile, combine curry paste, curry powder, turmeric, cumin, chili powder, salt, garlic, and ginger in a mixing bowl; mix well. Add curry mixture to onion/spinach mixture; cook over high heat, stirring constantly, just 1–2 minutes. Stir in tomato puree and reduce heat to simmer. (If any water has not been absorbed from the lentils, drain it off.) Stir into lentils and serve immediately. Makes 6 servings.

Nutritional information per serving:
Calories: 285
Fat: 2 g
Saturated fat: < 1 g
Carbohydrate: 49 g
Total sugars: 7 g
Protein: 17 g
Sodium: 405 mg
Cholesterol: 0 mg
Dietary fiber: 12 g

Lentil and Chickpea Stew

If you use red lentils, reduce the cooking time by about 15 minutes.

Ingredients:
1 tablespoon high-quality olive oil
1/2 cup celery, chopped
2 cups baby spinach
2 small yellow onions, chopped (about 1½ cups)
4 or 5 fingerling potatoes, diced
1 teaspoon cumin or mild yellow curry powder
1/2 teaspoon ground turmeric
1/4 teaspoon ground cinnamon
1/4 teaspoon ground nutmeg
1/2 teaspoon fine sea salt, divided
2½ cups fresh, ripe tomatoes (beefsteak or Roma), diced
8 cups water, more if needed
1 cup lentils, dried and rinsed (red or brown work best, but green
    are fine)
2 cans (15 ounces each) chickpeas, rinsed and drained, or 3½ cups
    cooked chickpeas
1/4 teaspoon black pepper, freshly ground
1 teaspoon fresh lemon juice
1 tablespoon balsamic vinegar

Preparation: Place a large soup pot over medium heat. Add oil and warm about 45 seconds. Add celery, spinach, onions, and potatoes; stir and heat about 1 minute. Add cumin or curry powder, turmeric, cinnamon, nutmeg, and 1/4 teaspoon salt. Heat for 7–8 minutes, stirring occasionally. Add tomatoes and heat another 10–12 minutes. Add water, lentils, chickpeas, pepper, and remaining 1/4 teaspoon salt; bring to a boil. Reduce heat and simmer, partially covered, for 50–60 minutes (35–45 minutes if using red lentils), stirring occasionally. Add additional water if all of it evaporates. Just before serving, add fresh lemon juice and balsamic vinegar. Makes 8 servings.

**Nutritional information
per serving:**
Calories: 285
Fat: 3 g
Saturated fat: < 1 g
Carbohydrate: 55 g
Total sugars: 2 g
Protein: 10 g
Sodium: 300 mg
Cholesterol: 0 mg
Dietary fiber: 15 g

The Anti–Breast Cancer Cookbook

Mahi Mahi Fisherman's Stew

*This is a rich and zesty stew full of healthful nutrients.
Note that crabmeat is low in calories and high in protein but also contains a
lot of sodium and cholesterol.*

Ingredients:
2 tablespoons olive oil
1 large yellow onion, chopped
1/4 cup canned green chiles, drained and chopped
3 small garlic cloves, finely chopped
4 large or 6 medium fresh tomatoes, chopped
2 cups dry white wine
1 tablespoon orange zest, grated
1⅓ cups orange juice
1 tablespoon sugar
1 tablespoon fresh cilantro, snipped
1 teaspoon dried basil
1/2 teaspoon salt
1/2 teaspoon black pepper, freshly ground
1/2 teaspoon dried oregano leaves
2 teaspoons seafood seasoning
1½ cups gluten-free, reduced-fat chicken broth
1 pound fresh mahi mahi fillets, chopped into chunks
1 can (6½ ounces) minced clams, drained
1½ pounds uncooked shrimp, shelled and deveined
1 pound fresh crabmeat

Preparation: Place a 6-quart Dutch oven over medium heat and
add oil. Add onion, chiles, and garlic; cook until onion and chiles
are tender and garlic is fragrant, about 5–6 minutes. Stir in tomatoes, wine, orange zest, orange juice, sugar, cilantro, basil, salt, pepper, oregano, seafood seasoning, and broth; heat to boiling. Reduce
heat to low and simmer uncovered for 15 minutes. Carefully stir in
fish, clams, and shrimp. Increase heat to boiling and then reduce
heat. Cover and simmer until shrimp are pink and fish flakes easily
with a fork, about 8–10 minutes. Makes 8 servings.

**Nutritional information
per serving:**
Calories: 275
Fat: 6 g
Saturated fat: 1 g
Carbohydrate: 17 g
Total sugars: 12 g
Protein: 38 g
Sodium: 925 mg
Cholesterol: 230 mg
Dietary fiber: 2 g

Miso Soup with Udon Noodles

You can add or change any of the vegetables in this soup—try it with thinly sliced zucchini or finely shredded cabbage. Add cubed, firm tofu for an extra burst of protein. If you use a darker miso, decrease the amount by a few tablespoons because it is more salty than white miso.

Ingredients:
1 package (12 ounces) fresh udon noodles
6 cups reduced-sodium vegetable stock or broth
3/4 cup carrots, sliced into very thin pieces
3/4 cup small fresh broccoli florets
3/4 cup fresh snow peas, sliced diagonally
1 cup fresh shiitake mushrooms, washed very well and thinly sliced
2 tablespoons white miso (also called shiro miso)
2 green onions, diced

Preparation: Cook udon noodles according to package directions. Drain and set aside. Meanwhile, place stock or broth in a large saucepan and bring to a boil. Lower heat to medium; add carrots and cook until crisp-tender, about 2–3 minutes. Add broccoli and snow peas; cook until slightly tender but still bright green, about 1 minute. Add mushrooms and cook for just 30–45 seconds, until a bit softened. Remove soup from heat. Place miso in a small ceramic bowl. Add a ladleful of hot broth to miso and whisk until miso is completely dissolved. Pour miso mixture into soup pot. Stir in noodles and green onions and serve. Makes 6 servings.

Nutritional information per serving:
Calories: 250
Fat: 2 g
Saturated fat: 0 g
Carbohydrate: 49 g
Total sugars: 9 g
Protein: 11 g
Sodium: 565 mg
Cholesterol: 0 mg
Dietary fiber: 6 g

The Anti–Breast Cancer Cookbook

Spiced Pumpkin Soup

Ingredients:
6 cups reduced-sodium and gluten-free chicken or vegetable broth
   (chicken broth makes richer soup)
2 cans (15 or 16 ounces each) 100 percent pure pumpkin
1 cup yellow onion, thinly sliced
1 garlic clove, minced
1 teaspoon salt
1/2 teaspoon nutmeg
1/2 teaspoon cinnamon
1/2 teaspoon thyme
1/2 teaspoon white pepper
1/2 cup reduced-fat sour cream, at room temperature
2 tablespoons fresh parsley, chopped

Preparation: Stir together broth, pumpkin, onion, garlic, salt, nutmeg, cinnamon, thyme, and pepper in a large saucepan; cover and cook at medium heat until boiling. Reduce heat and simmer, uncovered, 20–22 minutes. Stir in sour cream and heat about 1 minute. Divide into 6 soup bowls or mugs and garnish each with about 1 teaspoon parsley. Makes 6 servings.

Nutritional information per serving:
Calories: 115
Fat: 2 g
Saturated fat: 1 g
Carbohydrate: 17 g
Total sugars: 7 g
Protein: 6 g
Sodium: 475 mg
Cholesterol: 10 mg
Dietary fiber: 6 g

Turkey and Winter Vegetable Stew

Wondering what to do with your extra turkey meat from the holidays? This richly flavored stew is full of vitamins, minerals, and protein. It can be served as soup or over a whole grain for a heartier meal.

Ingredients:
1½ tablespoons olive oil
1 pound cooked turkey white meat, diced
2⅓ cups reduced-sodium chicken or vegetable broth
2/3 cup dry red wine
2 garlic cloves, minced
2 shallots, thinly sliced
1 tablespoon fresh thyme, chopped
1/4 teaspoon sea salt, ground
1/4 teaspoon black pepper, freshly ground
1 bay leaf
2 cups butternut squash, peeled, seeded, and diced
1 cup parsnips, peeled and sliced
1 medium-large yam, peeled and chopped
3 celery ribs, chopped
1 medium yellow onion, thinly sliced
1/2 cup reduced-fat sour cream
3 tablespoons whole-wheat flour

Preparation: Place a large saucepan over medium heat. Add oil and heat about 1 minute. Add chicken and brown on all sides. Stir in broth and wine. Add garlic, shallots, thyme, salt, pepper, and bay leaf; bring mixture to a boil. Reduce heat, cover, and simmer 20 minutes. Mix in squash, parsnips, yam, celery, and onion; bring to a boil. Reduce heat to low and simmer 30 minutes, or until vegetables are tender. In a small bowl, blend together sour cream and flour. Gradually stir 1/2 cup of the hot stew into the sour cream/flour mixture. Add the sour cream mixture to the saucepan. Remove bay leaf and continue to cook, stirring occasionally, until soup has thickened, about 6–8 minutes. Makes 6 servings.

Nutritional information per serving:
Calories: 298
Fat: 4 g
Saturated fat: 1 g
Carbohydrate: 20 g
Total sugars: 3 g
Protein: 20 g
Sodium: 260 mg
Cholesterol: 50 mg
Dietary fiber: 3 g

Vegetarian Vegetable Soup

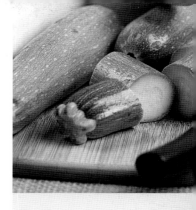

This soup is easy to make. It has loads of fiber and antioxidant vitamins and minerals. In a pinch, you can use frozen cauliflower, corn, and lima beans, and the soup will still turn out beautifully.

Ingredients:

1½ pounds ripe, fresh tomatoes, cored, seeded, and coarsely chopped
4½ cups gluten-free, reduced-sodium vegetable stock or broth
1/2 cup yellow onion, chopped
1/2 cup celery, diced
1 bay leaf
2 teaspoons dried basil leaves, divided
1/2 teaspoon fine sea salt
1/2 teaspoon dried oregano leaves
1/2 teaspoon black pepper, freshly ground
4 cups green or white cabbage, coarsely chopped
2 cups cauliflower florets
2 tablespoons fresh parsley, chopped
1 cup fresh corn kernels
1 cup fresh lima beans
2 cups carrots, peeled and diced
2 cups zucchini, cut lengthwise and diced
2 cups purple potatoes, peeled and diced

Preparation: Place tomatoes in a 5- or 6-quart Dutch oven with vegetable stock or broth and bring to a boil. Add onion, celery, bay leaf, 1½ teaspoons basil, salt, oregano, and pepper; reduce heat, cover, and simmer for 1 hour. Add cabbage, cauliflower, parsley, corn, beans, carrots, zucchini, potatoes; cover and simmer until vegetables are tender, 50–60 minutes longer. Add remaining 1/2 teaspoon basil; simmer 4–5 minutes longer and serve. Makes 10 servings.

Nutritional information per serving:
Calories: 160
Fat: < 1 g
Saturated fat: 0 g
Carbohydrate: 34 g
Total sugars: 9 g
Protein: 8 g
Sodium: 255 mg
Cholesterol: 0 mg
Dietary fiber: 9 g

White-Bean and Poblano Chili

Ingredients:
3 tablespoons olive oil, divided
2 garlic cloves, minced
1¼ cups yellow onion, chopped (about 1 large onion)
2 poblano chiles, seeded and minced
2 jalapeño chiles, seeded and minced
1 cup tomatillos, chopped
3/4 pound all-natural turkey sausage, casing removed, sliced into
    3/4-inch pieces
3/4 pound lean ground turkey
1 tablespoon chili powder
1 tablespoon cumin
1/2 teaspoon salt
1/2 teaspoon white pepper
1/4 teaspoon cayenne pepper
1 can (15½ ounces) small white beans, rinsed and drained
1 bunch fresh cilantro, chopped
1½ cups low-fat plain yogurt (preferably organic)

Preparation: Place a large soup pot or 4-quart Dutch oven over medium heat. Add 2 tablespoons oil; warm oil for about 45 seconds. Add garlic, onion, poblano chiles, jalapeño chiles, and tomatillos; sauté for about 15 minutes. Place a separate large skillet over medium heat and add remaining 1 tablespoon oil. Tip to coat all sides and heat about 30 seconds. Add sausage and heat 5 minutes, stirring occasionally. Add turkey; heat until browned, stirring occasionally. Add chili powder, cumin, salt, white pepper, and cayenne pepper; stir to combine. Add meat mixture and beans to a soup pot or Dutch oven. Lower heat to low-medium; simmer 30 minutes. Fold in cilantro; reduce heat and stir in yogurt. Serve warm. Makes 6 servings.

Nutritional information per serving:
Calories: 335
Fat: 14 g
Saturated fat: 4 g
Carbohydrate: 23 g
Total sugars: 9 g
Protein: 29 g
Sodium: 570 mg
Cholesterol: 90 mg
Dietary fiber: 5 g

Arugula and White-Bean Salad

This salad is rich in flavor and high in fiber as well as vitamin C and folate.
If you use organic arugula, you'll get lower pesticide exposure than with
conventionally grown arugula.

Ingredients:
2 cups dried white northern beans, soaked in water overnight (or 2
    cans white beans)
1 teaspoon light miso
1 small garlic clove, peeled and sliced in half
3-inch stem of rosemary (leaves removed) or 3/4 teaspoon dried
    rosemary
1½ tablespoons red wine vinegar
1½ tablespoons sherry vinegar
1/2 teaspoon black pepper, freshly ground
1/4 cup extra-virgin olive oil
1 bunch arugula de-stemmed, washed, and finely chopped (or 3
    cups baby arugula, chopped)
4 Roma tomatoes, finely diced
3 tablespoons pitted kalamata olives, chopped or sliced

Preparation: Rinse and drain beans twice and add to a large soup
pot, fully covered with water. Simmer for about 30 minutes. (For
canned beans, rinse and drain, then add to soup pot and heat 5
minutes, stirring occasionally.) Add miso and stir until blended.
Simmer until tender, about 10 additional minutes. Remove from
heat, drain, and let cool. To make dressing, place garlic, rosemary,
wine vinegar, sherry vinegar, and pepper into a blender or food processor and process until combined. Continue to blend while slowly
adding oil. Place beans, arugula, tomatoes, and olives in a large
bowl. Pour dressing on top and mix to combine. (You may not need
to use all the dressing; cover and refrigerate any leftover dressing
for up to 3 days.) Serve at room temperature. Makes 6 servings.

**Nutritional information
per serving:**
Calories: 220
Fat: 10 g
Saturated fat: 1 g
Carbohydrate: 25 g
Total sugars: 2 g
Protein: 8 g
Sodium: 200 mg
Cholesterol: 0 mg
Dietary fiber: 9 g

Asian Sesame Salad with Soba Noodles

You can substitute rice noodles for a gluten-free version. Add slices of seared tofu or tempeh to this soba noodle salad for a great dinner entrée.

Ingredients:
15 ounces dried soba noodles
2 teaspoons dark sesame oil
1/3 cup rice vinegar, more if needed
1/3 cup reduced-sodium wheat-free tamari, more if needed
2 tablespoons fresh lime juice
2 teaspoons fresh lime zest
2 tablespoons dark brown sugar
1 garlic clove, minced
Pinch red pepper flakes (or to taste)
1 cup carrots, peeled and finely grated
1/4 cup peanuts, coarsely chopped
1 green onion, thinly sliced
1/2 cup broccoli sprouts
1/4 cup fresh cilantro, chopped

Preparation: In a large soup pot, cook noodles according to package directions. Drain and set aside. Pour oil, vinegar, tamari, and lime juice into a large bowl. Mix in lime zest, brown sugar, garlic, and red pepper flakes; stir until sugar dissolves. Toss in carrots, peanuts, onion, broccoli sprouts, and cilantro. Slice noodles into 3-inch lengths and stir into dressing mixture. Cover and refrigerate at least 1 hour. Toss salad again before serving. If dry, add a splash of tamari and vinegar. Serve cold. Makes 6 servings.

Nutritional information per serving:
Calories: 335
Fat: 5 g
Saturated fat: < 1 g
Carbohydrate: 59 g
Total sugars: 6 g
Protein: 13 g
Sodium: 0 mg
Cholesterol: 580 mg
Dietary fiber: 6 g

The Anti–Breast Cancer Cookbook

Chicken and Navy Bean Salad

If you can't find grape-seed oil, feel free to substitute avocado or walnut oil, or just use all olive oil. Grape-seed oil is a polyunsaturated oil that emulsifies well and has a mild flavor.

Ingredients:

Vinaigrette
1 medium garlic clove, peeled and smashed
1/8 teaspoon sea salt
2 tablespoons high-quality culinary grape-seed oil
2½ tablespoons extra-virgin olive oil
5 tablespoons fresh orange juice
1/4 cup champagne or other white wine vinegar
1 tablespoon Dijon mustard

Salad
1 can (15½ ounces) navy or cannellini beans, rinsed and drained
2 cups cooked chicken breast, diced
1 cup zucchini, sliced lengthwise and diced
1 cup summer squash, sliced lengthwise and diced
2 celery ribs, diced
1/4 cup goat cheese, crumbled
1/4 cup oil-packed sun-dried tomatoes, drained and chopped
1 cup fresh basil leaves, coarsely chopped
1/4 teaspoon salt
1/4 teaspoon black pepper, freshly ground
4 cups romaine (or baby romaine) lettuce leaves, torn into thin strips
4 cups baby arugula

Preparation: To prepare vinaigrette, in a small bowl, use a fork or pestle to combine garlic and sea salt until it forms a coarse paste. Whisk in grape-seed oil and olive oil. Add orange juice, vinegar, and mustard; whisk until evenly blended. Set aside at room temperature. To prepare salad, put beans, chicken, zucchini, squash, celery, goat cheese, and tomatoes in a large bowl; blend well. Add basil and about 3/4 of the vinaigrette; toss. Season with salt and pepper and toss again. Toss remaining vinaigrette with romaine and arugula in medium bowl. Divide the romaine and arugula among 6 large plates. Serve the salad on top of the greens. Makes 6 servings.

Nutritional information per serving:
Calories: 265
Fat: 13 g
Saturated fat: 3 g
Carbohydrate: 16 g
Total sugars: 2 g
Protein: 21 g
Sodium: 410 mg
Cholesterol: 43 mg
Dietary fiber: 6 g

Grilled Corn and Shrimp Salad

Shrimp are low in calories and fat and high in protein. Corn is a great source of the antioxidant lutein, and high intake of lutein-rich foods has been shown to lower the risk of developing some cancers, as well as cataracts.

Ingredients:

Salad
4 ears fresh corn
1 pound fresh shrimp, peeled and deveined
Nonstick cooking spray
1¼ cups sweet red bell pepper, diced
3/4 cup red onion, diced
1 cup fresh, ripe tomato, seeded and diced
1 head romaine lettuce, washed and torn into bite-size pieces
8–10 basil leaves, torn into bite-size pieces

Dressing
3 tablespoons cider vinegar
3 tablespoons lime juice
1/8 teaspoon ground red pepper
1/4 cup fresh cilantro leaves
1/3 cup gluten-free, reduced-sodium, 99 percent fat-free chicken or
    vegetable broth
1 tablespoon olive oil

Preparation: To prepare salad, remove husks and silk from corn. Place a large pot or Dutch oven of salted water over medium heat and bring to a boil. Add corn and cook 12–15 minutes, until tender. Remove from heat and drain. Thread shrimp on 6 (12-inch-long) skewers. Coat grill with nonstick cooking spray; preheat grill to medium-high. Place corn on rack, and cook 8–10 minutes, turning frequently, until slightly charred on each side. Remove corn from grill and set aside. Place skewers of shrimp on grill and cook 6–8 minutes until heated through (about 3–4 minutes on each side). Remove shrimp from skewers and set aside. Cut corn from cobs, and place in a large bowl. Add shrimp, red pepper, onion, tomato, romaine, and basil; toss gently to combine. To prepare dressing, combine vinegar, lime juice, and red pepper in blender or food processor. Cover and process just 3–4 seconds. Add cilantro and process until pureed. With blender running, gradually add broth and oil; process until well blended. Pour dressing over shrimp salad and toss gently. Makes 4 servings.

Nutritional information per serving:
Calories: 225
Fat: 5 g
Saturated fat: < 1 g
Carbohydrate: 19 g
Total sugars: 5 g
Protein: 26 g
Sodium: 225 mg
Cholesterol: 195 mg
Dietary fiber: 3 g

The Anti–Breast Cancer Cookbook

Grilled Salmon Salad

Marinating salmon before grilling helps to significantly decrease the amount of charring and damaging chemicals that may be produced by the high temperature. This recipe doubles or triples easily to serve more guests. Try it with the Asian Ginger Dressing (see page 56) or the Herbed Flaxseed and Olive Oil Dressing (see page 64) instead of balsamic vinegar and olive oil. Using wheat-free tamari makes a gluten-free marinade.

Ingredients:
1/4 cup orange juice
2 tablespoons wheat-free tamari or reduced-sodium soy sauce
1 teaspoon fresh ginger root, minced (or 1/2 teaspoon ground ginger spice)
1 garlic clove, minced
2 skinless wild Alaskan salmon fillets (about 5–6 ounces each)
3 cups mixed baby greens (such as romaine, spinach, arugula, or frisée)
2 teaspoons balsamic vinegar
1 tablespoon extra-virgin olive oil
1 tablespoon walnuts, chopped
1 green onion, diced (pale green and white parts only)
1/4 cup bottled roasted red pepper in water, torn into thin strips (about 1/2 pepper)
1 tablespoon goat cheese, flaked

Preparation: To make the marinade, place orange juice, tamari or soy sauce, ginger, and garlic in a shallow, lipped dish and stir. Add salmon and place in the refrigerator for at least 1 hour, turning occasionally to coat each side. Meanwhile, prepare a charcoal grill with a bed of hot coals or preheat a gas grill (on high). Place salmon on grill; close lid on gas grill. Cook, turning once, until a thermometer inserted in center of thickest part reads 140°F, about 6–8 minutes total. Meanwhile, divide greens evenly between 2 dinner plates and sprinkle each with 1 teaspoon balsamic vinegar and 1/2 tablespoon oil; toss to coat. Divide onion, red pepper, and cheese between the 2 plates. Place a fillet on top. Makes 2 servings.

Nutritional information per serving:
Calories: 395
Fat: 20 g
Saturated fat: 5 g
Carbohydrate: 14 g
Total sugars: 4 g
Protein: 38 g
Sodium: 510 mg
Cholesterol: 95 mg
Dietary fiber: 3 g

Japanese Miso Cabbage Salad

Ingredients:
Nonstick cooking spray, olive-oil style
1 cup shallots, thinly sliced
2 dashes fine sea salt, divided
2 tablespoons plus 1 teaspoon mellow white miso
1 teaspoon brown mustard
2 tablespoons honey or brown sugar
1/4 cup rice vinegar
1/4 cup high-quality virgin olive oil
1 tablespoon toasted sesame oil
3 cups green cabbage, finely shredded (about 1/2 small cabbage)
3 cups red cabbage, finely shredded (about 1/2 small cabbage)
1/2 cup cashew pieces (preferably from raw cashews)
1/2 cup red onion, very thinly sliced
2 green onions, diced
10 ounces extra-firm tofu, at room temperature

Preparation: Spray a large skillet with nonstick cooking spray and place over medium heat. Add shallots and a dash of salt; cook, stirring every few minutes, for 12–15 minutes, until shallots have caramelized. Transfer shallots to a plate and let cool. To prepare dressing, whisk together miso, mustard, and honey or brown sugar until combined. Gradually whisk in rice vinegar, followed by olive oil and sesame oil. Season with remaining dash of salt. Place green cabbage, red cabbage, cashews, red onion, and green onion in a large bowl. Add shallots. Pour about half the dressing over the top and toss until dressing is evenly distributed. Add tofu and remaining dressing and toss again. Serve at room temperature. Makes 4 servings (or 8 side-salad servings).

Nutritional information per serving (based on 4 servings):
Calories: 276
Fat: 16 g
Saturated fat: 3 g
Carbohydrate: 24 g
Total sugars: 11 g
Protein: 9 g
Sodium: 250 mg
Cholesterol: 0 mg
Dietary fiber: 5 g

Jicama, Green Bean and Pomegranate-Pecan Salad

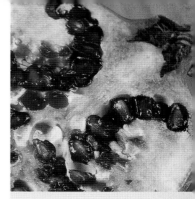

A jicama looks kind of like a big brown turnip. Beneath the thin skin is a sweet and crunchy vegetable that can be served raw or cooked. This salad is rich in antioxidants, such as selenium and luteolin, and is very high in fiber.

Ingredients:
1½ pounds jicama
1/4 cup pomegranate juice
3/4 pound French-cut green beans, rinsed and trimmed
1 fresh pomegranate
1/8 teaspoon salt
1/4 cup pecans, coarsely chopped
1 tablespoon fresh parsley, chopped
1 tablespoon extra-virgin olive oil
1 tablespoon fresh lemon juice
Salt and pepper to taste
2 cups mixed baby lettuce

Preparation: Peel and cut jicama into 1/4-inch-thick slices. Stack 2 or 3 slices on a cutting board and cut into 1/4-inch strips. Place strips in a bowl and toss with pomegranate juice. Cover and chill 30 minutes, tossing occasionally. Meanwhile, prepare a large bowl of ice water. Pour 3 cups water into a saucepan, add salt, and bring to a boil. Blanch beans for 3 minutes or until crisp-tender. With a slotted spoon, transfer beans into ice water to halt cooking. Drain in a colander. Dislodge seeds from pomegranate. (The easiest method is to peel underwater and strain, or cut in half, push center out, and whack on the back of each half with a wooden spoon.) Add green beans, pomegranate seeds, pecans, and parsley to jicama mixture. Stir in oil and lemon juice; toss. Season to taste with salt and pepper. Divide baby greens among 4 dinner plates and mound 1/4 of the jicama mixture in center of each. Makes 4 servings.

Nutritional information per serving:
Calories: 178
Fat: 8 g
Saturated fat: 1 g
Carbohydrate: 23 g
Total sugars: 12 g
Protein: 3 g
Sodium: 10 mg
Cholesterol: 0 mg
Dietary fiber: 8 g

Mango-Ginger-Carrot Salad

This light salad is rich in folate and beta-carotene as well as vitamin C. Serve it with lightly seared wild salmon or tuna.

Ingredients:
3 tablespoons rice vinegar
3 tablespoons toasted sesame oil
1 tablespoon extra-virgin olive oil
2 teaspoons fresh ginger, grated
2 carrots, peeled and finely grated
1/2 teaspoon lime juice
3 cups baby spinach
3 cups mixed baby greens
1 fresh, ripe mango, peeled, seeded, and diced
2 teaspoons sesame seeds

Preparation: In a small bowl, combine vinegar, sesame oil, olive oil, ginger, carrots, and lime juice. In a medium bowl, place spinach, baby greens, and mango. Add dressing and mix with tongs to combine. Sprinkle with sesame seeds and serve. Makes 4 servings.

Nutritional information per serving:
Calories: 169
Fat: 12 g
Saturated fat: 2 g
Carbohydrate: 14 g
Total sugars: 9 g
Protein: 2 g
Sodium: 38 mg
Cholesterol: 0 mg
Dietary fiber: 3 g

The Anti–Breast Cancer Cookbook

Mixed Greens and Papaya Salad with Cumin-Lime Vinaigrette

Papaya is rich in antioxidant carotenoids, especially lycopene, as well as vitamin C. A ripe papaya will be turning from green to yellow and often has some red to it as well.

Ingredients:
1/3 cup fresh lime juice
1 tablespoon honey
1 teaspoon ground cumin
1/8 teaspoon salt
1/8 teaspoon black pepper, freshly ground
1/2 cup flaxseed oil
1 ripe papaya, peeled, seeded, and cut into 1-inch pieces
1 head butter lettuce, washed and crisped
1 small bunch watercress, washed and chopped
1 ripe avocado, peeled and sliced lengthwise
2 tablespoons shelled pistachios

Preparation: To make vinaigrette, place honey and lime juice in a medium nonreactive bowl and whisk until the honey dissolves. Add cumin, salt, and pepper; whisk in flaxseed oil. Toss together papaya, lettuce, watercress, and vinaigrette. Divide among 6 salad plates and top each with avocado and pistachios. Makes 6 servings.

Nutritional information per serving:
Calories: 235
Fat: 18 g
Saturated fat: 2 g
Carbohydrate: 13 g
Total sugars: 6 g
Protein: 3 g
Sodium: 60 mg
Cholesterol: 0 mg
Dietary fiber: 4 g

Mushroom Barley Salad

Ingredients:
5 cups reduced-sodium vegetable broth
2 cups barley, rinsed in a strainer and drained
Nonstick cooking spray
8 ounces fresh mushrooms (button, cremini, or baby portobello),
   washed very well and chopped
1½ cups fresh leeks, washed, rinsed well, and diced
   (white part only)
1 cup carrots, shredded
1/2 cup red bell pepper, minced
2 tablespoons fresh lemon juice
2 tablespoons sesame or walnut oil
2 tablespoons reduced-sodium tamari or soy sauce
2 tablespoons cilantro, finely chopped

Preparation: Place broth in a large soup pot or 4-quart Dutch oven over medium heat; bring to a boil. Add barley and stir. Cover and reduce heat to low; simmer 35–40 minutes. Remove from heat and let cool. Spray a skillet with cooking spray and place over medium heat. Add mushrooms and heat for 2–3 minutes, until tender. Add leeks, carrots, and bell pepper; continue to heat, stirring, until soft and tender. Remove from heat and let cool. Refrigerate for faster cooling if necessary. Transfer to a large bowl. Add barley, lemon juice, oil, tamari or soy sauce, and cilantro; mix. Makes 6 servings.

Nutritional information per serving:
Calories: 315
Fat: 5 g
Saturated fat: < 1 g
Carbohydrate: 59 g
Total sugars: 5 g
Protein: 9 g
Sodium: 260 mg
Cholesterol: 0 mg
Dietary fiber: 13 g

The Anti–Breast Cancer Cookbook

Nutty Pea Salad

Many grocery stores sell tamari almonds in bulk, but they're expensive. You can make your own. Place about 4 cups almonds in a bowl and sprinkle with 1/3 cup reduced-sodium, wheat-free tamari and 1/2 teaspoon sugar. Turn until coated and bake in a 250°F oven for 25–30 minutes. Use wheat-free tamari for a gluten-free version.

Ingredients:
16 ounces frozen baby or petite peas (unthawed)
1/2 cup green onions, chopped
4 ounces tamari almonds, chopped
8 ounces water chestnuts, chopped
3 tablespoons olive oil mayonnaise
2 tablespoons reduced-fat sour cream
2 teaspoons yellow curry powder
1/4 teaspoon turmeric
Dash of salt and black pepper, freshly ground
6 large butter lettuce leaves, washed
1/4 cup watercress leaves, washed and patted dry

Preparation: In a medium bowl, combine peas, onions, almonds, and water chestnuts. In a separate small bowl, stir together mayonnaise, sour cream, curry powder, and turmeric. Fold mayonnaise mixture into pea mixture until combined. Season with a dash of salt and pepper. Place 1 lettuce leaf on each of 6 plates. Divide salad among plates and sprinkle with a few watercress leaves. Makes 6 servings.

Nutritional information per serving:
Calories: 250
Fat: 12 g
Saturated fat: 1 g
Carbohydrate: 26 g
Total sugars: 6 g
Protein: 9 g
Sodium: 150 mg
Cholesterol: 5 mg
Dietary fiber: 7 g

Panzanella Bread Salad

Vegetarian Virgin

Panzanella is a summery Italian salad made with leftover bread. It can be created with rustic white bread or Italian bread, but whole-wheat provides you with more slowly digested carbohydrates, which won't spike your insulin levels as much as white bread will.

Ingredients:

5 ripe tomatoes (any combination of red, orange, and yellow), cut into large chunks
4 cups day-old, crusty, whole-wheat French or Italian bread, cut into bite-size chunks
1 English cucumber, peeled and seeded, cut into large chunks
1/2 cup red onion, very thinly sliced and then cut into 1- to 2-inch pieces
1/4 cup fresh basil leaves, torn into small pieces
1/4 cup extra-virgin olive oil
2 tablespoons fresh lemon juice
1/8 teaspoon fine sea salt and pepper to taste

Preparation: Combine all ingredients in a large ceramic or other nonreactive bowl. Cover and let marinate for 1 hour to overnight (up to 12 hours). Do not refrigerate. Serve at room temperature. Makes 8 servings.

Nutritional information per serving:
Calories: 138
Fat: 7 g
Saturated fat: 1 g
Carbohydrate: 14 g
Total sugars: 3 g
Protein: 2 g
Sodium: 115 mg
Cholesterol: 0 mg
Dietary fiber: 2 g

Roasted Beets, Greens and Walnut Salad

You can make your own restaurant-style beet salad for a fraction of the cost. Beets are a great source of folate, phosphorus, magnesium, iron, and vitamin B6. Save the beet greens and sauté them with olive oil, sea salt, and thinly sliced garlic for a delicious side dish.

Ingredients:

Salad
1 pound baby beets (any mixture of golden and red)
1/2 teaspoon olive oil
Pinch of salt
4 cups mixed greens (such as romaine, spinach, watercress, or arugula)
1 medium green onion, thinly sliced
2 tablespoons unsalted walnuts, chopped
2 tablespoons goat cheese, crumbled or flaked

Vinaigrette
2 teaspoons grainy brown mustard
1½ tablespoons hazelnut or walnut oil
2 tablespoons olive oil
1/4 teaspoon fine sea salt
1/4 teaspoon black pepper, freshly ground

Preparation: Preheat oven to 400°F. Trim tops of the beets and wash them very well. Place beets on a heavy baking sheet and sprinkle with oil and salt; bake for about 30 minutes or until tender. Meanwhile, divide greens among 4 salad plates and place 1/4 of the sliced onion and 1/2 tablespoon walnuts on each. Add 1/2 tablespoon goat cheese to each plate. To make vinaigrette, whisk together all vinaigrette ingredients. When beets have finished cooking, remove baking sheet from oven and let sit about 5-6 minutes. Let beets cool enough to be peeled (skin should come off easily). Distribute evenly among salad plates. Drizzle each salad with about 1 tablespoon vinaigrette and serve. Makes 4 servings.

Nutritional information per serving:
Calories: 220
Fat: 15 g
Saturated fat: 2 g
Carbohydrate: 16 g
Total sugars: 9 g
Protein: 4 g
Sodium: 250 mg
Cholesterol: 2 mg
Dietary fiber: 5 g

Sesame Beef, Spinach and Watercress Salad

Ingredients:
2 teaspoons fresh ginger, grated
2 tablespoons light yellow miso
1/3 cup orange juice (preferably freshly squeezed)
2 tablespoons fresh lemon or lime juice
1 tablespoon sesame or olive oil
2 garlic cloves, finely chopped
1/4 teaspoon crushed red pepper flakes (more to taste)
2½ tablespoons sesame seeds (black or white or a mix), divided
1¼ pounds sirloin tip steak (about 1½ inches thick)
6 cups fresh baby spinach (typically 1 bag)
1 small bunch watercress, washed and chopped
1 cup roasted red pepper in water, cut in thin slices

Preparation: In a small bowl, whisk together ginger, miso, orange juice, and lemon or lime juice; set aside. Place a large sauté pan over medium heat; heat about 30 seconds, then add oil. Add garlic, pepper flakes, and 2 tablespoons sesame seeds. Cook, stirring frequently, until toasted and fragrant, 1–2 minutes. Transfer to a small bowl. Increase heat to medium-high and add steak. Sear steak for about 4 minutes on each side for medium-rare (preferable) or about 6 minutes on each side for medium doneness. Transfer to a platter and spread with garlic/sesame seed mixture. Cover with foil and let rest before slicing. Meanwhile, return pan to medium heat and stir in ginger/miso mixture, incorporating brown bits from bottom of pan. Stir in spinach and toss to coat; cook 1–2 minutes, until just wilted. To serve, divide spinach, watercress, and red pepper among 4 plates. Slice steak thinly and arrange on top of greens. Sprinkle with remaining sesame seeds and serve immediately. Makes 4 servings.

Nutritional information per serving:
Calories: 430
Fat: 15 g
Saturated fat: 4 g
Carbohydrate: 20 g
Total sugars: 7 g
Protein: 29 g
Sodium: 650 mg
Cholesterol: 70 mg
Dietary fiber: 6 g

Vegetarian Cobb Salad with Citrus-Miso Dressing

I call this a power salad. It has loads of protein and healthy, omega-3-rich fats, as well as fiber. I've used this citrus miso dressing on all different types of salads and as a marinade for chicken and fish.

Ingredients:

Dressing
2 tablespoons mellow white miso
3 tablespoons orange juice
2 tablespoons lemon juice
1/2 teaspoon fresh ginger, peeled and minced
1½ tablespoons olive oil
1 tablespoon flaxseed oil

Salad
4 cups mixed baby lettuce (such as baby spinach and baby arugula)
2 cups (about 1 head) loose, curly endive greens (using mostly tender inner leaves)
1¾ cups cooked kidney beans (rinsed and drained if using canned beans)
4 large omega-3-enriched eggs, hard-boiled and shelled
1/8 teaspoon sea salt
1/8 teaspoon black pepper, freshly ground
1 ripe but firm avocado, peeled, pitted, and sliced
1 cup grape tomatoes, halved
2 tablespoons goat cheese, crumbled
2 tablespoons walnuts, chopped

Preparation: To make dressing, stir together miso, orange juice, lemon juice, and ginger in a small ceramic bowl. Whisk in olive oil and flaxseed oil; set aside. In a large bowl, combine lettuce and endive. Add dressing; stir or fold together until dressing is evenly combined with lettuce. Divide dressed lettuce among 4 large plates or large salad bowls. Add 1/4 of beans to each salad. Slice each egg into fourths lengthwise and sprinkle with salt and pepper. Add egg slices to each salad. Place 1/4 of the avocado on each salad. Add 1/4 cup tomatoes, 1/2 tablespoon goat cheese, and 1/2 tablespoon walnuts to each salad. Serve immediately. Makes 4 servings.

Nutritional information per serving:
Calories: 420
Fat: 22 g
Saturated fat: 4 g
Carbohydrate: 35 g
Total sugars: 5 g
Protein: 20 g
Sodium: 675 mg
Cholesterol: 200 mg
Dietary fiber: 16 g

CASUAL DINING: BURGERS, TACOS, SANDWICHES AND MORE

Vegetarian　　**Vegan**　　**Gluten-Free**

Black Bean and Sweet Potato Enchiladas 133

Chickpea and Sunflower Tahini Burgers 134

Cranberry-Vegetable Baked Risotto 135

Easy, Speedy Chicken Tacos 136

Grilled Chicken Wraps with Cilantro Yogurt Dressing 137

Italian Halibut Sandwich 138

Joe Negri's Frittata à la Basilicata 139

Lentil Burgers 140

Portobello Burgers 141

Sautéed Onion and Pepper Pork Sandwiches 142

Shrimp, Peach and Bok Choy Satay 143

Spicy Turkey Relleno Burgers 144

Spinach, Onion and Mushroom Quesadillas with Manchego Cheese ...145

Sweet Potato Patties 146

West African Bean Fritters 147

Black Bean and Sweet Potato Enchiladas

Feel free to adjust the seasonings in the sauce and the enchilada filling to make it more or less spicy, depending on your tastes.

Ingredients:

Sauce

1 cup gluten-free, reduced-sodium vegetable broth
1 tablespoon arrowroot starch, dissolved in a little cold water
1¼ cups mild roasted green chiles, chopped
1 large garlic clove, peeled and minced
1/2 teaspoon ground cumin
1/2 teaspoon chili powder
Pinch cayenne pepper
1/4 teaspoon fine sea salt
1/4 teaspoon black pepper, freshly ground

Enchiladas

1 can (15½ ounces) black beans, rinsed and drained (or 1¾ cups cooked black beans)
2 garlic cloves, minced
1 teaspoon fresh lime juice
2¼ cups cooked sweet potatoes, peeled and diced
1 cup fresh spinach, chopped
1/4 cup roasted mild green chiles, chopped
1/4 cup yellow onion, finely diced
1/2 teaspoon ground cumin
1/4 teaspoon chili powder
1/4 teaspoon turmeric
1/8 teaspoon sea salt, ground
1/8 teaspoon black pepper, freshly ground
2–3 tablespoons fresh cilantro, chopped
1/2 teaspoon olive oil, divided
8 yellow corn tortillas
4 ounces shredded reduced-fat cheddar or Monterey Jack cheese

Preparation: Preheat oven to 350°F. To make sauce, combine broth, dissolved arrowroot, chiles, garlic, cumin, chili powder, cayenne pepper, salt, and black pepper in a saucepan; heat over medium-high heat; simmer until thickened. Set aside. To prepare filling, combine beans, garlic, and lime juice in a mixing bowl. Toss to coat and set aside. In a separate bowl, combine sweet potatoes, spinach, chiles, and onion. Stir in cumin, chili powder, and turmeric; season with salt and pepper. Pour about 1/4 cup sauce into the bottom of a baking dish large enough to hold 8 rolled enchiladas. To assemble enchiladas, place a skillet over medium-high heat. When the pan is very

Nutritional information per serving:
Calories: 430
Fat: 15 g
Saturated fat: 4 g
Carbohydrate: 56 g
Total sugars: 11 g
Protein: 18 g
Sodium: 755 mg
Cholesterol: 25 mg
Dietary fiber: 12 g

hot, add just 3–4 drops oil; immediately add a tortilla and flip to coat it. Cook 3–5 seconds on one side, flip, and cook another 3–5 seconds on second side. Stack tortillas between napkins and wrap with foil to keep them warm as you go. Lay the first hot tortilla in the sauced baking dish; top it with sauce. Spoon 1/8 of the sweet potato mixture along the center. Top with 1/8 black bean mixture. Wrap and roll the tortilla to the end of the baking dish. Repeat for remaining tortillas. Top with remainder of sauce and sprinkle with cheese. Bake for 20–25 minutes, until enchiladas are heated through and sauce is bubbling around the edges. Makes 4 servings of 2 enchiladas each.

Chickpea and Sunflower Tahini Burgers

These burgers are great served on a bed of baby greens or on a dressed, whole-grain bun with grilled vegetables and strips of roasted red bell pepper. They are rich in healthy fats, high in fiber, and very low in sugar.

Ingredients:

1¾ cups cooked chickpeas (rinsed and drained if using canned chickpeas)
2 small garlic cloves, roughly chopped
1/4 teaspoon fine sea salt
1/8 teaspoon black pepper, freshly ground
1/2 teaspoon dried oregano leaves
2 tablespoons nutritional yeast
2 tablespoons tahini, stirred so it has a uniform consistency
2 tablespoons ground flaxseed meal
1 tablespoon red wine vinegar

2 teaspoons grainy brown Dijon mustard
1/4 cup green onions, sliced (green portion only)
1/4 cup carrots, shredded
1/4 cup fresh basil, de-stemmed and finely chopped (or 1 teaspoon dried basil)
1 cup brown rice (small- or medium-grain), cooked and chilled
1/2 cup raw sunflower seeds
1 cup whole-grain rolled oats
Nonstick cooking spray
1 teaspoon sesame or olive oil

Nutritional information per serving:
Calories: 299
Fat: 11 g
Saturated fat: 1 g
Carbohydrate: 38 g
Total sugars: 1 g
Protein: 12 g
Sodium: 324 mg
Cholesterol: 0 mg
Dietary fiber: 8 g

Preparation: Place chickpeas, garlic, salt, pepper, oregano, yeast, tahini, flaxseed meal, vinegar, and mustard in a food processor; pulse/puree until well combined. Add onions, carrots, and basil; pulse to break up the larger pieces and until well combined. Add rice, sunflower seeds, and oats; pulse to incorporate and to break up seeds a bit. Remove blade and shape mixture into 6 patties. (It is helpful but not essential to refrigerate mixture for about 1/2 hour before shaping.) Place a nonstick skillet over medium heat and add oil. Add patties and cook 6–9 minutes on each side or until golden brown. Makes 6 burgers.

The Anti–Breast Cancer Cookbook

Cranberry-Vegetable Baked Risotto

For a vegan version, you can skip the Parmesan cheese or use soy cheese instead.

Ingredients:
Nonstick cooking spray
1 tablespoon olive oil
1 small yellow onion, diced
3/4 cup Arborio rice
1 cup gluten-free, low-sodium vegetable broth
1 cup portobello or baby portobello mushrooms, washed very well and thinly sliced
1 cup fresh asparagus, tough ends removed and diced
3/4 cup dried cranberries
2 tablespoons fresh basil, minced
1 tablespoon Parmesan cheese, freshly grated

Preparation: Preheat oven to 425°F. Spray a medium casserole dish with nonstick cooking spray (or lightly coat with a dab of oil). Set aside. Warm oil in a large saucepan over low-medium heat. Add onion, increase heat to medium, and cook until soft, about 5–6 minutes. Add rice; cook about 2 minutes. Add broth; bring to a boil. Lower heat slightly and cook 2 minutes. Stir in mushrooms, asparagus, cranberries, and basil. Pour mixture into casserole dish. Cover with foil and bake for 30–35 minutes. Remove from oven, stir in cheese and serve immediately. Makes 4 servings.

Nutritional information per serving:
Calories: 194
Fat: 6 g
Saturated fat: 4 g
Carbohydrate: 32 g
Total sugars: 16 g
Protein: 3 g
Sodium: 100 mg
Cholesterol: 16 mg
Dietary fiber: 4 g

Easy, Speedy Chicken Tacos

These tacos are high in fiber and protein. They contain antioxidants, such as lycopene in the tomatoes and anthocyanins in the black beans. You could also top them with diced, ripe avocado and any of the homemade salsas in this book.

Ingredients:
2 teaspoons chili powder
1/4 teaspoon ground cumin
1/8 teaspoon salt
1/8 teaspoon onion powder
1 boneless, skinless chicken breast (about 12 ounces), cut into
    thin strips
2 teaspoons olive oil
1/2 cup frozen whole-kernel corn, loosely packed
3/4 cup cooked black beans (rinsed and drained if using canned
    beans)
8 corn taco shells
1/2 cup romaine lettuce, shredded or chopped
2/3 cup fresh spinach, chopped
1 cup tomato, chopped
1/2 cup shredded reduced-fat cheddar cheese

Preparation: In a medium bowl, stir together chili powder, cumin, salt, and onion powder. Add chicken; toss to coat all sides. In a large nonstick skillet, warm oil over medium-high heat. Add chicken; cook, turning occasionally, for 2–4 minutes or until chicken is no longer pink inside. Stir in corn and beans. Heat through, stirring occasionally. Meanwhile, warm taco shells according to package directions. Fill taco shells with chicken mixture. Top with lettuce, spinach, tomato, and cheese. (Alternatively, add cheese before lettuce and tomato and rewarm tacos briefly to melt cheese.) Makes 4 servings of 2 tacos each.

Nutritional information per serving:
Calories: 370
Fat: 15 g
Saturated fat: 3 g
Carbohydrate: 30 g
Total sugars: 2 g
Protein: 29 g
Sodium: 473 mg
Cholesterol: 54 mg
Dietary fiber: 6 g

The Anti–Breast Cancer Cookbook

Grilled Chicken Wraps with Cilantro Yogurt Dressing

These wraps are a delicious combination of grilled chicken, summer veggies, and creamy dressing.

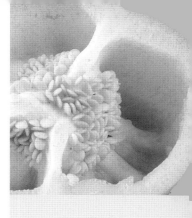

Ingredients:

Dressing

2 small garlic cloves, peeled and halved
1/2 cup cilantro leaves
1 cup low-fat plain yogurt (preferably organic)

2 tablespoons fresh lime juice
1/2 teaspoon chili powder
1/8 teaspoon fine sea salt
1/8 teaspoon black pepper, freshly ground

Wraps

4 boneless, skinless chicken breasts (about 4 ounces each) (preferably organic)
2 tablespoons olive oil, divided
1 teaspoon cumin
1 teaspoon chili powder
1 teaspoon sweet smoked paprika
1/2 teaspoon salt

1/2 teaspoon black pepper, freshly ground
3 summer squash, sliced lengthwise
3 zucchini, sliced lengthwise
1 small red onion, halved and sliced into 1/4-inch rings
1 red bell pepper, whole
1 yellow bell pepper, whole
4 large whole-wheat tortillas

Preparation: To make dressing, place garlic and cilantro into a food processor and chop to form semi-coarse pieces. Add yogurt, lime juice, chili powder, salt, and pepper; blend. Place in a ceramic bowl and chill. To prepare the wraps, season chicken by drizzling lightly with 2 teaspoons oil (about 1/2 teaspoon per breast), then rubbing with cumin, chili powder, paprika, salt, and black pepper. Let chicken breasts sit for 30–40 minutes to marinate. Meanwhile, prepare a charcoal grill or preheat a gas grill. Toss or lightly brush squash, zucchini, onion, red pepper, and yellow pepper with remaining oil. Place vegetables on grill and heat until softened and grilled through (turning once); about 4–5 minutes per side for squash, zucchini, and onion; peppers will take a few minutes longer and should be grilled until skin is charred. Let vegetables cool. Rinse charred skin off peppers and slice into strips. Slice squash halves into 1/2-inch pieces. Grill chicken, turning once, until heated through, about 6–8 minutes total. Let chicken cool and slice into strips. Tortillas can be warmed on grill for about 30 seconds, if desired. To serve, place grilled vegetables and chicken onto a tortilla and top with dressing. Makes 4 wraps.

Nutritional information per serving:
Calories: 398
Fat: 11 g
Saturated fat: 3 g
Carbohydrate: 38 g
Total sugars: 11 g
Protein: 37 g
Sodium: 332 mg
Cholesterol: 75mg
Dietary fiber: 5 g

Italian Halibut Sandwich

There is a rule in culinary circles that you should never mix cheese with fish. But these sandwiches are pretty tasty with fresh mozzarella on top. If you feel like breaking the rules, I won't tell.

Ingredients:
4 halibut fillets (about 6 ounces each)
2 teaspoons extra-virgin olive oil
1/8 teaspoon fine sea salt
1/8 teaspoon black pepper, freshly ground
Nonstick cooking spray
1 tablespoon Greek yogurt
2 tablespoons olive oil mayonnaise
2 tablespoons red onion, minced
1 teaspoon fresh rosemary, chopped
1/4 teaspoon dried thyme
1/2 teaspoon lemon juice
4 ciabatta or other crusty rolls (preferably whole grain)
12 medium, fresh basil leaves
2 tablespoons sun-dried tomatoes, reconstituted in water and
     thinly sliced
1 ripe avocado, pitted and thinly sliced

Preparation: Rinse fish and pat dry. Brush each side of each fillet with oil (1/2 teaspoon per fillet). Sprinkle each side with salt and pepper. Spray a skillet with nonstick cooking spray and place over medium-high heat. Add fish and cook about 4–6 minutes on each side, depending on thickness, until opaque and heated through. Meanwhile, in a small bowl, combine yogurt, mayonnaise, onion, rosemary, thyme, and lemon juice; whisk together and set aside. As fish finishes cooking, toast the rolls. Spread mayonnaise mixture on both sides of rolls. Place basil on each roll bottom (3 leaves per roll), followed by halibut, tomatoes, and avocado. Makes 4 servings of 1 sandwich each.

Nutritional information per serving:
Calories: 320
Fat: 12 g
Saturated fat: 3 g
Carbohydrate: 40 g
Total sugars: 15 g
Protein: 29 g
Sodium: 220 mg
Cholesterol: 35 mg
Dietary fiber: 6 g

The Anti–Breast Cancer Cookbook

Joe Negri's Frittata à la Basilicata

Joe Negri is a local celebrity where I live and an amazing jazz guitarist. He played Handyman Negri on Mister Rogers' Neighborhood. *I see him at the local gym, where we chat about lots of things, including food. This is one of his favorite recipes, handed down to him by his mother, Rose. He likes to make it on Easter Saturday to break the Lenten fast.*

Ingredients:
4 small Yukon Gold potatoes, scrubbed
Nonstick cooking spray
1/2 pound turkey sausage, with casing removed, diced or broken
    into small chunks
1/2 cup yellow onion, chopped
2 tablespoons celery, minced
1/4 teaspoon dried oregano leaves
1/4 teaspoon salt
1/4 teaspoon black pepper, freshly ground
3 large omega-3-enriched eggs plus 2 egg whites from large eggs,
    beaten together in a small bowl
1/4 teaspoon all-purpose unbleached white flour (just the tip of the
    spoon, per Joe)

Preparation: Parboil potatoes by placing them in a soup pot covered with cold water; bring to a boil. Boil 5 minutes and remove from heat. Drain and let cool. When cool, slice potatoes thinly. Meanwhile, spray an ovenproof skillet with nonstick cooking spray and place over medium heat. Add turkey sausage and cook until browned, about 5–6 minutes. Remove sausage from skillet and place in a small ceramic bowl or on a plate. Cover loosely with foil and set aside. Add onion and celery to skillet and return to medium heat; cook until onion begins to soften. Add potatoes and brown on both sides. Sprinkle oregano, salt, and pepper over vegetables. Add sausage and continue cooking about 2 minutes. Meanwhile, beat eggs in a small bowl; add flour and stir with a fork until combined. (The flour helps the frittata rise.) Preheat broiler to high. Add eggs to skillet; let cook until set on one side. Place entire skillet in the broiler and cook until light golden brown on top. Makes 3 servings.

Nutritional information per serving:
Calories: 295
Fat: 10 g
Saturated fat: 2 g
Carbohydrate: 25 g
Total sugars: 4 g
Protein: 25 g
Sodium: 750 mg
Cholesterol: 240 mg
Dietary fiber: 3 g

Lentil Burgers

These burgers can be served as appetizers, salad toppers, or healthy sliders (with mini whole-grain buns). You can use corn crumbs instead of bread crumbs for a gluten-free version.

Ingredients:
2 large omega-3-enriched eggs plus 3 egg whites from large eggs
3 cups cooked black lentils
1/4 teaspoon fine sea salt
1/4 teaspoon black pepper, freshly ground
1/2 teaspoon oregano
1/4 teaspoon cumin
1 sweet yellow onion (preferably Vidalia), finely chopped
1 cup fine whole-grain or whole-wheat bread crumbs
1/3 cup finely shredded carrot
1 tablespoon olive or peanut oil, divided

Preparation: Beat eggs and egg whites together in a small bowl. Add to food processor along with lentils, salt, pepper, oregano, and cumin. Puree until mixture is the texture of a thick dip or hummus. Pour into a ceramic bowl; stir in onion and bread crumbs. Let sit for a few minutes so that bread crumbs absorb some of the moisture. Shape into 12 patties about 1½ inches thick each. (If batter needs to be moistened, add a bit more water or egg. If it seems overly wet, add a few more bread crumbs.) Place a heavy skillet over medium-low heat and add 1 teaspoon oil. Add 4 patties, cover, and cook for 8–10 minutes, until bottoms begin to turn brown. Depending on your cook top, you may need to increase heat a bit to get them to brown. Flip burgers and cook on second side for 7–9 minutes or until golden. Remove burgers to a wire rack to cool. Repeat, heating 1 teaspoon oil with 4 patties twice more, until all patties are cooked. Makes 12 burgers, or 12 servings.

Nutritional information per serving:
Calories: 115
Fat: 3 g
Saturated fat : < 1 g
Carbohydrate: 15 g
Total sugars: 1 g
Protein: 7 g
Sodium: 45 mg
Cholesterol: 44 mg
Dietary fiber: 3 g

The Anti–Breast Cancer Cookbook

Portobello Burgers

You can also serve these portobello burgers with no bun, alone as an appetizer, or on a bed of baby spinach and arugula with balsamic vinaigrette.

Ingredients:
4 large portobello mushrooms, de-stemmed and washed very well
1 medium garlic clove, sliced into very thin slivers
1 small shallot, minced
1 teaspoon fresh rosemary (or 1/2 teaspoon dried rosemary)
1 teaspoon fresh thyme (or 1/2 teaspoon dried thyme)
2 tablespoons extra-virgin olive oil
3 tablespoons balsamic vinegar
1/2 teaspoon sea salt, freshly ground
1/2 teaspoon black pepper
4 whole-grain buns
1 cup baby arugula
1/2 cup roasted red peppers in water, torn into long pieces
4 slices (about 2 ounces) fresh mozzarella cheese

Preparation: Preheat broiler or grill. Pat mushrooms dry. With a paring knife, make slits in tops of caps. Stuff slivers of garlic, shallot, rosemary, and thyme into slits. In a small bowl, whisk together oil, vinegar, salt, and pepper. Brush mushrooms with oil mixture. Place them cap-side down on pan and broil or grill until soft and brown, about 4–5 minutes per side. Meanwhile, toast both sides of the buns. On each bun place 1/4 of the arugula and 1/4 of the red peppers; add a portobello then top with mozzarella. Makes 4 servings.

Nutritional information per serving:
Calories: 285
Fat: 11 g
Saturated fat: 2 g
Carbohydrate: 35 g
Total sugars: 1 g
Protein: 12 g
Sodium: 460 mg
Cholesterol: 18 mg
Dietary fiber: 3 g

Sautéed Onion and Pepper Pork Sandwiches

You can top these sandwiches with baby microgreens, roasted vegetables, and anything else that might add some crunch, flavor, and healthy nutrients. Slowly roasted, marinated pork doesn't contain the carcinogens you typically find in fried or grilled pork.

Ingredients:
1 medium yellow sweet onion, thinly sliced
1 cup carrots, shredded
1 large orange or red bell pepper, seeded and coarsely chopped
2 tablespoons quick-cooking tapioca, crushed
2 pounds boneless pork sirloin roast or boneless pork loin roast, trimmed of fat
3/4 cup Coffee Barbecue Sauce (see page 57)
6 whole-wheat hamburger buns, split and toasted

Preparation: In a 3½- or 4-quart slow cooker, combine onion, carrots, and pepper. Sprinkle with crushed tapioca. Place pork on top of vegetables. Pour barbecue sauce over meat. Cover and cook on low heat for 6–7 hours or on high heat for 3–3½ hours. Remove meat from slow cooker and thinly slice. Return sliced meat to slow cooker; stir to coat with sauce. Serve meat on hamburger buns. Makes 6 servings.

Nutritional information per serving:
Calories: 264
Fat: 6 g
Saturated fat: 1 g
Carbohydrate: 36 g
Total sugars: 7 g
Protein: 17 g
Sodium: 850 mg
Cholesterol: 42 mg
Dietary fiber: 3 g

The Anti–Breast Cancer Cookbook

Shrimp, Peach and Bok Choy Satay

Use wheat-free tamari to make a gluten-free version.

Ingredients:
1/2 cup mango or apricot nectar, divided
1/4 cup creamy natural peanut butter, stirred so that oil is evenly distributed
1/4 cup dark brown sugar
3 tablespoons rice vinegar
2 tablespoons reduced-sodium soy sauce or wheat-free tamari
3 ripe, firm peaches, sliced into 6 wedges
16 uncooked large shrimp, peeled and deveined
6 heads baby bok choy, halved lengthwise
1/8 teaspoon salt
1/8 teaspoon black pepper, freshly ground

Preparation: Preheat grill to medium-high. To make sauce, place 1/4 cup nectar, peanut butter, brown sugar, rice vinegar, and soy sauce or tamari in bowl and whisk until smooth. Arrange peaches, shrimp, and bok choy on grill. Brush with remaining 1/4 cup nectar and about 1/4 cup sauce. Sprinkle with salt and pepper. Grill until peaches are slightly charred, shrimp are just opaque in center, and bok choy halves are just tender, about 2 minutes per side for peaches and 3 minutes per side for shrimp and bok choy. Mound the shrimp, bok choy, and peaches on platter. Drizzle with a few teaspoons of sauce and serve with the remaining sauce. Makes 4 servings.

Nutritional information per serving:
Calories: 220
Fat: 9 g
Saturated fat: 2 g
Carbohydrate: 24 g
Total sugars: 18 g
Protein: 11 g
Sodium: 310 mg
Cholesterol: 0 mg
Dietary fiber: 3 g

Spicy Turkey Relleno Burgers

Ingredients:
1/4 cup millet
Water
2 large poblano peppers, halved lengthwise and seeded
2 plum tomatoes, cored and halved lengthwise
1 medium yellow onion, quartered
3 garlic cloves, unpeeled
6 whole button mushrooms, washed very well and patted dry
1/2 teaspoon kosher salt, divided
4 whole-wheat or nine-grain hamburger buns, split down the middle
3 egg whites from large eggs, lightly beaten, divided
1/2 teaspoon dried oregano
1/2 teaspoon ground cumin
1/2 teaspoon chili powder
1/4 teaspoon turmeric
1/4 teaspoon black pepper, freshly ground
3/4 pound lean ground turkey
5 ounces frozen, chopped spinach
Nonstick cooking spray
2 ounces fresh mozzarella, sliced into 4 slices

Preparation: Place millet in a dry skillet over medium-high heat; toast until it starts to pop. Meanwhile, boil a few cups of water in a small soup pan. Add 3/4 cup boiling water to millet and simmer until water is absorbed, about 15–17 minutes. While millet is cooking, preheat broiler. Remove millet from heat; cover and let stand. Place poblano peppers cut-side down on foil-lined broiler pan. Add tomatoes, onion, garlic, and mushrooms; broil until charred, about 7–8 minutes. Cool slightly. Peel garlic. Chop garlic, onion, tomatoes, and mushrooms; toss in a bowl with 1/4 teaspoon salt. Peel poblano peppers and cut each in half. Preheat oven to 375°F. Brush bun tops with 1/3 of beaten egg white. Combine oregano, cumin, and chili powder; sprinkle on bun tops; place bun tops and bottoms on baking sheet. Set aside. To prepare burgers, place millet, remaining egg whites, remaining kosher salt, and black pepper in a medium bowl; stir together until combined. Add turkey and mix (with hands or wooden spoon) until combined. Squeeze excess water from spinach and crumble into millet/turkey mixture; mix until just combined. Shape into 4 patties. Spray baking sheet with nonstick cooking spray. Arrange patties on baking sheet and bake 26–30 minutes, until cooked through. Remove from oven and place baking sheet with bun tops and bottoms into oven and bake about 4 minutes. Meanwhile, add 1/2 tomato mixture and 1 slice of cheese to each burger; return to oven and heat for 2–3 minutes. Serve on buns with poblano peppers and remaining tomato mixture. Makes 4 burgers.

Nutritional information per serving:
Calories: 424
Fat: 9 g
Saturated fat: 6 g
Carbohydrate: 52 g
Total sugars: 16 g
Protein: 32 g
Sodium: 450 mg
Cholesterol: 60 mg
Dietary fiber: 5 g

Spinach, Onion and Mushroom Quesadillas with Manchego Cheese

Serve with your favorite topping, such as salsa, diced avocados, or low-fat sour cream.

Ingredients:
2 teaspoons high-quality olive oil
8 ounces cremini mushrooms, washed very well, patted dry, and sliced
1 medium yellow onion, thinly sliced
1/2 teaspoon sea salt, divided
1 package (8 ounces) chopped, frozen spinach, thawed, drained, and squeezed dry
1/2 teaspoon cumin
1/4 teaspoon turmeric
1/4 teaspoon black pepper, freshly ground
8 large whole-wheat or gluten-free, brown-rice tortillas
1 tablespoon peanut or olive oil
5–6 ounces Manchego cheese (or any goat cheese)

Preparation: Preheat oven to 450°F. Place a large skillet over medium-high heat and add olive oil; warm oil about 30 seconds. Add mushrooms, onion, and 1/4 teaspoon salt. Cook, stirring from time to time, about 6–7 minutes, until mushrooms are brown and onions caramelize. Remove from heat and set aside. In a large bowl, combine spinach with remaining salt, cumin, turmeric, and pepper. Brush tortillas with peanut or olive oil. Place 4 tortillas on heavy, nonstick baking sheet and top evenly with mushroom mixture, spinach mixture, and cheese. Cover each tortilla with 1 of the remaining tortillas and press down firmly. Bake until lightly brown and crispy, about 10–12 minutes. Let cool. Cut into wedges. Makes 4 quesadillas, or 8 servings of 2 wedges each.

Nutritional information per serving:
Calories: 216
Fat: 12 g
Saturated fat: 4 g
Carbohydrate: 19 g
Total sugars: 2 g
Protein: 8 g
Sodium: 650 mg
Cholesterol: 18 mg
Dietary fiber: 1 g

Sweet Potato Patties

You can use yams for this recipe and it will be just as delicious. The rice can be cooked ahead of time and refrigerated; just bring it to room temperature before preparing the dish. The patties work great as salad toppers, burgers, or appetizers. The Miso Tahini Sauce (see page 66) is great for these patties.

Ingredients:
1 cup short-grain brown rice, rinsed a few times with cold water
Water, as needed
1 cup sweet potato, peeled and grated
1 medium yellow onion, diced
1/4 teaspoon sea salt
1/4 teaspoon black pepper, freshly ground
3/4 cup whole-wheat flour
2 teaspoons olive oil
3 cups mixed baby greens (such as spinach and arugula)
6 plum tomatoes, thinly sliced

Preparation: Place rice in a large soup pot and cover with water. Bring to a boil. Lower heat and simmer until tender, about 40–45 minutes. Remove from heat and let cool for at least 20 minutes. Stir together rice, potato, onion, salt, and pepper in a large bowl. Let sit for 5–10 minutes; salt will absorb some of the moisture. Stir in flour until batter becomes tacky. (Add 1 or 2 teaspoons water if necessary to prevent clumping.) Form mixture into 6 tight balls; flatten to form patties. Place oil in large skillet or fry pan; warm over medium heat. Add patties and let cook for 8–10 minutes. Flip and cook an additional 6–8 minutes. Serve on small plates with 1/2 cup mixed greens and tomato. Makes 6 servings.

Nutritional information per serving:
Calories: 322
Fat: 4 g
Saturated fat: < 1 g
Carbohydrate: 61 g
Total sugars: 5 g
Protein: 11 g
Sodium: 300 mg
Cholesterol: 0 mg
Dietary fiber: 7 g

The Anti–Breast Cancer Cookbook

West African Bean Fritters

I found this recipe via the Bean Education & Awareness Network and adapted it to my own tastes and health motivations. The fritters may be rolled and coated several hours before cooking; simply refrigerate them, covered.

Ingredients:
1 can (15½ ounces) black-eyed peas, rinsed and drained (or 1¾ cups cooked black-eyed peas)
2 egg whites from large eggs, lightly beaten
3 tablespoons yellow onion, chopped
2 teaspoons ginger root, minced (or 1/2 teaspoon ground ginger)
2 tablespoons red bell pepper, minced
1 tablespoon jalapeño chile pepper, seeded and minced
1/2 teaspoon cumin
1/4 teaspoon salt
1/4 cup whole-wheat panko bread crumbs
1/4 cup cornmeal
2 tablespoons sesame oil, divided
Ginger Tomato Dipping Sauce (see page 62)

Preparation: Preheat oven to 200°F. Place peas, egg whites, onion, ginger, red pepper, jalapeño pepper, cumin, and salt in food processor or blender; process until smooth. Transfer mixture to a medium bowl. Stir in bread crumbs. Roll about 1 tablespoon pea mixture into a ball; lightly coat with cornmeal. Repeat with remaining mixture until about 24 fritters have been prepared. Heat 1 teaspoon oil in a medium saucepan. Fry fritters 4 at a time, until browned, about 2–3 minutes. Drain on paper towels. Keep warm in oven until ready to serve. Spoon Ginger Tomato Dipping Sauce in center of small plates; arrange fritters in circle around the sauce. Makes 4 servings of 6 fritters each.

Nutritional information per serving:
Calories: 210
Fat: 11 g
Saturated fat: 1 g
Carbohydrate: 21 g
Total sugars: 1 g
Protein: 8 g
Sodium: 49 mg
Cholesterol: 0 mg
Dietary fiber: 4 g

MAIN DISHES

Vegetarian

Vegan

Gluten-Free

Beet-Kale-Carrot Pesto Pasta 149

Broccoli and Tomato Halibut ⊘ 150

Cajun Catfish with Broccoli and Brown Rice ⊘ 151

Cornmeal-Crusted Scallops with Lime-Chipotle Vinaigrette ∾ ⊘ 152

Curried Salmon with Lentils ⊘ 153

Dijon-Pecan Chicken ⊘ 154

Fusilli with Walnuts and Swiss Chard ∾ 155

Garlic Shrimp and Scallops ⊘ 156

Green Curry Shiitake Chicken ⊘ 157

Herb-Crust Margherita and Mushroom Pan Pizza ∾ 158

Herb Horseradish–Crusted Salmon ⊘ 159

Lamb Moussaka ⊘ 160

Lemon-Herb Salmon with Mango-Peach-Avocado Salsa ⊘ 161

Linguine with Spinach and Arugula ∾ ⊘ 162

Lychee Braised Chicken ⊘ 163

Mango-Nectarine Alaska Salmon ⊘ 164

Mozzarella and Spinach Stuffed Sole ⊘ 165

Orange-Glazed Yellowfin Tuna ⊘ 166

Oven-Top Gnocchi with Greens and Beans ∾ 167

Penne with Summer Squash, Zucchini and Sugar Snap Peas ∾ 168

Roasted Barbecued Wild Salmon ⊘ 169

Sautéed Swordfish Niçoise ⊘ 170

Sesame Tofu with Spinach and Chickpea Puree ∾ Ƴ ⊘ 171

Shrimp Étouffée 172

Sole Amandine ⊘ 173

Spanish Seafood Paella ⊘ 174

Spinach Tofu in Cashew-Coconut Sauce ∾ ⊘ 175

Steamed Asian Halibut with Sesame Kale ⊘ 176

Swordfish Florentine ⊘ 177

Tilapia with Cherry Cilantro Salsa ⊘ 178

Tofu and Bok Choy ∾ Ƴ 179

Tomato and Bacon Turkey Meatloaf ⊘ 180

Tomato Walnut Tilapia ⊘ 181

Vegetarian Pad Thai ∾ ⊘ 182

Walnut-Encrusted Halibut with Pear Chutney ⊘ 183

White Bean, Broccoli Rabe and Fontina Fusilli ∾ 184

The Anti–Breast Cancer Cookbook

Beet-Kale-Carrot Pesto Pasta

This recipe was created by Sherrie Flick—an amazing fiction writer living in Pittsburgh who is also an accomplished cook. She blogs at www.sherrieflick.com. In this dish, she uses her favorite basil pesto recipe, which is from Isa Chandra Moskowitz's Vegan with a Vengeance cookbook and can also be found on Sherrie's website, but any pesto will do. This beet-kale-carrot pasta dish is a delicious vegan meal when made with dry (not fresh) pasta.

Ingredients:

6 cups kale, de-stemmed and roughly chopped (Sherrie recommends dark green Tuscan kale)
2 tablespoons olive oil, plus an extra dash for the pasta
3 or 4 garlic cloves, thinly sliced
Few dashes of salt
3 medium carrots, peeled and cut into matchsticks
4 small beets (whole), rinsed and trimmed
2 tablespoons basil pesto (or more to taste)
8 ounces pasta (small whole-wheat penne works well)
Black pepper, freshly ground, to taste

Preparation: Place kale in a bowl of cold water. Heat oil in a large skillet over medium-high heat. Add garlic and sauté for approximately 2 minutes or until slices just start to turn tan. Add carrots, cover, and continue sautéing for 2 more minutes, making sure garlic doesn't stick. Drain kale slightly from water before adding to skillet. (The remaining water on the kale helps steam the greens right in the pan and also helps keep the garlic from sticking.) Add dash of salt and add lid to help with the steaming. Stir occasionally, until kale is vivid green, about 4 minutes, then turn heat to low. Bring some water and a dash of salt to boil in a medium saucepan. Add beets and boil until tender when pierced with a fork. (The time will vary depending upon the size of the beets.) Remove beets from water and let cool to the touch. Remove outer skin from beets and quarter them. Carefully add beets to the kale/carrot mixture in skillet. (Be gentle so they don't bleed over everything.) Bring some water to boil in a small soup pot. Add dash of oil and pasta. Cook per instructions on box. Turn heat under skillet back to medium-high. Add pesto, stir to combine, and heat through. Drain pasta and add to skillet. Stir and serve. Makes 4 servings.

Nutritional information per serving:
Calories: 380
Fat: 12 g
Saturated fat: 1 g
Carbohydrate: 59 g
Total sugars: 10 g
Protein: 12 g
Sodium: 232 mg
Cholesterol: 0 mg
Dietary fiber: 11 g

Broccoli and Tomato Halibut

Few vegetables rival broccoli and tomatoes in nutritional value. If you are watching your sugar and carbohydrate intake, this dish is perfect; it contains fewer than 10 grams of carbohydrates per serving.

Ingredients:
2 tablespoons olive oil
2 cups fresh broccoli florets, chopped
2½ cups fresh, ripe tomatoes, diced
2 tablespoons lemon juice
2 medium garlic cloves, minced
1 teaspoon dried tarragon
1/2 teaspoon sugar
1/4 teaspoon salt
1/4 teaspoon black pepper, freshly ground
4 halibut steaks (about 5–6 ounces each)

Preparation: Place oil in a large skillet over medium heat and warm for about 1 minute. Add broccoli and heat about 4–5 minutes, stirring occasionally. Add tomatoes, lemon juice, garlic, tarragon, sugar, salt, and pepper; cook 5 minutes, stirring occasionally. Add halibut, cover, and cook about 5–6 minutes on each side, until opaque. Divide halibut and vegetables among 4 dinner plates. Makes 4 servings.

Nutritional information per serving:
Calories: 220
Fat: 7 g
Saturated fat: 1 g
Carbohydrate: 8 g
Total sugars: 4 g
Protein: 29 g
Sodium: 85 mg
Cholesterol: 40 mg
Dietary fiber: 2 g

Cajun Catfish with Broccoli and Brown Rice

You can substitute the catfish with just about any other type of fish fillet, such as tilapia or trout.

Ingredients:

1/2 teaspoon cumin
1/2 teaspoon fine sea salt
1/4 teaspoon chipotle chili powder
1/4 teaspoon paprika
1/4 teaspoon black pepper, freshly ground
1/4 teaspoon cayenne pepper
2 cups gluten-free, reduced-sodium vegetable broth, divided

1 small yellow onion, chopped
1 small red bell pepper, chopped
1 cup uncooked brown rice, small- or medium-grain
3 cups small broccoli florets
2 tablespoons lime juice (from 2 or 3 limes), freshly squeezed
4 catfish fillets (4–5 ounces each)
1 lime or lemon, cut into wedges

Preparation: Place cumin, salt, chili powder, paprika, black pepper, and cayenne pepper in a small bowl; stir until well mixed. In a medium saucepan, heat 1/4 cup broth to a simmer over medium-high heat. Add onion, pepper, and 1 teaspoon of spice mixture. Cook about 3 minutes, or until onion begins to soften and becomes translucent. Stir in rice and cook 30 seconds. Add remaining 1¾ cups broth and bring to a boil. Reduce heat to low, cover, and simmer for about 30 minutes. Add broccoli florets and recover. Heat another 10–15 minutes or until liquid is absorbed. (Total cook time should be about 40–45 minutes.) Remove from heat and let sit covered for 10 minutes. Fluff rice with a fork and gently stir until ingredients are equally distributed. Add lime juice and stir. Meanwhile, preheat oven to 450°F. Place fish on parchment paper–lined baking sheet and sprinkle with remaining 1 teaspoon spice mixture. Bake fish 8–9 minutes or until flesh is opaque. Flake fish into bite-size pieces and serve over rice and broccoli mixture. Serve with lime or lemon wedges. Makes 4 servings.

Nutritional information per serving:
Calories: 195
Fat: 2 g
Saturated fat: < 1 g
Carbohydrate: 22 g
Total sugars: 3 g
Protein: 20 g
Sodium: 130 mg
Cholesterol: 45 mg
Dietary fiber: 4 g

Cornmeal-Crusted Scallops with Lime-Chipotle Vinaigrette

Ingredients:

Vinaigrette
2 tablespoons high-quality olive oil
2 tablespoons fresh lime juice
4 teaspoons sugar
1/4 teaspoon salt
1/4 teaspoon black pepper, freshly ground
1/2 teaspoon cumin
1 garlic clove, finely minced
1 whole chipotle chile, canned in adobo, minced
1/2 cup fresh corn kernels, cut from cob
1 tablespoon cilantro, finely chopped

Scallops
1 pound wild sea scallops, tough muscle removed
3/4 cup yellow cornmeal
1/4 teaspoon chili powder
1/4 teaspoon cumin
1/4 teaspoon fine sea salt
1/4 teaspoon black pepper, freshly ground
Nonstick olive oil cooking spray
1 lime, cut into wedges

Preparation: For vinaigrette, combine oil, lime juice, sugar, salt, pepper, 1/4 teaspoon cumin, garlic, chipotle pepper, corn, and cilantro in small bowl. Let sit for at least 30 minutes. Meanwhile, to prepare scallops, combine cornmeal, chili powder, cumin, salt, and pepper in a separate small bowl. Toss scallops in cornmeal mixture. Spray a large skillet with nonstick cooking spray and place over medium-high heat. Add scallops and cook 3–5 minutes, turning once, until browned on both sides and opaque in the middle. Drizzle scallops with vinaigrette and garnish with lime wedges. Makes 4 servings.

Nutritional information per serving:
Calories: 282
Fat: 8 g
Saturated fat: 1 g
Carbohydrate: 31 g
Total sugars: 5 g
Protein: 22 g
Sodium: 475 mg
Cholesterol: 3 mg
Dietary fiber: 3 g

The Anti–Breast Cancer Cookbook

Curried Salmon with Lentils

Ingredients:
1 teaspoon cumin
1 teaspoon chili powder
1/4 teaspoon turmeric
1/4 teaspoon fine sea salt
1 tablespoon plus 1 teaspoon high-quality olive oil, divided
4 salmon fillets (about 5 ounces each)
3/4 cup dried green lentils, rinsed and strained a few times
1/2 cup red onion, thinly sliced
2 tablespoons fresh lemon juice
1 medium garlic clove, crushed
1 small bunch cilantro leaves, chopped

Preparation: In a small bowl, combine cumin, chili powder, turmeric, and salt. Drizzle salmon with 1 teaspoon oil and rub with spice mixture; set aside for 15–20 minutes. Meanwhile, place lentils in a small soup pot, add water to cover, and simmer until tender, about 20–25 minutes. Drain lentils and, while still hot, toss with onion, lemon, garlic, and remaining 1 tablespoon oil. Preheat oven-top or stand-alone grill to medium. Grill salmon fillets 4–5 minutes on each side, until cooked through. Stir cilantro into lentils and serve with salmon. Makes 4 servings.

Nutritional information per serving:
Calories: 360
Fat: 15 g
Saturated fat: 2 g
Carbohydrate: 23 g
Total sugars: 1 g
Protein: 35 g
Sodium: 150 mg
Cholesterol: 42 mg
Dietary fiber: 6 g

Dijon-Pecan Chicken

This is a sweet and tangy way to prepare chicken that is rich in fiber and selenium. I like to serve it with a small green salad and steamed baby carrots on the side. Try to find free-range chicken for this recipe.

Ingredients:
Nonstick cooking spray
1/4 cup orange juice
6 tablespoons Dijon mustard
1/4 cup clover honey
2 tablespoons reduced-fat (2 percent) dairy milk
2 tablespoons nonhydrogenated buttery spread (such as Smart Balance or Fleischmann's Olive Oil Spread)
1 tablespoon lemon juice
1/8 teaspoon cumin
1/8 teaspoon salt
1/8 teaspoon black pepper, freshly ground
1/2 cup pecans, chopped
6 boneless, skinless chicken breasts (about 4–5 ounces each)

Preparation: Preheat oven to 350°F. Lightly coat a 9 x 13–inch baking dish with nonstick cooking spray. In a medium saucepan over medium heat, combine orange juice, mustard, honey, milk, spread, and lemon juice. Season with cumin, salt, and pepper. Stir in pecans. Place chicken breasts in baking dish and bake for 10 minutes. In the meantime, stir mustard/pecan sauce occasionally. Cover chicken with mustard/pecan sauce and bake an additional 20–22 minutes or until chicken is no longer pink inside and juices run clear. Makes 6 servings.

Nutritional information per serving:
Calories: 278
Fat: 12 g
Saturated fat: 2 g
Carbohydrate: 14 g
Total sugars: 12 g
Protein: 28 g
Sodium: 365 mg
Cholesterol: 68 mg
Dietary fiber: 3 g

The Anti–Breast Cancer Cookbook

Fusilli with Walnuts and Swiss Chard

Ingredients:
1/4 cup walnuts
1½ tablespoons olive oil
4 medium shallots
2 or 3 small garlic cloves, minced
2 tablespoons white wine vinegar
1/2 teaspoon ground cumin
1/4 teaspoon turmeric
1½ cups reduced-sodium vegetable broth
1/4 teaspoon sea salt, ground
1/3 cup water
6 cups Swiss chard stems, cut into 1-inch pieces
1/2 cup evaporated skim milk
1/3 cup dried currants (or raisins)
16 ounces whole-grain fusilli
3 tablespoons Pecorino Romano cheese, grated
3 tablespoons walnuts, chopped

Preparation: Place walnuts in a dry skillet and toast over medium heat, stirring or shaking frequently, for about 5–6 minutes. Transfer to a nonreactive bowl. Place oil in a large skillet over medium-high heat and warm about 1 minute. Add shallots and cook until golden brown, about 5–6 minutes. Add garlic and cook about 1 minute. Remove from heat and stir in vinegar, cumin, and turmeric. Let vinegar evaporate (about 20–30 seconds) and return skillet to medium-high heat. Add broth, salt, and water; bring to a simmer. Stir in chard stems; cover and reduce heat to medium-low. Simmer about 12–15 minutes or until chard stems are tender. Stir in milk and currants; simmer about 10 minutes or until thickened. Meanwhile, cook fusilli according to instructions on package. Drain pasta and add to chard mixture; stir until blended. Transfer to serving bowl or plate and top with cheese and walnuts. Makes 6 servings.

Nutritional information per serving:
Calories: 350
Fat: 10 g
Saturated fat: 2 g
Carbohydrate: 59 g
Total sugars: 11 g
Protein: 17 g
Sodium: 475 mg
Cholesterol: 4 mg
Dietary fiber: 8 g

Garlic Shrimp and Scallops

This garlicky seafood dish is low in calories and sugar content but very high in protein. Serve over brown rice or whole-grain couscous with a small spinach salad topped by one of the delicious vinaigrettes in this book.

Ingredients:
1 teaspoon olive oil
4 garlic cloves, minced
1/4 teaspoon crushed red pepper flakes, or to taste (they are spicy!)
1/2 pound shrimp, peeled and deveined
1/2 pound bay scallops
1/2 teaspoon paprika
1/4 cup gluten-free, reduced-sodium, 99 percent fat-free chicken broth
1 teaspoon fresh lime juice
1/2 cup fresh Italian parsley, finely chopped
1/4 teaspoon salt
1/4 teaspoon black pepper, freshly ground

Preparation: In a large, heavy skillet, heat oil over low-medium heat. Add garlic and sauté until light brown. Remove garlic with a slotted spoon and set aside. Add pepper flakes and increase heat to medium-high; warm about 30 seconds. Add shrimp, scallops, and paprika; stir. Return garlic to skillet; sauté 1–2 minutes while stirring. Add chicken broth and cook 1 minute. Remove shrimp and scallops with a slotted spoon. Place on a platter; set aside and keep warm. Add lime juice, parsley, salt, and pepper to skillet and heat just through. Pour sauce over shrimp and scallops and serve immediately. Makes 4 servings.

Nutritional information per serving:
Calories: 165
Fat: 5 g
Saturated fat: < 1 g
Carbohydrate: 3 g
Total sugars: trace
Protein: 27 g
Sodium: 270 mg
Cholesterol: 122 mg
Dietary fiber: 1 g

Green Curry Shiitake Chicken

This recipe comes courtesy of my former Exeter schoolmate Alex Ankeles. He notes, "There are so many variations—the protein can change, the veggies can change, and the type of curry paste can change. Have fun experimenting!" Coconut milk is rich in fiber as well as a dozen vitamins and minerals, including potassium and selenium. Serve hot over rice.

Ingredients:
2 tablespoons sesame oil
1 tablespoon green curry paste (more if desired)
2 boneless, skinless medium chicken breasts (about 4 ounces each), chopped into 1-inch chunks
1/2 cup carrots, peeled and diced
12 ounces shiitake mushrooms, washed very well and sliced
1 medium yellow onion, sliced
1 cup Thai eggplant, sliced and cut into quarters
1/2 cup corn kernels, cut off cooked cob
1–1½ tablespoons fish sauce (less if brand is very pungent)
1 can (13 ounces) coconut milk (Alex likes the Thai brand Chaokoh)
1 green chile, sliced (optional—this will make the dish *very* spicy)
2 cups brown rice, short- or medium-grain, cooked

Preparation: In a nonstick soup pot, heat oil and curry paste on high until the paste bubbles. Add chicken, carrots, mushrooms, onions, eggplant, corn, and fish sauce. Stir for about 1 minute and then add coconut milk. Lower heat to medium and cook for about 6 minutes. (If you prefer a thicker curry, let it reduce for another couple of minutes.) Add green chile. Makes 4 servings.

Nutritional information per serving:
Calories: 439
Fat: 19 g
Saturated fat: 13 g
Carbohydrate: 45 g
Total sugars: 8 g
Protein: 22 g
Sodium: 335 mg
Cholesterol: 30 mg
Dietary fiber: 8 g

Herb-Crust Margherita and Mushroom Pan Pizza

Ingredients:
3/4 cup lukewarm water (105°–115° F)
1 package (1/4 ounce) active dry yeast
1 cup all-purpose unbleached white flour (more if needed)
1 cup whole-wheat flour
2 teaspoons dried oregano leaves
2 teaspoons dried basil
1/2 teaspoon salt
1/2 teaspoon garlic powder
1/2 teaspoon dried thyme
1/4 teaspoon white pepper
2 tablespoons olive oil, divided
1 tablespoon yellow or white cornmeal
1 medium, ripe beefsteak tomato, thinly sliced
5 or 6 large leaves fresh basil, washed and torn into strips
3 ounces fresh mozzarella, sliced and cut into half moons
1 cup shiitake mushrooms, washed very well and thinly sliced

Preparation: In a small bowl, stir together water and yeast. Let stand about 10 minutes, until foamy. In a large bowl, combine white flour, wheat flour, oregano, basil, salt, garlic powder, thyme, and pepper. Add 1 tablespoon oil to yeast mixture. Pour yeast mixture into flour mixture; mix until doughlike. Knead for 5–6 minutes. (Add more flour if dough is sticky.) Cover and let stand about 1½ hours in a warm and protected place (with little airflow). When dough has risen, preheat oven to 425°F. Add 1½ teaspoon oil to a deep-dish pan, 8–9 inches in diameter, turning pan to coat. Spread cornmeal on a dry, flat surface. Roll out dough on top of cornmeal until it measures about 8½–9 inches in diameter. Place in pan. Brush with remaining oil and add layers of tomatoes, basil, mozzarella, and mushrooms. Bake for 18–20 minutes, until edges of pizza dough are lightly browned and cheese has melted. Makes 4 servings.

Nutritional information per serving:
Calories: 420
Fat: 11 g
Saturated fat: 3 g
Carbohydrate: 58 g
Total sugars: 1 g
Protein: 22 g
Sodium: 270 mg
Cholesterol: 10 mg
Dietary fiber: 11 g

Herb Horseradish–Crusted Salmon

Horseradish is rich in glucosinolates, the same cancer-fighting antioxidant compounds found in broccoli and cauliflower.

Ingredients:
4 boneless wild salmon fillets (about 5-6 ounces each)
1/2 teaspoon fine sea salt, divided
1/2 teaspoon dried rosemary
1/4 teaspoon black pepper, freshly ground
1/2 cup parsley leaves, lightly packed
1/3 cup basil leaves
1/4 cup fresh horseradish root, peeled and finely grated
1 shallot, chopped
1½ teaspoons olive oil
1½ teaspoons Dijon mustard
1½ teaspoons lemon zest, finely grated
3/4 teaspoon lemon juice

Preparation: Preheat oven to 450°F. Line a large baking sheet with foil and spray with nonstick cooking spray. Place fish skin-side down on foil; sprinkle with 1/4 teaspoon salt, rosemary, and pepper. In a food processor, combine parsley, basil, horseradish, shallot, oil, mustard, lemon zest, lemon juice, and remaining 1/4 teaspoon salt. Pulse until mixture is very finely ground. Spread mixture evenly over top of fish, pressing down so that it adheres. Bake in top third of oven until cooked through and crust begins to brown, about 20-22 minutes. Makes 4 servings.

Nutritional information per serving:
Calories: 268
Fat: 16 g
Saturated fat: 3 g
Carbohydrate: 2 g
Total sugars: 0 g
Protein: 29 g
Sodium: 330 mg
Cholesterol: 80 mg
Dietary fiber: 1 g

Lamb Moussaka

This dish can be made with ground turkey, ground chicken, or a vegetarian ground-meat substitute. You can also use a combination of cooked lentils and brown rice seasoned with cumin, cinnamon, and turmeric instead of meat—just leave out the meat-browning step.

Ingredients:

2 large eggplants, thinly sliced into rounds
Salt as needed
2 teaspoons olive oil
1 pound lean ground lamb
1 teaspoon cumin
1/4 teaspoon ground cinnamon
2 medium yellow onions, halved and thinly sliced
2 garlic cloves, peeled and finely chopped
1 can (14 ounces) diced tomatoes, undrained

3 teaspoons fresh parsley, chopped
1/4 teaspoon dried oregano leaves
2 large omega-3-enriched eggs
8 ounces low-fat plain Greek yogurt
Black pepper, freshly ground as needed
1/2 cup mozzarella cheese, finely grated
1/4 cup Parmesan cheese, finely grated

Preparation: Lay eggplant slices in a single layer on paper towels. Lightly salt both sides of each slice and let sit for 30 minutes. Pat dry. Place a skillet over medium-high heat. Brush a very thin layer of oil on each side of each eggplant slice. In batches, add eggplant in a single layer to the skillet and brown on both sides. Remove to a plate. Add lamb to skillet and brown for 5 minutes, crumbling with spatula and stirring as needed. Season with cumin, cinnamon, onion, and garlic; sauté for 7–8 minutes, until onion is soft and translucent. Add tomatoes, parsley, and oregano; bring to a boil, then quickly reduce heat to low. Let simmer for 15–20 minutes, stirring occasionally, until ingredients are tender. Meanwhile, preheat oven to 350°F. Arrange half the eggplant slices in a single layer in an ovenproof 13 x 9-inch baking dish. Add lamb/tomato mixture and layer remaining eggplant slices on top. Beat eggs in a bowl until foamy, preferably using a stand mixer. Add yogurt and continue beating until mixture is fluffy. Add a sprinkle of salt and pepper. Pour egg mixture over eggplant slices, spreading out in an even layer. Sprinkle mozzarella and Parmesan on top. Bake 40–45 minutes, or until golden brown on top and cooked through. Makes 6 servings.

Nutritional information per serving:
Calories: 330
Fat: 14 g
Saturated fat: 6 g
Carbohydrate: 18 g
Total sugars: 8 g
Protein: 33 g
Sodium: 400 mg
Cholesterol: 140 mg
Dietary fiber: 7 g

The Anti–Breast Cancer Cookbook

Lemon-Herb Salmon
with Mango-Peach-Avocado Salsa

This tasty dish is full of the flavonoid luteolin, omega-3 fatty acids, and vitamin C, all of which have antioxidant and cancer-fighting properties.

Salsa
1 ripe avocado, pitted and chopped
1 ripe peach, peeled, pitted, and chopped
1 mango, seeded and chopped
1 jalapeño pepper, seeded and minced
1½ tablespoons red onion, minced
2 tablespoons fresh cilantro, chopped
2 tablespoons fresh lemon or lime juice

Salmon
1 tablespoon olive oil
1 garlic clove, minced
4 Alaska salmon fillets (about 4–5 ounces each)
2 teaspoons fresh lemon juice
1/8 teaspoon salt
1/8 teaspoon black pepper, freshly ground
2 tablespoons fresh parsley
Lemon wedges

Preparation: Combine all salsa ingredients in a large bowl and set aside. Place large skillet over medium heat and add oil. Stir in garlic and heat about 1 minute. Drizzle lemon juice over fillets and then dust with salt and pepper. Add salmon to skillet. Cook for 10 minutes per inch of thickness, measured at thickest part, or until fish flakes when tested with a fork. Turn halfway through cooking to brown on both sides. (I typically cook about 5 minutes on one side, flip with a spatula, and cook another 4–5 minutes on the other side.) Sprinkle with parsley and serve with lemon and salsa. Makes 4 servings.

Nutritional information per serving:
Calories: 335
Fat: 19 g
Saturated fat: 4 g
Carbohydrate: 17 g
Total sugars: 10 g
Protein: 25 g
Sodium: 125 mg
Cholesterol: 65 mg
Dietary fiber: 5 g

Linguine with Spinach and Arugula

Use brown rice linguine to make a gluten-free version.

Ingredients:
12 ounces whole-grain linguine (such as Barilla) or gluten-free
    brown rice linguine
2 tablespoons olive oil
2½ cups (4 ounces) arugual or baby arugula, trimmed and packed
2½ cups (4 ounces) baby spinach, packed
3 tablespoons Parmesan cheese, freshly grated
1/2 teaspoon dried basil
1/2 teaspoon dried oregano
Salt and black pepper, freshly ground to taste
3 tablespoons pine nuts

Preparation: Cook linguine in a large pot of boiling water per
package instructions, stirring occasionally, until al dente. Meanwhile, place a large, heavy skillet over medium heat and add oil.
Warm oil about 1 minute. Add arugula and spinach; stir until
greens are just wilted, about 30 seconds. Remove from heat. Drain
pasta and return to pot. Add greens to pasta and toss well. Add
Parmesan, basil, and oregano. Salt and pepper to taste; toss well.
Transfer to bowl. Sprinkle with pine nuts. Serve immediately.
Makes 6 servings.

**Nutritional information
per serving:**
Calories: 240
Fat: 8 g
Saturated fat: 1 g
Carbohydrate: 41 g
Total sugars: 2 g
Protein: 2 g
Sodium: 50 mg or more
    (depending on
    amount of salt used)
Cholesterol: 2 mg
Dietary fiber: 7 g

The Anti–Breast Cancer Cookbook

Lychee Braised Chicken

A lychee (or litchi) is a sweet, exotic pinkish fruit from southern China. It is rich in dietary fiber, as well as vitamin C, thiamin, niacin, and folate.

Ingredients:
1 tablespoon olive oil
4 boneless, skinless chicken breast halves (about 1 pound total)
1 cup orange juice
3 teaspoons sugar
1 garlic clove, minced
1 teaspoon dried rosemary
2 teaspoons cornstarch
1/4 cup dry white wine
1/4 teaspoon salt
1/4 teaspoon black pepper, freshly ground
15 fresh lychees, peeled and sectioned

Preparation: Heat oil in a large skillet over medium heat. Add chicken. Cook until chicken is browned on both sides and no longer pink in center, about 9–11 minutes (turning after 4–5 minutes). Remove chicken from skillet and place on a serving plate; cover with foil to keep warm. Add orange juice, sugar, garlic, and rosemary to skillet; bring to a boil. Combine cornstarch and wine; add to skillet. Cook, stirring constantly, until sauce is clear and thickened. Season with salt and pepper. Add lychees; heat thoroughly, stirring occasionally. Serve lychee sauce over chicken. Makes 4 servings.

Nutritional information per serving:
Calories: 220
Fat: 5 g
Saturated fat: 3 g
Carbohydrate: 17 g
Total sugars: 14 g
Protein: 27 g
Sodium: 185 mg
Cholesterol: 45 mg
Dietary fiber: 1 g

Mango-Nectarine Alaska Salmon

Try to find wild, not farmed, salmon to make this dish, as studies have shown that farmed varieties of salmon may contain higher levels of chemical contaminants such as mercury. This recipe is rich in omega-3 fatty acids and the antioxidants quercetin, lycopene, and beta-carotene.

Ingredients:
Nonstick cooking spray
1/4 cup yellow onion, diced
1/2 cup red bell pepper, diced
1 medium tomato, diced, seeds and membrane removed
1¾ cups water plus 3 tablespoons, divided
1/4 cup clover honey
3 tablespoons gluten-free tomato paste (such as Glen Muir Organic)
2 teaspoons cornstarch
1/2 teaspoon salt
1 tablespoon white wine or gluten-free chicken broth
Pinch red pepper flakes (optional)
2 ripe but firm avocados, peeled and diced
2 ripe but firm nectarines, peeled and diced
1 ripe but firm mango, peeled and diced
1 whole wild Alaska salmon, filleted (about 3 pounds total)

Preparation: Preheat oven to 350°F. Spray a large skillet with nonstick cooking spray and place over medium heat. Sauté onion, pepper, and tomato in 3 tablespoons water, stirring frequently, until vegetables are softened, about 5 minutes. Combine 1¾ cups water, honey, tomato paste, cornstarch, salt, wine or broth, and pepper flakes in a medium bowl. Allow cornstarch to dissolve. Add mixture to vegetables and cook over medium heat, stirring, until sauce thickens slightly. Remove mixture from heat and gently stir in avocados, nectarines, and mango. Lightly coat 9 x 13–inch baking dish with cooking spray. Place salmon fillets side by side, skin-side down in dish. Pour sauce over salmon and bake about 30–35 minutes, depending on size of fish, until fish flakes easily with a fork. Makes 8 servings.

Nutritional information per serving:
Calories: 408
Fat: 14 g
Saturated fat: 2 g
Carbohydrate: 24 g
Total sugars: 16 g
Protein: 46 g
Sodium: 225 mg
Cholesterol: 120 mg
Dietary fiber: 5 g

The Anti–Breast Cancer Cookbook

Mozzarella and Spinach Stuffed Sole

Ingredients:
Nonstick cooking spray
2 teaspoons olive oil
1/2 pound fresh cremini mushrooms, washed very well and sliced
1 small yellow onion, diced
1 garlic clove, minced
2 cups fresh spinach, chopped
1/4 teaspoon oregano leaves, crushed
1/4 teaspoon dried basil
1½ pounds sole fillets or other whitefish
1 tablespoon sherry or other red wine
1/3 cup fresh mozzarella cheese, finely grated

Preparation: Preheat oven to 400°F. Coat a 10 x 6-inch baking dish with nonstick cooking spray. Place a medium skillet over medium heat and add oil. Heat about 45–60 seconds; add mushrooms and sauté for about 2 minutes or until tender. Add onion and garlic; heat about 3 minutes more, until onion is translucent. Add spinach and continue cooking for about 1 minute or until spinach is barely wilted. Remove from heat and drain liquid from skillet into baking dish. Add oregano and basil to mushroom mixture. Stir to combine. Spread 1/4 of mixture in center of each fillet, roll up, and place seam-side down in baking dish. Sprinkle with sherry and then cheese. Bake for 16–20 minutes, until fish is heated through. Makes 4 servings.

Nutritional information per serving:
Calories: 273
Fat: 9 g
Saturated fat: 4 g
Carbohydrates: 6 g
Total sugar: 3 g
Protein: 39 g
Sodium: 163 mg
Cholesterol: 95 mg
Dietary fiber: 2 g

Orange-Glazed Yellowfin Tuna

This recipe also works well with halibut, catfish, or grouper. The first steps can be done ahead of time or the entire recipe can be made at once. It is delicious served with whole-grain couscous and a mixed-green salad with berries, pecans, and goat cheese.

Ingredients:
4 firm yellowfin tuna fillets, about 1 inch thick (5–6 ounces each)
1/3 cup olive oil, divided
Black pepper, freshly ground
1/4 cup plus 1 tablespoon fresh orange juice
3 tablespoons fresh lemon juice
1/4 cup champagne or other white wine vinegar
2 tablespoons natural orange marmalade
1 teaspoon fresh ginger, minced
2 small garlic cloves, minced
1/2 teaspoon ground white pepper
1/2 teaspoon fine sea salt

Preparation: Place fish in a dish large enough to hold them side by side. Brush with 2 tablespoons oil. Sprinkle a small amount of black pepper over both sides of fillets. Cover dish with plastic wrap or foil and refrigerate until ready to cook. To prepare glaze, place nonreactive saucepan over medium-high heat. Add orange juice, lemon juice, vinegar, marmalade, ginger, garlic, and white pepper; stir. Bring mixture to a boil. Lower heat slightly and continue boiling until mixture reduces to about 1/2 cup, about 5½–7 minutes. Remove pan from heat and let mixture cool. Whisk in remaining oil except for about 1–2 teaspoons. Transfer glaze to a nonreactive bowl, cover, and refrigerate until ready to use (if not using immediately). Preheat grill or broiler. Return glaze to a small saucepan (if chilled); warm it over low heat. Brush fish with glaze and season lightly with salt. Carefully brush grill's cooking surface with remaining oil to prevent sticking. Grill fish until browned, about 4–5 minutes per side. Serve immediately. Makes 4 servings.

**Nutritional information
per serving:**
Calories: 330
Fat: 18 g
Saturated fat: 3 g
Carbohydrate: 10 g
Total sugars: 8 g
Protein: 33 g
Sodium: 305 mg
Cholesterol: 65 mg
Dietary fiber: < 1 g

The Anti–Breast Cancer Cookbook

Oven-Top Gnocchi
with Greens and Beans

A friend passed this recipe along to me; I changed a few ingredients to make it healthier. You can make this dish using all chard or all spinach. You can also use spinach gnocchi instead of whole-wheat gnocchi. It might seem strange to brown the gnocchi rather than boiling it, but trust me, it turns out beautifully. Feel free to experiment with different types of greens and beans.

Ingredients:

1 tablespoon plus 1 teaspoon high-quality olive oil, divided
1 package (16 ounces) shelf-stable whole-wheat gnocchi
1 medium sweet yellow onion, thinly sliced
2 medium garlic cloves, minced (more if you like a garlicky flavor)
1/2 cup reduced-sodium vegetable broth or water
3 cups chard leaves, chopped (1/2 small bunch)
4 cups fresh spinach or baby spinach (about 7 ounces)
4 medium, vine-ripened tomatoes, diced
1 can (15½ ounces) white beans, rinsed and drained
1/2 teaspoon dried basil
1/2 teaspoon dried oregano leaves
1/2 teaspoon fine sea salt
1/4 teaspoon black pepper, freshly ground
1/3 cup part-skim mozzarella cheese, shredded
1/4 cup Parmesan cheese, finely shredded

Preparation: Heat 1 tablespoon oil in a large nonstick skillet over medium heat. Add gnocchi and cook, stirring often, until plumped and starting to brown, about 6–7 minutes. Transfer to a ceramic bowl. Add remaining 1 teaspoon oil and onion; cook over medium heat, stirring, for about 2 minutes. Stir in garlic and broth or water. Cover and cook until onion is soft, about 4–6 minutes. Add chard and spinach; cook, stirring, until greens start to wilt, 1–2 minutes. Stir in tomatoes, beans, basil, oregano, salt, and pepper; bring to a simmer. Stir in gnocchi and sprinkle with mozzarella and Parmesan. Cover and cook until the cheese is melted and the sauce bubbles, about 3–3½ minutes. Serve warm. Makes 6 servings.

Nutritional information per serving (using vegetable broth):
Calories: 270
Fat: 6 g
Saturated fat: 2 g
Carbohydrate: 32 g
Total sugars: 13 g
Protein: 12 g
Sodium: 425 mg
Cholesterol: 10 mg
Dietary fiber: 7 g

Penne with Summer Squash, Zucchini and Sugar Snap Peas

Vegetarian

Ingredients:

1 pound whole-grain penne
1 cup reduced-sodium vegetable broth
1/2 pound summer squash, seeded and julienned
1/2 pound zucchini, seeded and julienned
1/4 pound fresh sugar snap peas
1/2 teaspoon olive oil

1/4 cup Parmesan or Romano cheese, freshly grated
1/4 cup fresh basil leaves, thinly sliced
2 tablespoons pine nuts
1/2 teaspoon salt
1/2 teaspoon black pepper, freshly ground

Preparation: Bring 2 quarts salted water to a boil. Add penne and cook until al dente, about 7–9 minutes, or according to package instructions. Drain and set aside. Meanwhile, place broth in a skillet large enough to hold all the vegetables; bring to a boil. Add squash, zucchini, and peas; steam, covered, for about 4 minutes. When vegetables are just tender, add cooked penne and oil; toss until heated through. Divide pasta and vegetables evenly among 6 warmed plates or pasta bowls. Sprinkle each with cheese, basil, and pine nuts. Sprinkle with salt and pepper. Makes 6 servings.

Nutritional information per serving:
Calories: 348
Fat: 16 g
Saturated fat: 3 g
Carbohydrate: 20 g
Total sugars: 11 g
Protein: 36 g
Sodium: 295 mg
Cholesterol: 60 mg
Dietary fiber: 6 g

Roasted Barbecued Wild Salmon

This salmon dish is infused with citrus and spices and is rich in omega-3 fatty acids. Try it with some wilted spinach warmed in a skillet with a dab of olive oil, garlic, and sea salt.

Ingredients:
Nonstick cooking spray
1/4 cup orange juice
2 tablespoons fresh lemon juice
1 tablespoon light brown sugar
1 tablespoon chili powder
1 tablespoon lemon zest, finely grated
1 teaspoon ground cumin
1/8 teaspoon salt
Pinch cayenne pepper
4 medium wild salmon fillets, about 1-inch thick

Preparation: Preheat oven to 400° F. Coat a shallow baking dish with nonstick cooking spray. In a small bowl, whisk together orange juice, lemon juice, sugar, chili powder, lemon zest, cumin, salt, and pepper. Use tongs to place fish in baking dish. Pour orange juice mixture over salmon and turn to coat both sides. Roast for about 15–16 minutes, until a fork can be inserted easily into salmon. Serve on a large platter or 4 dinner plates. Makes 4 servings.

Nutritional information per serving:
Calories: 275
Fat: 8 g
Saturated fat: 1 g
Carbohydrate: 7 g
Total sugars: 4 g
Protein: 44 g
Sodium: 244 mg
Cholesterol: 120 mg
Dietary fiber: < 1 g

Sautéed Swordfish Niçoise

Ingredients:
2 small garlic cloves, peeled
1/4 teaspoon fine sea salt
4 swordfish steaks, fresh or thawed frozen, 1 inch thick (about 5-6
    ounces each)
4 tablespoons olive oil, divided
1/4 cup bottled roasted red pepper, drained and diced
1/3 cup pitted kalamata olives, finely chopped
1/4 cup fresh flat-leaf parsley, finely chopped
2 tablespoons bottled capers, drained
1 flat anchovy fillet, minced
1 scallion, minced
3 tablespoons balsamic or red wine vinegar
1/4 teaspoon dried oregano leaves
1/4 teaspoon black pepper, freshly ground
1 lemon, cut into wedges

Preparation: In a small bowl, mash garlic with a fork and add salt.
Mash again until a paste forms. Set aside. Rinse and pat fish dry.
In a large skillet, heat 1 tablespoon oil over medium heat until hot
but not smoking. Add fish and sauté for about 4–5 minutes on
each side or until just cooked through. While fish is cooking, in
the small bowl with the garlic paste, add red pepper, olives, parsley, capers, anchovy, scallion, vinegar, remaining 3 tablespoons oil,
oregano, and black pepper; stir until uniformly mixed. Transfer
fish to 4 dinner plates and spoon sauce over each. Serve with lemon
wedges on the side. Makes 4 servings.

**Nutritional information
per serving:**
Calories: 280
Fat: 16 g
Saturated fat: 3 g
Carbohydrate: 2 g
Total sugars: < 1 g
Protein: 29 g
Sodium: 450 mg
Cholesterol: 55 mg
Dietary fiber: 1 g

The Anti–Breast Cancer Cookbook

Sesame Tofu with Spinach and Chickpea Puree

Ingredients:

3 tablespoons toasted sesame oil
3 tablespoons wheat-free tamari
 or reduced-sodium soy sauce
2 tablespoons mirin
2 tablespoons rice or cider
 vinegar
2 garlic cloves, minced
1/4 cup shallots, minced
1½ teaspoons fresh ginger,
 grated
1/3 cup water
1 pound firm tofu, cut into
 1/2-inch slices
1 cup cooked or canned

chickpeas (rinsed and
 drained if using canned)
Nonstick cooking spray
2 shallots, diced
2 garlic cloves, sliced
2 teaspoons fresh lemon juice
1/4 teaspoon sweet paprika
1/4 teaspoon salt
1/4 teaspoon black pepper,
 freshly ground
2 tablespoons olive oil
1 tablespoon flaxseed oil (or
 olive oil)
4 cups baby spinach

Preparation: Preheat oven to 375°F. Stir together sesame oil, tamari or soy sauce, mirin, vinegar, garlic, shallots, ginger, and water in a small bowl. Place tofu in a large shallow baking dish and pour contents of bowl on top. Flip tofu slices over so that marinade coats all sides. Bake for about 20 minutes. Turn tofu slices and bake for an additional 20–25 minutes or until liquid is absorbed. Meanwhile, place chickpeas and some water (about 1/2 cup) in a small soup pot or saucepan. Cook, stirring, over medium heat for about 10 minutes. While chickpeas cook, place a nonstick skillet over medium heat and spray with nonstick cooking spray. Add shallots and garlic; heat, stirring, until fragrant and softened, about 5–6 minutes. Remove from heat. Drain chickpeas and rinse with cool water. Place chickpeas, shallot mixture, lemon juice, paprika, salt, and pepper in a blender or (preferably) a food processor. Pulse and add olive oil and flaxseed oil until mixture is smooth. Place the same nonstick skillet over medium heat and spray with nonstick cooking spray. Add spinach; heat about 3–4 minutes, turning with a fork or spatula, until wilted. Place 1/4 of chickpea puree and 1/4 of spinach on each of 4 dinner plates. Top each with 1/4 of the tofu slices. Makes 4 servings.

Nutritional information per serving:
Calories: 420
Fat: 24 g
Saturated fat: 4 g
Carbohydrate: 28 g
Total sugars: 2 g
Protein: 24 g
Sodium: 550 mg
Cholesterol: 0 mg
Dietary fiber: 6 g

Shrimp Étouffée

This delicious Creole dish is full of healthy vegetables and antioxidant spices. Serve it over brown rice, red rice, or couscous for a heavenly dinner.

Ingredients:
3 tablespoons olive oil
1/4 cup all-purpose unbleached white flour
2 small yellow onions, diced
1 green bell pepper, cored, seeded, and diced (about 1 cup)
1 red bell pepper, seeded and diced (about 1 cup)
3 celery stalks, finely diced
3 or 4 medium garlic cloves, minced
2 cups fresh tomatoes (plum or beefsteak), chopped
2 cups reduced-sodium, 99 percent fat-free chicken stock
1/4 cup parsley, finely chopped
1 teaspoon dried thyme
1 teaspoon dried oregano leaves
1/8 teaspoon cayenne pepper
1 bay leaf
1/8 teaspoon sea salt, freshly ground
1/8 teaspoon black pepper, freshly ground
2 pounds medium shrimp, peeled and deveined
3 scallions, chopped

Preparation: Add oil to a large, heavy-bottomed pot and place over medium heat. Warm about 1 minute. Whisk in flour to create a roux with the consistency of wet sand. Reduce heat to medium-low and cook gently, stirring occasionally, until roux takes on a lightly toasted aroma and has the color of peanut butter, about 14–22 minutes. Add onions, peppers, celery, and garlic; stir frequently so that mixture does not get lumpy. Increase heat to medium and sauté mixture, stirring often, about 10–12 minutes or until vegetables reduce. Stir in tomatoes, stock, parsley, thyme, oregano, cayenne pepper, bay leaf, salt, and pepper; bring to a boil. Reduce heat to medium-low and simmer for about 30 minutes. Stir in shrimp and simmer for another 6–8 minutes, until shrimp is just cooked through. Garnish with scallions. Makes 6 servings.

Nutritional information per serving:
Calories: 275
Fat: 9 g
Saturated fat: 1 g
Carbohydrate: 15 g
Total sugars: 5 g
Protein: 33 g
Sodium: 355 mg
Cholesterol: 225 mg
Dietary fiber: 3 g

The Anti–Breast Cancer Cookbook

Sole Amandine

This light and flavorful fish recipe is amazingly easy to prepare. Serve it with a rich grain, such as Roasted Beets, Baby Greens and Walnut Salad (see page 129).

Ingredients:
4 boneless sole fillets (4–5 ounces each)
1/4 cup lemon juice
1 tablespoon olive oil
1 teaspoon lemon zest
1 large garlic clove, peeled and minced
1/2 teaspoon dried thyme, crushed
1/4 teaspoon fine sea salt
1/4 teaspoon black pepper, freshly ground
3 tablespoons slivered almonds
1/4 cup parsley, freshly chopped

Preparation: Preheat oven to 375°F. Rinse fish and pat dry. Place in a single layer in a 13 x 9 x 2–inch baking dish. In a small bowl, whisk together lemon juice, oil, lemon zest, garlic, thyme, salt, and pepper. Pour evenly over fish; turn once to coat. Sprinkle with almonds. Bake, uncovered, 9–11 minutes or until fish is opaque and flakes easily with a fork. Top with parsley before serving. Makes 4 servings.

Nutritional information per serving:
Calories: 195
Fat: 7 g
Saturated fat: 1 g
Carbohydrate: 4 g
Total sugars: 1 g
Protein: 28 g
Sodium: 215 mg
Cholesterol: 70 mg
Dietary fiber: 1 g

Spanish Seafood Paella

Ingredients:
2 tablespoons olive oil
4 medium garlic cloves, roughly chopped
1 shallot, chopped
2 teaspoons paprika
1/2 teaspoon dried thyme (optional)
1 cup fresh tomatoes, chopped
5 cups gluten-free, reduced-sodium, organic chicken broth
1 cup green beans, washed and cut in half
1 cup green peas, fresh or frozen (thawed)
Large pinch saffron (optional)
3/4 teaspoon fine sea salt
3/4 teaspoon black pepper, freshly ground
3 cups short-grain brown rice, rinsed
1 pound large uncooked shrimp, peeled and deveined
1 pound squid, cleaned, with bodies cut into 1/2-inch rings
12 clams, scrubbed
12 mussels, scrubbed and debearded
1 lemon, cut into wedges

Preparation: Heat oil in a large, wide skillet over medium-high heat. Add garlic, shallot, paprika, and thyme to the middle of the skillet. Sauté until garlic just begins to brown, 2–3 minutes. Stir in tomatoes; simmer for another 3–4 minutes. Add broth, beans, peas, and saffron; bring to a boil. Season well with salt and pepper; simmer for 15–20 minutes or until liquid is reduced by almost half. Stir in rice and simmer, uncovered and without stirring, for about 5 minutes. Add shrimp, squid, clams, and mussels. Push seafood down into the rice and liquid and cook 20–25 minutes (add a little water or broth if necessary). Remove from heat and let sit for about 5 minutes. Serve in a deep, wide bowl accompanied by lemon wedges to squeeze on top. Makes 8 servings.

Nutritional information per serving:
Calories: 405
Fat: 6 g
Saturated fat: 1 g
Carbohydrate: 58 g
Total sugars: 1 g
Protein: 30 g
Sodium: 435 mg
Cholesterol: 225 mg
Dietary fiber: 4 g

The Anti–Breast Cancer Cookbook

Spinach Tofu in Cashew-Coconut Sauce

At first glance, this dish appears pretty high in fat, but coconut milk contains medium-chain fatty acids, which are known to keep weight in check. Cashew butter and tofu are high in protein and antioxidants as well as healthy fats. For variety, try this dish with almond butter or natural peanut butter in place of the cashew butter.

Ingredients:
1 can (13 or 13½ ounces) coconut milk
1/3 cup cashew butter
2 teaspoons fresh ginger, grated
2 teaspoons brown sugar or honey
1 tablespoon fresh lime juice
1 tablespoon wheat-free tamari
1/8 teaspoon paprika
1/8 teaspoon cumin
1/8 teaspoon turmeric
Pinch cayenne pepper
1 pound extra-firm tofu, sliced into 1-inch cubes
4 cups regular or baby spinach leaves
1/4 teaspoon fine sea salt
1/4 teaspoon black pepper, freshly ground
2 cups cooked short-grain brown rice

Preparation: Place coconut milk, butter, ginger, sugar, lime juice, tamari, paprika, cumin, turmeric, and pepper in slow cooker; stir well to combine. Add tofu; cook on low setting for 2½ hours. Add spinach and stir until leaves wilt and blend into mixture. Season with salt and pepper. Serve spinach and tofu in 4 bowls or soup plates over 1/2 cup brown rice. Makes 4 servings.

Nutritional information per serving:
Calories: 404
Fat: 24 g
Saturated fat: 8 g
Carbohydrate: 39 g
Total sugars: 22 g
Protein: 24 g
Sodium: 275 mg
Cholesterol: 0 mg
Dietary fiber: 5 g

Steamed Asian Halibut
with Sesame Kale

This sesame kale side dish is a favorite recipe of my friend Holly Conti and her son, Alex.

Ingredients:

Kale
1 pound fresh kale
2 tablespoons wheat-free tamari
    or reduced-sodium soy sauce
1 garlic clove, minced
2 teaspoons honey

1 tablespoon red wine vinegar or
    white balsamic vinegar
Pinch of red pepper flakes
2 tablespoons toasted sesame
    seeds

Halibut
4 halibut fillets (about 5–6 ounces each) or 1½ pounds halibut cut
    into 4 pieces
3 green onions, cut into 3-inch-long pieces
4 ounces fresh white mushrooms, washed very well and thinly sliced
5 or 6 leaves Napa cabbage, sliced into 4-inch pieces
1 teaspoon fresh ginger root, minced
1 garlic cloves, chopped
1/8 teaspoon paprika
1/8 teaspoon cayenne pepper
3½ tablespoons wheat-free tamari
1/8 cup water
2 tablespoons cilantro, chopped (optional)

Preparation: To prepare kale, separate leaves from stems. Chop stems and greens separately. Steam stems 2–3 minutes over about 1 inch boiling water. Add greens and steam until just tender, about 3–4 minutes more. Drain kale and allow it to cool until it can be handled. Squeeze out as much water as possible and place in a serving bowl. In a small bowl, combine soy sauce or tamari, garlic, honey, vinegar, and pepper flakes. Mix with kale in serving bowl and top with sesame seeds. Chill. In the meantime, arrange fish and 1/2 of onions on bottom of steaming basket or bowl. Then layer 1/2 of mushrooms and 1/2 of cabbage. Add fish. Sprinkle ginger, garlic, paprika, and pepper over fish. Top with remaining onions, mushrooms, and cabbage. Drizzle tamari and water over everything. Place steam basket in steamer over 1 inch of boiling water; cover. Steam for 15–20 minutes or until fish flakes easily. Garnish with cilantro. Makes 4 servings.

**Nutritional information
per serving of halibut:**
Calories: 185
Fat: 3 g
Saturated fat: < 1 g
Carbohydrate: 5 g
Total sugars: 2 g
Protein: 34 g
Sodium: 290 mg
Cholesterol: 45 mg
Dietary fiber: 2 g

**Nutritional information
per serving of kale:**
Calories: 100
Fat: 3 g
Saturated fat: < 1 g
Carbohydrate: 13 g
Total sugars: 3 g
Protein: 5 g
Sodium: 380 g
Cholesterol: 0 mg
Dietary fiber: 3 g

The Anti–Breast Cancer Cookbook

Swordfish Florentine

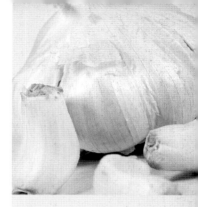

Ingredients:

Aioli Sauce
Pinch saffron
1 tablespoon water
1/2 cup low-fat sour cream
2 tablespoons olive oil mayonnaise
1 tablespoon lemon juice
2 small garlic cloves, crushed
1/4 teaspoon salt
1/4 teaspoon black pepper, freshly ground
Pinch of cayenne pepper (optional)

Swordfish
4 swordfish steaks (about 5–6 ounces each)
1 teaspoon lemon juice
1 teaspoon olive oil
Sea salt to taste
Black pepper, freshly ground, to taste
1½ pounds or 3 bags (10 ounces each) of fresh spinach, washed and
    placed on paper towels

Preparation: To prepare sauce, stir together saffron and water. Let
stand 30 minutes. Add sour cream, mayonnaise, lemon juice, garlic,
salt, black pepper, and cayenne pepper. Cover and chill. Meanwhile,
preheat broiler or prepare outdoor charcoal grill. To prepare fish,
brush each steak with lemon juice and oil; sprinkle with salt and
pepper. Broil or grill about 3–4 minutes on each side. While fish is
cooking, shred spinach finely with a sharp knife. Place spinach in
a large saucepan over medium heat, add dash of salt; cook about
2 minutes or until leaves are only slightly wilted. (The water still
clinging to the spinach leaves will help "steam" them.) Remove
saucepan from heat. Set out 4 dinner plates. Place 1/4 warmed
spinach on each plate; top each with a steak and about 2 tablespoons sauce. Makes 4 servings.

**Nutritional information
per serving:**
Calories: 274
Fat: 10 g
Saturated fat: 3 g
Carbohydrate: 11 g
Total sugars: 2 g
Protein: 35 g
Sodium: 460 mg
Cholesterol: 65 mg
Dietary fiber: 5 g

Tilapia with Cherry Cilantro Salsa

Ingredients:
2 cups Bing cherries, pitted and coarsely chopped (about 8 ounces)
3 tablespoons red onion, finely chopped
1/4 cup fresh cilantro, chopped
3 tablespoons orange or yellow bell pepper, finely chopped
1/2 jalapeño pepper, seeded and minced
1 tablespoon fresh lime juice
1/4 teaspoon kosher salt
1/4 teaspoon black pepper, freshly ground
1/4 teaspoon ground coriander
4 tilapia fillets (4–5 ounces each)
1 tablespoon high-quality olive oil
Nonstick cooking spray, olive-oil style

Preparation: To prepare salsa, combine cherries, onion, cilantro, bell pepper, jalapeño pepper, and lime juice in a medium bowl. Toss to combine and set aside. In a small bowl, stir together salt, pepper, and coriander. Rub fish with oil and sprinkle with spice mixture. Spray a grill pan with nonstick cooking spray and place over medium-high heat. Add fish; cook 3–4 minutes or until opaque. Flip with a thin spatula and cook another 2–3 minutes, until heated through. Top with salsa and serve. Makes 4 servings.

Nutritional information per serving:
Calories: 198
Fat: 5 g
Saturated fat: 1 g
Carbohydrate: 12 g
Total sugars: 8 g
Protein: 27 g
Sodium: 260 mg
Cholesterol: 55 mg
Dietary fiber: 2 g

Tofu and Bok Choy

Ingredients:
8 ounces udon noodles
3 tablespoons cooked black beans
1/2 teaspoon salt, divided
2 tablespoons mirin
1 package (12–13 ounces) firm tofu
1 tablespoon toasted sesame oil, divided
1 teaspoon fresh ginger, minced
1 small head bok choy, thinly sliced, stems and leaves separated
2 cups carrots, julienned
Dash black pepper, freshly ground
1/4 cup daikon radish, shredded (optional)

Preparation: Cook udon noodles according to package directions. Meanwhile, combine beans, 1/4 teaspoon salt, and mirin in a small bowl. Crush beans with back of a spoon and mix well with salt and mirin. Press block of tofu between paper towels to absorb excess moisture. (I sometimes set a cutting board on top of the paper towels to compress the tofu.) Cut tofu into 3/4-inch slices; cut slices into 1-inch squares. Toss tofu with bean mixture and set aside. Place large, deep, nonstick skillet over medium-high heat. Add 1 teaspoon oil, garlic, and bok choy stems; stir-fry for 2 minutes. Add bok choy leaves, carrots, and tofu mixture; stir-fry for 2 minutes or until vegetables are crisp-tender. Sprinkle with pepper and remaining 1/4 teaspoon salt. Drain noodles; toss with bean mixture and remaining 2 teaspoons oil. Transfer to serving plates. Spoon tofu mixture over noodles. Garnish with radish. Makes 4 servings.

Nutritional information per serving:
Calories: 430
Fat: 11 g
Saturated fat: 1 g
Carbohydrate: 56 g
Total sugars: 12 g
Protein: 27 g
Sodium: 390 mg
Cholesterol: 0 mg
Dietary fiber: 10 g

Tomato and Bacon Turkey Meatloaf

This dish is great with traditional fare, such as potato salad and green beans. Use nitrite-free bacon, if possible, to decrease your potential exposure to carcinogens that can be created when bacon is cooked.

Ingredients:
Nonstick cooking spray
4 slices organic bacon (such as Applegate Farms)
1 large omega-3-enriched egg
3 sun-dried tomatoes packed in oil, chopped (or soften dry-packed sun-dried tomatoes in boiling water)
1/4 cup red bell pepper, diced
1/4 cup green bell pepper, diced
1/2 cup yellow onion, finely chopped
1/2 cup fine, whole-grain bread crumbs or gluten-free bread crumbs
1/3 cup reduced-sodium V8 juice
1 teaspoon wheat-free tamari or Bragg Liquid Aminos
1/2 teaspoon dried basil
1/2 teaspoon dried oregano leaves
1/4 teaspoon salt
1/4 teaspoon black pepper
1½ pounds ground lean turkey
2 beefsteak tomatoes, sliced about 1/4 inch thick
1 teaspoon olive oil

Preparation: Preheat oven to 350°F. Spray a skillet with nonstick cooking spray and place over medium-high heat. Add bacon and heat for about 6–7 minutes, until crisp. Let cool briefly and drain on paper towels. Place egg in large bowl and beat gently. Crumble bacon. Add bacon, sun-dried tomatoes, red pepper, green pepper, onion, bread crumbs, juice, tamari or Bragg Liquid Aminos, basil, oregano, salt, and pepper. Stir in turkey and mix until uniformly blended. Press into 8 x 4–inch loaf pan. Lay tomato slices on top, overlapping slightly, and brush with oil. Bake 60–70 minutes, until tomato slices are roasted and meat is cooked through. Drain off fat if necessary. Makes 8 servings.

Nutritional information per serving:
Calories: 195
Fat: 8 g
Saturated fat: 3 g
Carbohydrate: 10 g
Total sugars: 4 g
Protein: 21 g
Sodium: 395 mg
Cholesterol: 55 mg
Dietary fiber: 3 g

The Anti–Breast Cancer Cookbook

Tomato Walnut Tilapia

You can use any type of whitefish fillet to make this light and healthy dish. Walnuts are full of fiber, magnesium, and healthy omega-3 fatty acids.

Ingredients:
1/2 cup whole-wheat bread crumbs or gluten-free bread crumbs
1/4 cup walnuts, chopped
2 tablespoons lemon juice
1/2 tablespoon olive oil
4 tilapia fillets (about 4–5 ounces each)
Salt and black pepper, freshly ground, to taste
Nonstick cooking spray
1 medium tomato, thinly sliced

Preparation: Preheat broiler. In a medium bowl, stir together bread crumbs, walnuts, lemon juice, and oil. Rinse and dry fish; sprinkle with salt and pepper to taste. Spray a large ovenproof skillet with nonstick cooking spray and place over medium heat. Cook fish about 2–3 minutes on each side or until lightly browned. Place tomato slices over fish and spoon bread crumb mixture on top. Broil 3–4 inches from the heat for about 2½–3 minutes or until topping is lightly browned. Makes 4 servings.

Nutritional information per serving:
Calories: 252
Fat: 9 g
Saturated fat: 2 g
Carbohydrate: 13 g
Total sugars: 2 g
Protein: 29 g
Sodium: 168 mg
Cholesterol: 64 mg
Dietary fiber: 2 g

Vegetarian Pad Thai

Ingredients:
8 ounces dried rice noodles
3 tablespoons fresh lime sauce
2 tablespoons reduced-sodium, wheat-free tamari
1 tablespoon brown sugar
1/8 teaspoon red pepper flakes, crushed
1 teaspoon water
Nonstick cooking spray
3 large omega-3-enriched eggs
Dash of salt and pepper
2½ teaspoons sesame oil
2 medium garlic cloves, minced
1–2 teaspoons fresh ginger, peeled and minced
2 small or 1 medium carrot, peeled and cut into narrow strips
5–6 green onions, chopped
1 cup mung bean sprouts
2 tablespoons peanuts, chopped
1 cup red cabbage, shredded
1 lime, sliced (optional)
2 tablespoons fresh cilantro, chopped (optional)

Preparation: Place rice noodles in a bowl, cover with some warm water, and soak about 20 minutes, until they become limp. Meanwhile, combine lime juice, tamari, brown sugar, pepper flakes, and water in small bowl. Place small nonstick skillet over low to medium heat and spray with nonstick cooking spray. Crack eggs onto small skillet and sprinkle with salt and pepper. Cook eggs until firm but still moist; flip and turn off heat. Meanwhile, place large, deep skillet or wok over high heat and add oil. Add garlic and ginger; stir-fry for 30–40 seconds. Add carrot and onions; stir-fry for 1 minute. Add lime juice mixture to garlic/vegetable mixture. Drain noodles and add to wok, tossing with tongs until they soften and curl, about 1 minute. Chop eggs into small strips with spatula. Add eggs and sprouts to wok. Place on serving platter, sprinkle with peanuts, and garnish with cilantro and lime. Makes 4 servings.

Nutritional information per serving:
Calories: 239
Fat: 10 g
Saturated fat: 4 g
Carbohydrate: 30 g
Total sugars: 3 g
Protein: 7 g
Sodium: 520 mg
Cholesterol: 170 mg
Dietary fiber: 4 g

Walnut-Encrusted Halibut
with Pear Chutney

Ingredients:

Halibut
1 cup walnuts
1½ pounds fresh halibut fillets or other whitefish (such as
    tilapia or cod)
1 teaspoon dried basil
1 teaspoon dried oregano leaves
1/4 teaspoon fine sea salt
1/4 teaspoon black pepper, freshly ground
1/4 cup rice flour
1 egg white from a large egg
1 tablespoon olive oil

Chutney
2 medium Bosc or A'njou pears, peeled, cored, and chopped
1/2 small jalapeño pepper, seeded and minced
1/2 cup white wine
1 shallot, minced
1 teaspoon cinnamon
1/2 teaspoon cumin
1/2 teaspoon nutmeg
Pinch cayenne pepper (optional)

Preparation: Preheat oven to 350°F. Place walnuts on a heavy
baking sheet and roast for 5 minutes. In the meantime, place all
chutney ingredients in a saucepan over medium-high heat. Bring
mixture to a boil, reduce heat to low, cover, and simmer. Remove
walnuts from oven, transfer to a bowl, and set aside to cool. Change
oven setting to broil. Remove skin from fish (if necessary) and cut
into 4 equal-size fillets. Grind walnuts in coffee grinder or food
processor. (Alternatively, place walnuts in a resealable plastic bag
and use a meat tenderizer to pound nuts to a medium-fine texture.)
Transfer walnuts to a shallow dish. Add basil, oregano, salt, pepper, and flour; blend well. Brush egg white onto fish and carefully
roll each fillet in walnut mixture, making sure to coat thoroughly.
Place fish on baking sheet. Drizzle or baste with oil and cook for
approximately 15–17 minutes, until opaque but still moist. Top
with chutney and serve. Makes 4 servings.

**Nutritional information
per serving:**
Calories: 398
Fat: 14 g
Saturated fat: 1 g
Carbohydrate: 26 g
Total sugars: 9 g
Protein: 42 g
Sodium: 208 mg
Cholesterol: 54 mg
Dietary fiber: 5 g

White Bean, Broccoli Rabe and Fontina Fusilli

Vegetarian

You can substitute spinach for the broccoli rabe.

Ingredients:
10 ounces whole-wheat pasta shells, fusilli, chiocciole, or gluten-
    free rice spirals
1 large bunch broccoli rabe, trimmed and cut into 1-inch pieces
1½ cups reduced-sodium vegetable broth
1 tablespoon all-purpose unbleached white flour
2 tablespoons high-quality olive oil
2 medium garlic cloves, minced
1 can (15½ ounces) cannellini beans, rinsed and drained
2 tablespoons red wine vinegar
1/4 teaspoon salt
1/4 teaspoon black pepper, freshly ground
1/2 cup fontina cheese, shredded
1/3 cup pine nuts, toasted

Preparation: Place a large pot of water over medium-high heat and bring to a boil. Add pasta and cook according to package directions, stirring occasionally. Stir in broccoli rabe during last 2–3 minutes of recommended cooking. Drain and dry pot. Place broth and flour in a small bowl and whisk until smooth. Place dry pot back over medium-high heat and add oil; warm oil for 45–60 seconds. Add garlic; cook, stirring constantly, until fragrant, about 30–60 seconds. Add broth/flour mixture; bring to a simmer, whisking constantly, until it thickens, about 3–4 minutes. Add beans, vinegar, salt, pepper, pasta, and broccoli rabe; cook, stirring, until mixture is heated through, about 1 minute. Remove from heat. Add cheese and stir until it melts. Serve immediately, topped with pine nuts. Makes 6 servings.

Nutritional information per serving:
Calories: 365
Fat: 13 g
Saturated fat: 3 g
Carbohydrate: 43 g
Total sugars: 3 g
Protein: 19 g
Sodium: 385 mg
Cholesterol: 10 mg
Dietary fiber: 7 g

The Anti–Breast Cancer Cookbook

DESToday — DESSERTS

Vegetarian

Vegan

Gluten-Free

Almond Polenta Cake   186
Apple-Nut Cake 187
Apple-Strawberry Pie   188
Avocado Gelato with Peach-Cherry Sauce   189
Blueberry Yogurt Tart 190
Bread Pudding with Apple-Cranberry Sauce 191
Carrot-Walnut Cookies   192
Chocolate-Almond Biscotti 193
Chocolate-Hazelnut Cheesecake 194
Cinnamon Black Rice Pudding with Tart Cherry Sauce   195
Coconut Pudding   196
Coffee Frozen Yogurt   196
Cream Cheese and Walnut Crumble 197
Gingerbread 198
Granola Cookies 199
Lemon Yogurt Cake with Mixed Berries 200
Light Chocolate Cake 201
Oatmeal-Cherry-Chocolate Chip Cookies   202
Pumpkin–Black Rice Pudding   203
Raspberry-Strawberry-Lime Yogurt Tart 204
Raspberry Pudding   205
Ruby Red Grapefruit Brûlée   205
Walnut-Raspberry Tart 206
Whole-Wheat Dark Chocolate Chip-Nut Cookies 207

Almond Polenta Cake

This rich and delicious cake contains valuable omega-3 fatty acids, fiber, and magnesium. Many online purveyors carry roasted almond oil; I get mine at the local Marshall's discount department store. To make this recipe vegan, use 3 tablespoons ground flaxseed meal mixed with about 8–9 tablespoons water as an egg replacer.

Ingredients:
Nonstick cooking spray
1/2 cup sliced almonds, toasted, divided
1/2 cup ground almonds
1/2 cup finely ground polenta (or grind regular polenta in a
    food processor)
1/2 cup whole-wheat pastry flour or all-purpose gluten-free
    baking flour
1½ teaspoons cornstarch
1 teaspoon baking powder or gluten-free baking powder
1/2 teaspoon salt
1/2 cup nonhydrogenated buttery spread (such as Smart Balance
    or Fleischmann's Olive Oil Spread)
1/4 cup roasted almond oil
2/3 cup sugar
3 large omega-3-enriched eggs
3 tablespoons orange juice
1/2 teaspoon vanilla extract

Preparation: Preheat oven to 325°F. Coat 8-inch round spring-form pan with nonstick cooking spray (or tiny dab of oil). Sprinkle a few almonds on bottom of pan. Whisk together remaining almonds, polenta, flour, cornstarch, baking powder, and salt. Using a hand mixer, cream together spread, oil, and sugar until fluffy. Beat in eggs one at a time, making sure each egg is combined before the next one is added. Beat in orange juice and vanilla. Add dry ingredients; stir until just combined. Pour into springform pan; bake 45–50 minutes, or until toothpick inserted in the center comes out clean. Cool for 15 minutes and then turn out on wire rack to cool completely. Makes 12 servings.

Nutritional information per serving:
Calories: 225
Fat: 13 g
Saturated fat: 1 g
Carbohydrate: 22 g
Total sugars: 12 g
Protein: 5 g
Sodium: 165 mg
Cholesterol: 50 mg
Dietary fiber: 2 g

The Anti–Breast Cancer Cookbook

Apple-Nut Cake

You can use dried cherries, dried cranberries, or raisins in place of the currants for variation.

Ingredients:
Nonstick cooking spray
4 medium sweet-tart apples (such as Granny Smith or Fuji), shredded
2/3 cup brown sugar
1/3 cup cold-pressed canola oil
1/2 teaspoon vanilla extract
1 extra large omega-3-enriched egg, beaten
3/4 cup all-purpose unbleached white flour, unsifted
3/4 cup whole-wheat pastry flour, unsifted
3 tablespoons ground flaxseed meal
1 teaspoon baking powder
1 teaspoon baking soda
1 teaspoon cinnamon
1/4 teaspoon nutmeg
1/4 teaspoon salt
1/3 cup dried currants
1/2 cup walnuts, chopped

Preparation: Preheat oven to 350°F. Spray an 8-inch square cake pan with nonstick cooking spray. In a large bowl, combine apples and sugar; let stand about 10 minutes. Add oil, vanilla, and egg; blend. In a separate bowl, stir together white flour, wheat flour, flaxseed meal, baking powder, baking soda, cinnamon, nutmeg, and salt. Add apple mixture and stir until evenly distributed and well mixed. Stir in currants and walnuts. Pour into cake pan and bake 35–40 minutes or until a toothpick comes out clean. Makes 10 servings.

Nutritional information per serving:
Calories: 325
Fat: 16 g
Saturated fat: 2 g
Carbohydrate: 40 g
Total sugars: 21 g
Protein: 5 g
Sodium: 235 mg
Cholesterol: 22 mg
Dietary fiber: 4 g

Apple-Strawberry Pie

This recipe also works well with raspberries, cranberries, or blueberries instead of strawberries. For a vegan pie, substitute rice or almond milk for the nonfat dairy milk in the crust.

Ingredients:

Filling
5 sweet-tart apples (such as Granny Smith), peeled and thinly sliced (5½ cups)
1 tablespoon lemon juice
1/8 teaspoon ground cinnamon
1/8 teaspoon ground nutmeg
2/3 cup sugar
3 tablespoons cornstarch
2½ cups fresh strawberries, chopped or sliced

Crust
1⅓ cups all-purpose unbleached white flour
1⅓ cups whole-wheat pastry flour
1/2 teaspoon salt
2/3 cup high-oleic safflower oil
6 tablespoons plus 1 teaspoon nonfat (skim) dairy milk, divided
1 teaspoon sugar

Preparation: Preheat oven to 400°F. For the filling, combine apples, lemon juice, cinnamon, nutmeg, sugar, and cornstarch in a large bowl; gently fold in strawberries. For the crust, whisk together white flour, wheat flour, and salt in a medium bowl. Pour oil into glass measuring cup; add 6 tablespoons milk without stirring. Pour into flour mixture and stir briefly, just until combined. Divide dough in half and form two balls. Place a 15-inch-long piece of wax paper on your work surface. (Put a few drops of water under the paper or place it on top of a textured surface to keep it from sliding around.) Place one ball on the paper and press into a 6-inch circle. Top with another piece of wax paper and roll out with a rolling pin to make a 12-inch circle. (The edges may extend beyond the top and bottom of the wax paper slightly; you can loosen it with a knife when you lift the dough.) If necessary, tear uneven edges to make a smooth and even circle. Remove top sheet and turn dough into a 9-inch pie pan. Add filling. Roll out the second dough ball between fresh pieces of wax paper. Place it on top to form top crust of pie. Fold top crust under bottom crust all the way around and crimp the edges. Cut slits in the top; brush very lightly with remaining 1 teaspoon milk; sprinkle with sugar. Bake for 10 minutes. Reduce heat to 350°F and bake 45–50 minutes, until crust is lightly golden and filling bubbles. Cool 3 or more hours before serving. Makes 10 servings.

Nutritional information per serving:
Calories: 359
Fat: 14 g
Saturated fat: 1 g
Carbohydrate: 55 g
Total sugars: 24 g
Protein: 4 g
Sodium: 85 mg
Cholesterol: 0 mg
Dietary fiber: 5 g

The Anti–Breast Cancer Cookbook

Avocado Gelato with Peach-Cherry Sauce

You'll need an ice-cream maker for this dessert.

Ingredients:

Gelato
2 cups reduced-fat (2 percent) dairy milk (preferably organic), divided
2/3 cup granulated white or raw (turbinado) sugar, divided
3 strips (4 x 1 inch) fresh orange zest
Pinch of salt
2 tablespoons cornstarch
2 ripe but firm California avocados (1–1¼ pounds total), peeled, pitted, and quartered
3 tablespoons mango nectar

Sauce
1 ripe peach, pitted and chopped
1 cup fresh dark cherries, pitted
2 teaspoons brown sugar
1/4 cup mango nectar

Preparation: To make gelato, bring 1¾ cups milk, 1/2 cup sugar, orange zest, and pinch of salt to a simmer in a 2-quart heavy saucepan over moderate heat. Whisk together cornstarch and remaining 1/4 cup milk in small bowl until smooth; whisk into simmering milk. Bring to a boil, whisking constantly; boil 1 minute. Transfer mixture to a metal bowl. Set metal bowl in a larger bowl filled with ice and cold water and cool completely, stirring frequently. Discard orange zest. Puree avocado, mango nectar, and remaining sugar in a food processor until smooth. Add milk mixture and blend well. Freeze avocado mixture in ice-cream maker. Transfer to airtight container and freeze until hardened, about 1 hour. To make sauce, combine peach, cherries, and sugar in a sauté pan. Bring to a simmer and cook over medium-high heat, stirring occasionally, until fruit is soft, 6–8 minutes. Transfer mixture to a food processor and puree until completely smooth. Return mixture to sauté pan over medium-high heat. Add mango nectar; simmer until reduced to about 1/4 cup, 1–2 minutes. Makes 4 servings of gelato topped with sauce.

Nutritional information per serving:
Calories: 379
Fat: 12 g
Saturated fat: 3 g
Carbohydrate: 65 g
Total sugars: 50 g
Protein: 7 g
Sodium: 15 mg
Cholesterol: 10 mg
Dietary fiber: 8 g

Blueberry Yogurt Tart

Make sure the graham crackers you use for the crust are free of trans fat. If you see "partially hydrogenated" in the ingredient list, the crackers contain trans fat.

Ingredients:

Crust
1/2 cup pecans, lightly toasted
12–14 whole-wheat graham cracker sheets (enough to make 1 cup cracker crumbs)
1 egg white from a large egg

1 tablespoon unsalted butter, melted
1 tablespoon sunflower or cold-pressed canola oil
1/8 teaspoon salt

Custard
1 cup low-fat plain or vanilla yogurt
1/4 cup sugar

2 large omega-3-enriched eggs
1 teaspoon vanilla extract

Topping
2 cups fresh blueberries
1/2 cup water
1/4 cup sugar (raw or granulated white)

1/2 teaspoon lemon zest
1/2 teaspoon ground cinnamon
1/4 teaspoon ground ginger

Preparation: Preheat oven to 425°F. For the crust, coarsely chop pecans in a food processor. Add graham cracker crumbs and process until crumbs become fine. (If you do not have a food processor, you can grind pecans in a coffee grinder and crumble graham crackers by placing them in a plastic bag and crushing them with a rolling pin.) Whisk egg white in a medium bowl until frothy. Add crumb mixture, butter, oil, and salt; toss to combine. Press mixture into the bottom and 1/2 inch up the sides of a 9-inch removable-bottom tart pan. Set pan on a baking sheet. Bake until shell is dry and slightly dark around the edges, about 8–9 minutes. Cool on a wire rack. Reduce oven temperature to 325°F. Combine all ingredients for the custard and pour into cooled pie shell. Bake 15–20 minutes, until custard is firm. Let cool in refrigerator for at least 1 hour and preferably overnight. To make topping, combine blueberries, water, sugar, lemon zest, cinnamon, and ginger; bring to a boil. Reduce to a simmer. Allow mixture to reduce until thickened (resembling jam). Allow mixture to cool and spread evenly over tart surface. Keep refrigerated before serving. Makes 8 servings.

Nutritional information per serving:
Calories: 195
Fat: 8 g
Saturated fat: 3 g
Carbohydrate: 27 g
Total sugars: 23 g
Protein: 4 g
Sodium: 138 mg
Cholesterol: 16 mg
Dietary fiber: 1 g

The Anti–Breast Cancer Cookbook

Bread Pudding
with Apple-Cranberry Sauce

Ingredients:

Bread Pudding
Nonstick cooking spray
10 slices thick whole-wheat or nine-grain (whole-grain) bread
1 large omega-3-enriched egg plus 3 egg whites from large eggs
1½ cups nonfat dairy milk (preferably organic)
3 tablespoons plus 2 teaspoons raw (turbinado) sugar, divided
2 tablespoons Splenda Brown Sugar Blend
1 teaspoon vanilla extract
1/2 teaspoon cinnamon
1/4 teaspoon nutmeg
1/4 teaspoon ground cloves

Sauce
1¼ cups vitamin C–enriched apple juice
1/2 cup natural apple butter
2 tablespoons molasses
1/2 cup fresh cranberries, chopped
1/4 teaspoon ground cinnamon
1/4 teaspoon ground nutmeg
1 teaspoon orange zest

Preparation: Preheat oven to 350°F. To make bread pudding, spray an 8 x 8–inch baking dish with nonstick cooking spray (or lightly coat with oil). Lay slices of bread in baking dish in two rows, overlapping like shingles on a roof. In a medium bowl, beat together egg, egg whites, milk, 3 tablespoons raw sugar, Splenda, and vanilla. Pour egg mixture over bread. In small bowl, stir together cinnamon, nutmeg, cloves, and 2 teaspoons raw sugar. Sprinkle sugar mixture over bread pudding; bake for 30–35 minutes, until it has browned on top and is firm to the touch. Meanwhile, to prepare sauce, place apple juice, apple butter, molasses, cranberries, cinnamon, nutmeg, and orange zest in a medium saucepan. Stir together and bring to a simmer over low heat. Let simmer for 5–6 minutes. Serve bread pudding warm or at room temperature with warm sauce. Makes 8 servings, about 1/2 cup bread pudding with 1/4 cup sauce each.

Nutritional information per serving:
Calories: 230
Fat: 3 g
Saturated fat: < 1 g
Carbohydrate: 44 g
Total sugars: 21 g
Protein: 7 g
Sodium: 250 mg
Cholesterol: 24 mg
Dietary fiber: 3 g

Carrot-Walnut Cookies

I adapted this recipe from one published many years ago in a Whole Foods newsletter, changing a number of ingredients to suit my tastes and health motivations. You can use just about any type of nut in place of the walnuts; I prefer raw nuts because they retain their healthy oil better than roasted ones. Make this dish gluten-free by substituting Bob's Red Mill gluten-free all-purpose baking flour for the whole-wheat pastry flour and using ground almonds instead of wheat germ.

Ingredients:
3/4 cup walnuts
1 cup old-fashioned rolled oats
1 cup dried currants, cherries, cranberries, or raisins
1/2 cup whole-wheat pastry flour or gluten-free all-purpose baking flour
3 tablespoons ground flaxseed meal
2 tablespoons wheat germ or ground almonds
1¼ teaspoons baking powder or gluten-free baking powder
1¼ teaspoons ground cinnamon
1/2 teaspoon ground ginger
1/4 teaspoon nutmeg
2 carrots, grated
1 Fuji or Golden Delicious apple, grated
1 ripe banana, mashed with a fork
1/4 cup apple juice

Preparation: Preheat oven to 350°F. Line 2 baking sheets with parchment paper or use 2 heavy, nonstick baking sheets. Combine walnuts, oats, and dried fruit in a food processor; pulse until finely ground. Transfer to a bowl and stir in wheat flour or baking flour, flaxseed meal, wheat germ or almonds, baking powder, cinnamon, ginger, and nutmeg. Add carrots, apples, banana, and apple juice; stir until combined. Drop by rounded tablespoon at least 1 inch apart on baking sheets. Press down on cookies with the back of a fork or a spatula to flatten slightly. Bake until tops and bottoms are lightly browned, about 22–25 minutes. Makes about 24 cookies.

Nutritional information per cookie:
Calories: 100
Fat: 4 g
Saturated fat: 0 g
Carbohydrate: 15 g
Total sugars: 6 g
Protein: 2 g
Sodium: 30 mg
Cholesterol: 0 mg
Dietary fiber: 2 g

The Anti–Breast Cancer Cookbook

Chocolate-Almond Biscotti

This recipe was in my first cookbook and got such wonderful feedback that I felt the need to include it again. The trick is getting all the dry ingredients moistened and using a very thin, serrated knife to cut the logs into cookies after the first baking. These delicious biscotti are full of antioxidants such as epicatechin and selenium.

Ingredients:
2 tablespoons brewed espresso or very strong coffee, at room
    temperature
3 egg whites from large or extra large eggs
1/3 cup cold-pressed canola oil
1¼ teaspoons vanilla extract
1⅔ cups all-purpose white flour
2/3 cup sugar
1/2 cup unsweetened, unprocessed dark cocoa powder
1 teaspoon baking powder
1/4 teaspoon baking soda
1/8 teaspoon salt
1/2 cup almonds, sliced, chopped, or ground
1/4 cup dried tart cherries

Preparation: Preheat oven to 350°F. In a small bowl, beat together espresso or coffee, egg whites, oil, and vanilla. In a large bowl, combine flour, sugar, cocoa powder, baking powder, baking soda, salt, almonds, and cherries; stir until well blended. Add coffee mixture; stir until well mixed and evenly moistened. Shape dough into 2 12 x 2–inch logs. (You might want to oil your fingers a bit to prevent sticking.) Place logs on nonstick baking sheet and flatten slightly, so each is about 1-inch high. Bake 30 minutes, remove from oven, and cool 10 minutes. Transfer 1 log to cutting board and slice diagonally into 1-inch-thick pieces. Arrange cut-side up, on baking sheet. Repeat with second log; use additional baking sheet if necessary. Bake 20 minutes; transfer to wire rack to cool. Store in airtight container up to 1 month. Makes about 24 biscotti.

Nutritional information per biscotti:
Calories: 110
Fat: 5 g
Saturated fat: < 1 g
Carbohydrate: 14 g
Total sugars: 6 g
Protein: 2 g
Sodium: 35 mg
Cholesterol: 0 mg
Dietary fiber: 1 g

Chocolate-Hazelnut Cheesecake

Vegetarian

Ingredients:

Crust
6 whole sheets graham crackers (use a brand that does not contain
    trans fat), broken into pieces
1/2 cup hazelnuts (about 2 ounces), loose skins rubbed off
2 tablespoons dark brown sugar
1/4 cup coconut or sunflower oil

Filling
16 ounces reduced-fat cream cheese, at room temperature
1/2 cup plus 1/3 cup sugar, divided
4 large omega-3-enriched eggs, separated
1 cup reduced-fat sour cream
1/2 cup whole-wheat pastry flour
1/4 cup unprocessed dark cocoa powder
2 tablespoons Frangelico liqueur
1 teaspoon vanilla extract

Preparation: Preheat oven to 350°F. To prepare crust, lightly oil
a springform pan, 9 inches in diameter with sides 2¾ inches high.
Finely grind graham crackers, hazelnuts, and brown sugar in a food
processor. Add oil and process until crumbs are evenly moistened.
Press crumb mixture onto bottom of pan. Bake 10 minutes. Cool
on wire rack. To prepare filling, with an electric mixer, beat cream
cheese with 1/2 cup sugar until light and fluffy. Add egg yolks one
at a time, beating after each yolk is added until just blended. Add
sour cream, flour, cocoa powder, liqueur, and vanilla; beat just until
mixture is smooth. Using clean, dry beaters, beat egg whites until
soft peaks form. Gradually add remaining 1/3 cup sugar and beat
until stiff but not dry. Fold egg whites into cream cheese mixture,
half at a time. Pour filling into crust; bake until center is just set,
about 50 minutes. Turn off oven but leave cheesecake in oven 40
minutes longer; transfer cheesecake to wire rack and cool to room
temperature. Cut around pan sides with small sharp knife to loosen
cheesecake. Cover and refrigerate overnight. Makes 10 servings.

**Nutritional information
per serving:**
Calories: 360
Fat: 21 g
Saturated fat: 10 g
Carbohydrate: 38 g
Total sugars: 24 g
Protein: 9 g
Sodium: 300 mg
Cholesterol: 110 mg
Dietary fiber: 3 g

The Anti–Breast Cancer Cookbook

Cinnamon Black Rice Pudding with Tart Cherry Sauce

I designed this recipe by combining a recipe I found online with one from a 2005 edition of Gourmet *magazine. Black rice is commonly eaten in southeastern Asia and is gaining recognition elsewhere for its high levels of anthocyanins, the same antioxidants in blackberries. This rice contains almost no simple sugars. Coconut milk is rich in lauric acid, which may have immune boosting properties. For a lower-fat version, use dairy, rice, or soy milk.*

Ingredients:

Pudding
1 cup black rice
3 cups water
1/8 teaspoon salt
1/3 cup raw (turbinado) sugar
1½ cups unsweetened coconut
 milk (or 2 cups organic

2 percent fat dairy milk, rice
 milk, or soy milk)
1 teaspoon ground cinnamon
1 teaspoon vanilla extract
1/4 teaspoon almond extract

Sauce
1¼ cups dried tart cherries
1¾ cups plus 1 tablespoon water
2 tablespoons raw (turbinado)
 sugar

1 teaspoon cornstarch
3/4 teaspoon vanilla extract

Preparation: To prepare pudding, place rice, water, and salt in a 3- or 4-quart heavy saucepan and bring to a boil. Reduce heat to low and cover with a tight-fitting lid; simmer 45 minutes (rice will be cooked but still wet). Stir in sugar and milk; bring to a boil over high heat. Reduce heat to low and simmer, uncovered, stirring occasionally, until mixture is thick and rice is tender but still slightly chewy, about 30 minutes. Meanwhile, to prepare sauce, combine cherries and water in a medium saucepan. Place over medium-high heat; bring to a boil. Reduce heat and simmer 20 minutes. Stir in sugar; cook 5 minutes. Combine remaining 1 tablespoon water with cornstarch. Add to cherry mixture; bring to a boil. Cook 1 minute or until slightly thick, stirring consistently. Remove from heat; stir in vanilla. Serve pudding topped with sauce. Makes 6 servings.

Nutritional information per serving:

Made with coconut milk
Calories: 440
Fat: 12 g
Saturated fat: 10 g
Carbohydrate: 80 g
Total sugars: 51 g
Protein: 5 g
Sodium: 50 mg
Cholesterol: 0 mg
Dietary fiber: 1 g

Made with 2 percent fat dairy milk
Calories: 365
Fat: 3 g
Saturated fat: 1 g
Carbohydrate: 80 g
Total sugars: 56 g
Protein: 7 g
Sodium: 45 mg
Cholesterol: 6 mg
Dietary fiber: 1 g

Coconut Pudding

For an extra treat, serve this pudding topped with dark chocolate sauce.

Nutritional information per serving:
Calories: 183
Fat: 7 g
Saturated fat: 3 g
Carbohydrate: 24 g
Total sugars: 20 g
Protein: 6 g
Sodium: 30 mg
Cholesterol: 0 mg
Dietary fiber: < 1 g

Ingredients:
1 pound silken tofu
1/3 cup raw (turbinado) sugar
1/2 teaspoon vanilla extract
1/2 cup shredded coconut

Preparation: In a blender or food processor, whip together tofu, sugar, and vanilla until stiff and creamy. In a bowl, fold coconut into tofu mixture. Pour into parfait glasses or individual dessert bowls and chill. Makes 4 servings.

Coffee Frozen Yogurt

You will need an ice-cream maker for this recipe.

Nutritional information per serving:
Calories: 124
Fat: 4 g
Saturated fat: 2 g
Carbohydrate: 18 g
Total sugars: 8 g
Protein: 4 g
Sodium: 55 mg
Cholesterol: 15mg
Dietary fiber: 0 g

Ingredients:
1/2 cup strong espresso, chilled
1/2 cup granulated white sugar
1 quart organic low-fat plain yogurt (such as Stonyfield or Brown Cow)

Preparation: In a bowl, combine espresso, sugar, and yogurt; stir until smooth. Churn in an ice-cream maker until mixture has the consistency of soft-serve ice cream, about 20 minutes, depending on the machine. Makes 8 servings.

Cream Cheese and Walnut Crumble

Just a handful of walnuts has close to 3 grams of omega-3 fatty acids, crucial for enhancing immunity and fighting inflammation.

Ingredients:

Crust
1/2 cup brown sugar
2 cups whole-wheat pastry flour
1 cup walnuts, finely chopped (with a food processor or nut chopper)
1/2 cup nonhydrogenated buttery spread (such as Smart Balance or Fleischmann's Olive Oil Spread), melted
1/3 cup natural applesauce

Filling
1/4 cup brown sugar, packed
1 package (16 ounces) reduced-fat cream cheese, at room temperature
2 large omega-3-enriched eggs
2 tablespoons lemon juice
1 tablespoon vanilla extract
2 tablespoons reduced-fat (2 percent) dairy milk

Preparation: Preheat oven to 350°F. For the crust, combine sugar, wheat flour, and walnuts in a medium bowl. Add spread and applesauce; stir until mixture is light and crumbly. Set aside 1½ cups to be used as topping. Use a spatula or pancake turner to press remainder of mixture firmly into a 9 x 13–inch baking pan. Bake 12–13 minutes, or until light brown. For the filling, use an electric hand mixer set to low to cream together sugar and cream cheese until smooth. Add eggs one by one, lemon juice, vanilla, and milk; stir or blend gently until mixed. Spoon batter into crust; sprinkle reserved 1½ cups crumbs on top. Bake for 23–25 minutes, until set. Cool in pan on wire rack. Cut into squares or rectangles and refrigerate for several hours before serving. Makes about 16 servings.

Nutritional information per serving:
Calories: 202
Fat: 12 g
Saturated fat: 4 g
Carbohydrate: 23 g
Total sugars: 8 g
Protein: 1 g
Sodium: 130 mg
Cholesterol: 40 mg
Dietary fiber: 3 g

Gingerbread

A high-fat diet has been linked to obesity, and obesity has been shown to increase the risk of numerous cancer types, including postmenopausal breast cancer. This gingerbread contains less than 1 gram of fat per serving. It is low in calories but rich in flavor.

Ingredients:
Nonstick cooking spray
1½ cups all-purpose unbleached white flour
1 cup whole-wheat flour
2/3 cup granulated white sugar
2½ teaspoons baking soda
1 teaspoon ground ginger
1 teaspoon ground cinnamon
1 teaspoon allspice
1½ cups natural (unsweetened) applesauce
1 cup dark molasses
3 egg whites from large eggs

Preparation: Preheat oven to 325°F. Spray a 9 x 13-inch pan with nonstick cooking spray or oil lightly. Combine white flour, wheat flour, sugar, baking soda, ginger, cinnamon, and allspice in large bowl. Mix well. Add applesauce, molasses, and egg whites; stir until well blended. Spread evenly in the pan; bake 35–40 minutes, until a toothpick comes out clean. Serve warm. Makes 18 servings of 1 slice each.

Nutritional information per serving:
Calories: 156
Fat: < 1 g
Saturated fat: 0 g
Carbohydrate: 36 g
Total sugars: 13 g
Protein: 2 g
Sodium: 20 mg
Cholesterol: 0 mg
Dietary fiber: 2 g

The Anti–Breast Cancer Cookbook

Granola Cookies

Feel free to substitute dried tart cherries, chopped dates, or raisins for the dried cranberries. If you can't find ground flaxseed meal, try wheat germ instead.

Ingredients:
3/4 cup all-purpose unbleached white flour
3/4 cup whole-wheat flour
3 tablespoons ground flaxseed meal
1 teaspoon baking powder
1/2 teaspoon baking soda
1/2 teaspoon ground cinnamon
1/2 teaspoon salt
3 tablespoons cold-pressed canola or sunflower oil
1/2 cup Splenda Brown Sugar Blend (or 2/3 cup regular brown sugar, packed)
1 large omega-3-enriched egg
Zest of 1 orange
1/4 cup orange juice (preferably freshly squeezed)
1 cup high-protein granola cereal (such as Bear Naked Peak Protein)
1/2 cup whole-grain rolled oats
1/4 cup walnuts, chopped
1/3 cup dried cranberries

Preparation: Preheat oven to 350°F. In small bowl, stir together white flour, wheat flour, flaxseed meal, baking powder, baking soda, cinnamon, and salt; set aside. In a bowl, use a hand mixer to cream together oil and sugar. Add egg and beat until fluffy. Beat in orange zest and juice. Beat in flour mixture; stir in cereal, oats, walnuts, and cranberries. Line baking sheets with parchment paper or use nonstick baking sheets. Drop batter by 1½–2 tablespoons onto baking sheets, leaving space in between for batter to spread. Bake for 11–13 minutes, until lightly browned. Remove from oven and transfer to wire racks to cool completely. Makes 24 cookies.

Nutritional information per cookie:
Calories: 112
Fat: 4 g
Saturated fat: 1 g
Carbohydrate: 16 g
Total sugars: 7 g
Protein: 3 g
Sodium: 80 mg
Cholesterol: 8 mg
Dietary fiber: 2 g

Lemon Yogurt Cake with Mixed Berries

Vegetarian

You can also make this cake in a vanilla version, using vanilla yogurt and vanilla extract and no lemon extract. The vanilla version is simply fantastic, although I prefer the lemon. Any combination of fresh berries works well as a topping.

Ingredients:
Nonstick cooking spray
1⅓ cups all-purpose unbleached white flour
2/3 cup whole-wheat pastry flour
1½ teaspoons baking powder
1/2 teaspoon baking soda
1/4 teaspoon salt
1 cup low-fat lemon yogurt (preferably organic)
3/4 cup raw (turbinado) sugar
3 large omega-3-enriched eggs
1/3 cup cold-pressed canola or olive oil
1/2 teaspoon pure lemon extract
1/2 teaspoon pure vanilla extract
2/3 cup fresh strawberries, hulled and sliced
2/3 cup fresh blueberries
2/3 cup fresh blackberries

Preparation: Preheat oven to 350°F. Spray a 9-inch cake pan with nonstick cooking spray and line the bottom with a circle of parchment paper. Also spray parchment paper with cooking spray. Set pan aside. In a medium bowl, whisk together white flour, wheat flour, baking powder, baking soda, and salt. In a separate bowl, whisk together yogurt, sugar, eggs, oil, lemon extract, and vanilla extract. Gently whisk flour mixture into yogurt mixture until just blended and smooth. Pour batter into pan and bake for 45–50 minutes, until cake is golden brown and top has formed a thin crust. The cake should be just firm in the center when done. Cool cake on a wire rack for 15 minutes. Remove cake from pan and peel off parchment paper. Continue cooling on rack. Decorate top with strawberries, blueberries, and blackberries. Refrigerate or serve immediately. Makes 10 servings.

Nutritional information per serving:
Calories: 295
Fat: 9 g
Saturated fat: 1 g
Carbohydrate: 48 g
Total sugars: 20 g
Protein: 7 g
Sodium: 195 mg
Cholesterol: 60 mg
Dietary fiber: 4 g

The Anti–Breast Cancer Cookbook

Light Chocolate Cake

Vegetarian

Instead of butter or oil, this cake relies on chunky applesauce for its moistness, keeping it relatively low in fat and calories.

Ingredients:

Topping
1 tablespoon raw (turbinado) sugar
1 teaspoon cinnamon

Cake
Nonstick cooking spray
1 cup all-purpose unbleached white flour
1 cup whole-wheat pastry flour
1/2 cup granulated white sugar
1/4 cup brown sugar, loosely packed
3 tablespoons unprocessed cocoa powder
1 teaspoon baking soda
1 teaspoon baking powder
1/4 teaspoon salt
1 teaspoon cinnamon
1/4 teaspoon ground ginger
2 cups chunky natural (unsweetened) applesauce
4 egg whites from large eggs

Preparation: Preheat oven to 350°F. To make topping, stir together sugar and cinnamon in small bowl. Set aside. Spray a 9 x 13-inch pan with nonstick cooking spray or lightly oil it. In large bowl, add white flour, wheat flour, white sugar, brown sugar, cocoa powder, baking soda, baking powder, salt, cinnamon, and ginger; mix gently to distribute. Stir in applesauce and egg whites; mix lightly, until just moistened. Pour batter into pan and sprinkle with topping; bake 40–45 minutes, until a toothpick inserted in center comes out dry. Remove from oven and cool before serving. Makes 12 servings.

Nutritional information per cookie:
Calories: 100
Fat: 3 g
Saturated fat: 2 g
Carbohydrate: 14 g
Total sugars: < 1 g
Protein: 2 g
Sodium: 45 mg
Cholesterol: 0 mg
Dietary fiber: 2 g

Oatmeal-Cherry-Chocolate Chip Cookies

You can make this recipe with any dried fruit or nuts and with or without the coconut. Feel free to experiment with dates, raisins, currants, and dried cranberries, as well as hazelnuts and macadamia nuts. For gluten-free cookies, try using a mixture of Bob's Red Mill almond flour and oat flour instead of white and whole-wheat flour.

Ingredients:
3½ cups whole-grain rolled oats
3/4 cup dried tart cherries
1 cup unsweetened dried shredded coconut
1/2 cup dark chocolate chips
1/3 cup walnuts or pecans, chopped
1 cup all-purpose unbleached white flour
3/4 cup whole-wheat flour or whole-wheat pastry flour
1 teaspoon baking soda
1/2 teaspoon sea salt
1/2 cup Splenda Brown Sugar Blend
2/3 cup natural (unsweetened) applesauce
3 tablespoons sunflower oil
2 teaspoons vanilla extract

Preparation: Combine rolled oats, cherries, coconut, chocolate chips, walnuts or pecans, white flour, wheat flour, baking soda, sea salt, and Splenda in large bowl. In a separate small bowl, stir together applesauce, oil, and vanilla. Add wet mixture to dry mixture; stir until just incorporated and moisture is evenly distributed. Cover and refrigerate for at least 30 minutes. Meanwhile, preheat oven to 350°F. Line 2 heavy baking sheets with parchment paper or use nonstick baking sheets. Roll chilled dough into balls and stagger in rows on baking sheets. Bake 13–16 minutes or until just set and light brown around the edges. Makes about 48 cookies.

Nutritional information per serving:
Calories: 170
Fat: < 1 g
Saturated fat: 0 g
Carbohydrate: 38 g
Total sugars: 20 g
Protein: 4 g
Sodium: 175 mg
Cholesterol: 0 mg
Dietary fiber: 2 g

The Anti–Breast Cancer Cookbook

Pumpkin–Black Rice Pudding

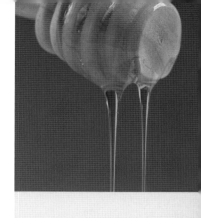

This pudding is an excellent source of vitamin A, phosphorus, and calcium. If you use black Arborio rice, you are getting a nice dose of antioxidant anthocyanins, the same great nutrient found in blueberries, blackberries, and purple grapes. Regular Arborio rice will work too. Serve with a dollop of yogurt and sliced strawberries or chopped nuts.

Ingredients:
2 cups water
1 cup black Arborio rice
3 cups organic reduced-fat (2 percent) dairy milk or enriched
    vanilla soy milk
1 cup solid-pack 100 percent pure pumpkin (not pumpkin pie filling)
1/2 cup clover honey or pure maple syrup
1 teaspoon vanilla extract
3/4 teaspoon ground cinnamon
1/4 teaspoon ground ginger
1/4 teaspoon ground nutmeg
1/4 teaspoon allspice
1/4 teaspoon salt

Preparation: Preheat oven to 375°F. Place water in an ovenproof 4-quart saucepan and bring to a boil. Stir in rice and cover. Reduce heat to low and simmer until rice is nearly cooked, about 20–22 minutes. Meanwhile, whisk together milk, pumpkin, honey, vanilla, cinnamon, ginger, nutmeg, allspice, and salt in a large bowl. While rice is still hot, add pumpkin mixture to the saucepan; stir well to combine. Cover and transfer to the oven. Bake until liquid has reduced by about 1/3 and mixture is bubbling and foamy, about 45–50 minutes. Remove from oven and stir well to combine all ingredients. Transfer to a large bowl. Cover and chill in refrigerator for at least 8 hours or overnight. The pudding will keep for up to 4 days in an airtight container in the refrigerator. Makes 8 servings.

Nutritional information per serving:
Calories: 145
Fat: 5 g
Saturated fat: 1 g
Carbohydrate: 19 g
Total sugars: 12 g
Protein: 6 g
Sodium: 115 mg
Cholesterol: 0 mg
Dietary fiber: 2 g

Raspberry-Strawberry-Lime Yogurt Tart

Vegetarian

For this recipe, I recommend using graham crackers that do not contain trans fats (partially hydrogenated oil). For the vanilla yogurt filling, you can mix 1 cup regular low-fat yogurt with 1 cup Greek yogurt to make a thicker texture. You can grind the almonds in a food processor or coffee grinder.

Ingredients:
1¼ cups graham cracker crumbs (about 16 sheets graham crackers ground in a food processor or crushed in a plastic bag)
1/4 cup ground almonds
1 tablespoon Splenda Brown Sugar Blend
5 tablespoons nonhydrogenated spread (such as Smart Balance or Fleischmann's Olive Oil Spread), melted
2 cups low-fat organic vanilla yogurt
2 tablespoons maple syrup or clover honey
Zest of 1 lime
1 cup fresh strawberries, sliced
1 cup fresh raspberries

Preparation: Preheat oven to 350°F. In large bowl, combine graham cracker crumbs, almonds, and sugar; mix well. Add melted spread; mix until all crumbs are coated. Press into a 9-inch tart pan with a removable bottom; bake for 8–10 minutes, until crust is set and light brown. Let cool for at least 20 minutes. Meanwhile, stir maple syrup or honey and lime zest into yogurt in small bowl. Pour into cooled crust. Chill for at least 1 hour. Top with strawberries and raspberries. Makes 10 servings.

Nutritional information per serving:
Calories: 186
Fat: 3 g
Saturated fat: 2 g
Carbohydrate: 36 g
Total sugars: 14 g
Protein: 4 g
Sodium: 120 mg
Cholesterol: 20 mg
Dietary fiber: 2 g

The Anti–Breast Cancer Cookbook

Raspberry Pudding

This pudding is great served with fresh blueberries and sliced kiwi or shaved dark chocolate.

Ingredients:
2 cups frozen raspberries without sugar
2 teaspoons vanilla extract
3 tablespoons sugar-free raspberry syrup (such as DaVinci)
2 cups low-fat ricotta cheese

Preparation: Place raspberries, vanilla extract, and syrup in a food processor or blender. Process until mostly smooth. Add cheese and process again until fully blended. Refrigerate, covered, for at least 1 hour but preferably overnight. Makes 8 servings of about 1/2 cup each.

Nutritional information per serving:
Calories: 155
Fat: 5 g
Saturated fat: 3 g
Carbohydrate: 20 g
Total sugars: 14 g
Protein: 8 g
Sodium: 80 mg
Cholesterol: 20 mg
Dietary fiber: 3 g

Ruby Red Grapefruit Brûlée

Grapefruit and other citrus fruits contain fiber as well as vitamin C. Pink and red grapefruit also contain the cancer-fighting antioxidant lycopene.

Ingredients:
3 large ruby red grapefruits
1/4 cup dark brown sugar, divided
1 tablespoon unsalted butter, cut into tiny pieces
1/2 teaspoon ground cinnamon

Preparation: Place oven rack about 5 inches from broiler and preheat broiler. Slice stem and opposite end off each grapefruit. Stand each grapefruit on a cutting board and slice off rind and pith with a very sharp knife. Cut each grapefruit into 4 round, parallel slices, about 1/2-inch thick. Place slices in a single layer on large baking sheet. Top each slice with 1 teaspoon sugar (more if desired) and dot with butter; sprinkle cinnamon on top. Broil grapefruit 6–8 minutes, until bubbling and beginning to brown. Drizzle pan juices over each slice when serving. Makes 6 servings of 2 grapefruit slices each.

Nutritional information per serving:
Calories: 110
Fat: 2 g
Saturated fat: 1 g
Carbohydrate: 22 g
Total sugars: 17 g
Protein: 1 g
Sodium: 4 mg
Cholesterol: 5 mg
Dietary fiber: 2 g

Walnut-Raspberry Tart

The bottom crust and walnut filling used for this tart make a wonderful base for an assortment of fresh fruit tarts, such as strawberry, blueberry, or kiwi. This recipe makes a 10-inch tart, but it can be used to make any size tart, from petite fours to 5-inch tartlets.

Ingredients:

Crust
3/4 cup all-purpose unbleached white flour
3/4 cup whole-wheat pastry flour
1/2 cup nonhydrogenated buttery spread (such as Smart Balance),
    at room temperature
1/4 teaspoon salt
1 large omega-3-enriched egg
1 tablespoon sugar

Filling
1/2 cup Splenda Brown Sugar
    Blend
2 large omega-3-enriched eggs
    plus 1 omega-3-enriched egg
    yolk from a large egg

1/2 cup all-purpose unbleached
    white flour
1/2 teaspoon cinnamon
1/2 teaspoon baking powder
2 cups walnuts, chopped or pieces

Topping
1/2 cup all-natural red raspberry preserves
1½ pints fresh raspberries

Preparation: Preheat oven to 400°F. To prepare crust, combine all crust ingredients. Using a paddle in a stand mixer, mix at low speed until just combined. Press into the bottom and 1 inch up the sides of a 10-inch fluted tart pan with a removable bottom. Bake approximately 8 minutes. Remove from oven and decrease heat to 350°F. For filling, combine Splenda Brown Sugar Blend, eggs, and egg yolk in a bowl. Mix with a spoon or stand mixer until light and fluffy. Add flour, cinnamon, baking powder, and walnuts. Pour into crust. Bake 30–35 minutes or until filling is firm. Remove from oven and let cool 30 minutes. Refrigerate at least 2 hours. To make topping, place small saucepan over low heat and add preserves. Heat until preserves melt; gently stir in fresh raspberries. Spread topping evenly on cooled tart filling. Makes about 12 servings.

Nutritional information per serving:
Calories: 310
Fat: 15 g
Saturated fat: 2 g
Carbohydrate: 37 g
Total sugars: 10 g
Protein: 8 g
Sodium: 115 mg
Cholesterol: 66 mg
Dietary fiber: 6 g

The Anti–Breast Cancer Cookbook

Whole-Wheat Dark Chocolate Chip-Nut Cookies

Vegetarian

Most recipes that use whole-wheat flour combine it with a larger portion of white flour. This recipe goes a bold step further, using only whole-wheat flour and including antioxidant-rich dark chocolate and mixed nuts.

Ingredients:
1 cup granulated white sugar
1/2 cup Splenda Brown Sugar Blend
1 cup nonhydrogenated buttery spread (such as Smart Balance or Fleischmann's Olive Oil Spread), softened
3 large omega-3-enriched eggs
1 cup natural peanut butter, stirred so that oil is mixed in
1 cup whole-grain rolled oats
2¼ cups whole-wheat flour
3 teaspoons baking soda
1/2 cup pecans, chopped
1/2 cup walnuts, chopped
1 cup dark chocolate chips
Nonstick cooking spray

Preparation: Preheat oven to 350°F. Cream together white sugar, Splenda Brown Sugar Blend, and nonhydrogenated spread with a hand or stand mixer. Beat in eggs and peanut butter. Switch to a dough hook. Add rolled oats and mix on low speed. Slowly add wheat flour, baking soda, pecans, walnuts, and chocolate chips (in that order), thoroughly mixing each ingredient as added. Spray 2 heavy baking sheets with nonstick cooking spray (or use nonstick baking sheets). Spoon dough by tablespoons onto baking sheets, staggering diagonally at least 1½ inches apart. Bake about 13–15 minutes, until golden brown around the edges and set in the middle. Let cookies rest a few minutes before moving from baking sheets onto a cooling rack. Makes about 48 cookies.

Nutritional information per cookie:
Calories: 125
Fat: 6 g
Saturated fat: 3 g
Carbohydrate: 15 g
Total sugars: 9 g
Protein: 3 g
Sodium: 110 mg
Cholesterol: 23 mg
Dietary fiber: 2 g

BEVERAGES

Vegetarian

Vegan

Gluten-Free

Almond-Date Shake ❧ ⊘ 209

Blackberry-Blueberry Burst Smoothie ❧ ℣ ⊘ 209

Blueberry-Lemon Smoothie ❧ ⊘ 210

Chai Tea ❧ ⊘ 210

Cherry-Banana Smoothie ❧ ⊘ 211

Chocolate-Cherry Smoothie ❧ ⊘ 211

Chocolate Cream Soda ❧ ℣ ⊘ 211

Chocolate-Strawberry-Banana Shake ❧ ℣ ⊘ 212

Cranberry-Banana Smoothie ❧ ⊘ 212

Dark Hot Chocolate ❧ ⊘ 213

Eggnog ❧ ⊘ 213

Ginger-Lemon Iced Green Tea ❧ ℣ ⊘ 214

Iced Raspberry Sun Tea ❧ ℣ ⊘ 214

Malibu Beach Bum ❧ ℣ ⊘ 215

Orange-Mango Smoothie ❧ ⊘ 215

Orange Blast ❧ ℣ ⊘ 216

Peachy Melon Blend ❧ ℣ ⊘ 216

Pomegranate Slush ❧ ℣ ⊘ 216

Raspberry-Cherry Smoothie ❧ ⊘ 217

Silken Berry Smoothie ❧ ⊘ 217

Strawberry-Peach Smoothie ❧ ⊘ 217

Almond-Date Shake

Ingredients:
6–7 dates
1 cup almond milk
1/2 cup (about 5 ounces) low-fat Greek vanilla yogurt
1 ripe banana, cut in pieces and frozen
2–3 ice cubes or about 1/3 cup crushed ice
Sprinkle of cinnamon or nutmeg

Preparation: In a bowl, cover dates with some warm water for about 25 minutes to soften. Remove from water, pat dry, and chop. Place all ingredients in a blender; blend until smooth. Serve topped with a sprinkle of cinnamon or nutmeg. Makes 2 servings.

Nutritional information per serving:
Calories: 169
Fat: 1 g
Saturated fat: 0 g
Carbohydrate: 37 g
Total sugars: 27 g
Protein: 7 g
Sodium: 98 mg
Cholesterol: 0 mg
Dietary fiber: 4 g

Blackberry-Blueberry Burst Smoothie

This is a refreshing smoothie with berries that contain cancer-fighting antioxidants.

Ingredients:
1 cup fresh blackberries
1/2 cup fresh or frozen (unsweetened) blueberries
1 teaspoon vanilla extract
6 ice cubes
1 teaspoon clover honey or pure maple syrup

Preparation: Place all ingredients in a blender and blend until smooth. Makes 2 servings.

Nutritional information per serving:
Calories: 85
Fat: < 1 g
Saturated fat: 0 g
Carbohydrate: 19 g
Total sugars: 14 g
Protein: 1 g
Sodium: 5 mg
Cholesterol: 0 mg
Dietary fiber: 0 g

Blueberry-Lemon Smoothie

This recipe's vitamin C and vitamin D may help prevent breast cancer as well as other forms of cancer.

Ingredients:
1 cup fresh or frozen (unsweetened) blueberries
3/4 cup low-fat lemon yogurt (preferably organic)
3/4 cup nonfat milk (preferably organic)
2 teaspoons honey or pure maple syrup

Preparation: Place all ingredients in a blender and blend until smooth. Makes 2 servings.

Nutritional information per serving:
Calories: 130
Fat: 2 g
Saturated fat: < 1 g
Carbohydrate: 22 g
Total sugars: 18 g
Protein: 7 g
Sodium: 90 mg
Cholesterol: 5 mg
Dietary fiber: 2 g

Chai Tea

This recipe makes traditional chai tea. If you use decaffeinated tea leaves, increase the amount of tea by either 1 teaspoon of loose tea or 1 tea bag to make up for the lost flavor. You can also make the tea/spice mixture ahead of time and store it. Add the milk and reheat when you're ready to serve.

Ingredients:
2¼ cups water
3 black tea bags or 1 tablespoon loose organic black tea
1 cinnamon stick
6 whole green cardamom pods, crushed, or about 1/4 teaspoon cardamom seeds
4 whole cloves
1/8 teaspoon nutmeg
1/2 teaspoon fresh ginger root, peeled and minced
1 teaspoon pure vanilla extract
2 tablespoons brown sugar
2 cups reduced-fat (2 percent) dairy milk (preferably organic)

Preparation: Boil water and brew tea until well steeped. In a large saucepan, place brewed tea with cinnamon stick, cardamom, cloves, nutmeg, ginger, vanilla, and sugar. Bring just to a boil; cover and reduce heat to low. Let simmer for approximately 5 minutes (longer if you prefer stronger, spicier chai). Add milk and slowly bring just to a simmer; do not boil. Remove from heat and strain mixture through strainer or coffee filters; press on the residue bits with a spoon to extract spice essences. Serve hot or let cool a bit and then serve over ice. Makes 3 servings.

Nutritional information per serving:
Calories: 100
Fat: 3 g
Saturated fat: 2 g
Carbohydrate: 14 g
Total sugars: 14 g
Protein: 5 g
Sodium: 82 mg
Cholesterol: 13 mg
Dietary fiber: 0 g

The Anti–Breast Cancer Cookbook

Cherry-Banana Smoothie

Ingredients:
2 ripe bananas, cut in chunks and frozen
2 cups frozen, unsweetened, tart cherries
2 cups nonfat milk (preferably organic)

Preparation: Place banana, cherries, and milk in a blender and puree until smooth. Serve immediately. Makes 2 servings.

Nutritional information per serving:
Calories: 145
Fat: < 1 g
Saturated fat: 0 g
Carbohydrate: 30 g
Total sugars: 22 g
Protein: 6 g
Sodium: 65 mg
Cholesterol: 2 mg
Dietary fiber: 3 g

Chocolate-Cherry Smoothie

Ingredients:
1 cup frozen cherries
1 ripe banana, cut in chunks
3/4 cup nonfat plain yogurt (preferably organic)
1/4 cup peach or mango nectar
2 tablespoons sugar-free, reduced-calorie chocolate syrup

Preparation: Freeze banana at least 2 hours before preparing, preferably overnight. Place all ingredients in a blender and blend until smooth. Makes 2 servings.

Nutritional information per serving:
Calories: 165
Fat: 0 g
Saturated fat: 0 g
Carbohydrate: 34 g
Total sugars: 23 g
Protein: 7 g
Sodium: 62 mg
Cholesterol: 4 mg
Dietary fiber: 4 g

Chocolate Cream Soda

This beverage is somewhat misnamed, since it doesn't contain any actual cream. But its soy milk fortified with calcium and vitamin D provides valuable nutrients and isoflavones.

Ingredients:
2 tablespoons sugar-free chocolate syrup
1¼ cups vanilla or chocolate soy milk, fortified with calcium and vitamin D
1¼ cups seltzer water or club soda

Preparation: Stir chocolate syrup into soy milk until blended. Divide soy milk/syrup mixture between 2 tall, chilled glasses. Add seltzer or club soda to fill glasses. Makes 2 servings.

Nutritional information per serving:
Calories: 86
Fat: 3 g
Saturated fat: < 1 g
Carbohydrate: 11 g
Total sugars: 7 g
Protein: 4 g
Sodium: 42 mg
Cholesterol: 0 mg
Dietary fiber: 1 g

Chocolate-Strawberry-Banana Shake

You can reduce the milk by half and add a scoop of low-fat chocolate frozen yogurt for extra-chocolaty flavor. Instead of whey protein powder, use soy protein powder for a vegan version.

Nutritional information per serving:
Calories: 210
Fat: 4 g
Saturated fat: 1 g
Carbohydrate: 26 g
Total sugars: 16 g
Protein: 17 g
Sodium: 179 mg
Cholesterol: 25 mg
Dietary fiber: 3 g

Ingredients:
1 cup organic reduced-fat (2 percent) dairy milk or enriched
    original or vanilla soy milk
1 banana, cut in chunks and frozen
2/3 cup frozen strawberries
2 teaspoons chocolate whey or soy protein powder
1/2 teaspoon vanilla extract

Preparation: Place all ingredients in a blender and blend until smooth. Makes 2 servings.

Cranberry-Banana Smoothie

Nutritional information per serving:
Calories: 180
Fat: < 1 g
Saturated fat: 0 g
Carbohydrate: 36 g
Total sugars: 27 g
Protein: 8 g
Sodium: 116 mg
Cholesterol: 8 mg
Dietary fiber: 1 g

Ingredients:
1 medium banana, peeled and sliced
1 cup vanilla nonfat yogurt (preferably organic)
3/4 cup 100 percent cranberry juice, chilled
1 cup nonfat milk (preferably organic)

Preparation: Freeze banana for at least 2 hours, preferably overnight. Place all ingredients in a blender and blend until smooth. Makes 2 servings.

Dark Hot Chocolate

Ingredients:
1/2 cup unsweetened cocoa powder
3 ounces dark chocolate, 70 percent cacao or greater, chopped (or dark chocolate chips, 70 percent cacao)
4 cups organic reduced-fat (2 percent) dairy milk
1 tablespoon clover honey or raw (turbinado) sugar

Preparation: In a medium saucepan, stir cocoa powder and chocolate pieces over medium heat. Whisk in milk and honey or raw sugar. Heat just until boiling, whisking constantly. Serve in mugs. Makes 4 servings.

Nutritional information per serving:
Calories: 180
Fat: 5 g
Saturated fat: 3 g
Carbohydrate: 26 g
Total sugars: 23 g
Protein: 9 g
Sodium: 100 mg
Cholesterol: 5 mg
Dietary fiber: 0 g

Eggnog

Ingredients:
1 banana, cut into chunks
2½ cups organic reduced-fat (2 percent) dairy milk or enriched vanilla soy milk
1/2 cup pasteurized egg white product (I use Egg Beaters)
1 single-serve packet Truvia or Splenda
1/2 teaspoon vanilla extract
1/2 teaspoon almond extract

Preparation: Freeze banana overnight. Place banana and milk in a blender; process until smooth. Add egg white, Truvia or Splenda, vanilla, and almond; blend again until well mixed. Serve in chilled mugs. Makes 3 servings.

Nutritional information per serving:
Calories: 235
Fat: 6 g
Saturated fat: 4 g
Carbohydrate: 29 g
Total sugars: 23 g
Protein: 17 g
Sodium: 270 mg
Cholesterol: 25 mg
Dietary fiber: 0 g

Nutritional information per serving:

Made with sugar
Calories: 126
Fat: 0 g
Saturated fat: 0 g
Carbohydrate: 32 g
Total sugars: 31 g
Protein: 0 g
Sodium: 0 mg
Cholesterol: 0 mg
Dietary fiber: 0 g

Made with Splenda or other low-calorie sweetener
Calories: 2
Fat: 0 g
Saturated fat: 0 g
Carbohydrate: < 1 g
Total sugars: 0 g
Protein: 0 g
Sodium: 0 mg
Cholesterol: 0 mg
Dietary fiber: 0 g

Nutritional information per serving:
Calories: 17
Fat: < 1 g
Saturated fat: 0 g
Carbohydrate: 4 g
Total sugars: 2 g
Protein: < 1 g
Sodium: < 1 mg
Cholesterol: 0 mg
Dietary fiber: < 1 g

Ginger-Lemon Iced Green Tea

Ingredients:
2 cups water
1 cup sugar; or Splenda or other low-calorie sweetener equal to 1 cup sugar
1 teaspoon ground ginger
1½ teaspoons lemon peel, grated
6 green tea bags
4 teaspoons fresh lemon juice
Sparkling or seltzer water, as needed

Preparation: In a medium saucepan, add water, sugar or Splenda, ginger, and lemon peel; bring to a boil over medium heat. Reduce heat to gentle boil; cook about 7–8 minutes. Remove from heat and add tea bags. Steep 10 minutes, stirring or dunking tea bags frequently. Remove tea bags and stir lemon juice into tea mixture. Cover and refrigerate. (Refrigerated mixture lasts up to 2 weeks.) Pour 1/4 cup tea mixture into tall glass; stir in 3/4 cup sparkling or seltzer water. Add ice cubes and serve. Makes 1½ cups of tea mixture—enough for about 6 glasses of iced tea.

Iced Raspberry Sun Tea

This drink requires sunlight, so it's best to make it in the warm summer months, unless you live in a sunny, tropical region.

Ingredients:
6 raspberry-flavored black tea bags
1/4 cup fresh mint leaves
4 cups cold water
12 whole fresh raspberries
4 mint sprigs

Preparation: Add tea bags, mint, and water to a loosely capped glass container. Place container in the sun; steep 2–4 hours, depending on desired strength. Strain tea into a pitcher, cover, and refrigerate until ready to serve. To serve, fill 4 tall glasses with ice. Add tea. Garnish each glass with 3 raspberries and 1 mint sprig. Makes 1 quart, or 4 servings of 8 ounces each.

The Anti–Breast Cancer Cookbook

Malibu Beach Bum

This smooth drink is really refreshing after a good workout.

Ingredients:
2 medium, ripe bananas, cut into chunks
1 medium orange, peeled and sliced into chunks
1/2 cup frozen unsweetened peaches
1/3 cup frozen unsweetened blueberries
1/2 cup enriched soy, rice, or almond milk
1/2 cup coconut milk

Preparation: Place bananas, orange, peaches, and blueberries in a blender; blend 30–45 seconds. Add soy milk and coconut milk and blend about 30 more seconds. Serve immediately. Makes 3 servings.

Nutritional information per serving:
Calories: 200
Fat: 9 g
Saturated fat: 7 g
Carbohydrate: 28 g
Total sugars: 17 g
Protein: 4 g
Sodium: 25 mg
Cholesterol: 0 mg
Dietary fiber: 4 g

Orange-Mango Smoothie

This recipe is made with a calorie-free sweetener; if you use raw sugar, the nutritional information will be different.

Ingredients:
1½ cups mango chunks, frozen
1 large, ripe orange, peeled and sectioned
1½ cups low-fat, organic vanilla yogurt
1 cup nonfat milk (preferably organic)
2 tablespoons vanilla whey protein powder
1 single-serve packet Truvia, Splenda, or raw sugar (optional)

Preparation: Place all ingredients in a blender. Blend until smooth. Makes 3 servings.

Nutritional information per serving:
Calories: 250
Fat: 2 g
Saturated fat: 1 g
Carbohydrate: 43 g
Total sugars: 36 g
Protein: 20 g
Sodium: 120 mg
Cholesterol: 2 mg
Dietary fiber: 3 g

Orange Blast

Nutritional information per serving:
Calories: 88
Fat: 0 g
Saturated fat: 0 g
Carbohydrate: 21 g
Total sugars: 16 g
Protein: 3 g
Sodium: 78 mg
Cholesterol: 0 mg
Dietary fiber: 1 g

Ingredients:
2/3 cup carrot juice
2/3 cup fresh orange juice
1/4 cup 100 percent pure pumpkin

Preparation: Place all ingredients in a blender or food processor; blend until smooth. Serve in chilled highball glasses. Makes 2 servings.

Peachy Melon Blend

Use dairy, soy, rice, or almond milk instead of orange juice to make this drink richer.

Nutritional information per serving:
Calories: 125
Fat: 0 g
Saturated fat: 0 g
Carbohydrate: 30 g
Total sugars: 25 g
Protein: 2 g
Sodium: 20 mg
Cholesterol: 0 mg
Dietary fiber: 3 g

Ingredients:
1 cup fresh orange juice
1 cup unsweetened frozen peaches
1 cup fresh cantaloupe
1/2 cup fresh honeydew

Preparation: Place all ingredients in a blender; blend until smooth. Makes 2 servings.

Pomegranate Slush

This drink contains antioxidants, such as ellagic acid and vitamin C, that may help prevent cancers such as breast cancer.

Nutritional information per serving:
Calories: 92
Fat: 0 g
Saturated fat: 0 g
Carbohydrate: 23 g
Total sugars: 22 g
Protein: < 1 g
Sodium: 12 mg
Cholesterol: 0 mg
Dietary fiber: 0 g

Ingredients:
1½ cups 100 percent pomegranate juice
1¼ cups grapefruit juice
1/4 cup white grape juice
1½–2 cups crushed ice

Preparation: Place all ingredients in a blender and blend until slushy. Serve in tall, chilled glasses. Makes 4 servings.

The Anti–Breast Cancer Cookbook

Raspberry-Cherry Smoothie

Ingredients:
1/2 cup low-fat frozen vanilla yogurt
3 ice cubes
1 cup frozen unsweetened raspberries
1 cup tart cherry juice
1 ripe banana, cut into chunks (frozen if desired)

Preparation: Place all ingredients in a blender and blend until smooth. Serve immediately. Makes 2 servings.

Nutritional information per serving:
Calories: 235
Fat: 1 g
Saturated fat: 0 g
Carbohydrate: 50 g
Total sugars: 32 g
Protein: 6 g
Sodium: 38 mg
Cholesterol: 22 mg
Dietary fiber: 4 g

Silken Berry Smoothie

Ingredients:
2 cups frozen mixed berries (any mixture of blueberries, raspberries, blackberries, strawberries)
1 cup plain low-fat yogurt (preferably organic)
1/2 cup silken tofu
1 ripe banana, cut in chunks and frozen
1/2 cup mango or pear nectar
5 or 6 ice cubes, or about 1 cup crushed ice

Preparation: Place all ingredients in a blender and blend until smooth. Serve immediately. Makes 2 servings.

Nutritional information per serving:
Calories: 170
Fat: 2 g
Saturated fat: < 1 g
Carbohydrate: 30 g
Total sugars: 20 g
Protein: 7 g
Sodium: 65 mg
Cholesterol: 5 mg
Dietary fiber: 4 g

Strawberry-Peach Smoothie

Ingredients:
1 cup frozen unsweetened peaches
1 cup frozen whole or sliced unsweetened strawberries
1 cup low-fat frozen vanilla yogurt (preferably organic)
1 cup organic reduced-fat (2 percent) dairy milk or organic soy milk (such as Silk or Edensoy)
1/2 teaspoon vanilla extract

Preparation: Place all ingredients in a blender and blend until smooth. Serve immediately. Makes 2 servings.

Nutritional information per serving:
Calories: 190
Fat: 3 g
Saturated fat: 1 g
Carbohydrate: 31 g
Total sugars: 21 g
Protein: 10 g
Sodium: 32 mg
Cholesterol: 30 mg
Dietary fiber: 2 g

Index

A

Acorn squash
maple-roasted, 86
soup, apple-, 99
Almonds
chocolate biscotti with, 193
dip, hazelnut-, 55
maple-nut granola, 44
muffins, pear-, 26
nutty pea salad, 127
polenta cake with, 186
raspberry-strawberry-lime yogurt tart, 204
salsa verde–Italian style, 69
sole amandine, 173
soup with celery and, 100
Apples
carrot-walnut cookies, 192
conserve, cranberry-pecan-, 59
maple-roasted acorn squash, 86
nut cake with, 187
oatmeal quick bread, cranberry-, 27
oat muffins, carrot, 32
pie, strawberry-, 188
soup, acorn squash-, 99
sweet potatoes with pecans and, 89
whole-wheat muffins, raspberry-, 50
Arugula
chicken and navy-bean salad, 119
linguine with spinach and, 162
portobello burgers, 141
salad with white beans and, 117
squash risotto with, 95
Asparagus
cranberry-vegetable baked risotto, 135
Avocados
creamy dressing, 60
gelato with peach-cherry sauce, 189
Italian halibut sandwiches, 138
lemon-herb salmon with mango-
peach-avocado salsa, 161
mango-nectarine salmon, 164
mixed greens and papaya salad
with cumin-lime vinaigrette, 125
salsa with corn, black beans and, 58
salsa with tomatillos and, 56
vegetarian cobb salad with citrus-
miso dressing, 131

B

Bananas
blueberry-banana flax pancakes with
strawberry yogurt topping, 31
carrot-walnut cookies, 192
chocolate-cherry smoothie, 211
chocolate shake with strawberries
and, 212
dark chocolate banana bread with
pecans, 39
eggnog, 213
Malibu beach bum, 215

muffins, blackberry-, 28
pancakes, oat bran-, 29
raspberry-cherry smoothie, 217
silken berry smoothie, 217
smoothie of cherries and, 211
smoothie of cranberries and, 212
Beef
spinach and watercress salad with
sesame, 130
stew with sun-dried tomatoes, 102
Beets
greens and walnut salad with
roasted, 129
pasta with pesto of kale, carrots and, 149
Bell peppers
baked potatoes, cauliflower and, 80
basmati rice, 74
chipotle turkey and bean chili, 106
cocoa-scented black bean chili, 107
dip with feta and, 61
dressing, 68
grilled chicken wraps with cilantro
dressing, 137
grilled corn and shrimp salad, 120
Italian pasta salad, 84
mango-nectarine salmon, 164
Moroccan potato casserole, 88
polenta and roasted vegetables, 94
quinoa tabbouleh, 93
quinoa with edamame, 91
sautéed onion and pork sandwiches, 142
shrimp étouffée, 172
tomato and bacon turkey meatloaf, 180
tricolored pepper salsa, 72
Berries
silken berry smoothie, 217
See also specific varieties
Black beans
bean salad with creamy herb
dressing, 75
chipotle turkey and bean chili, 106
cocoa-scented chili, 107
easy, speedy chicken tacos, 136
enchiladas with sweet potatoes and,
133-134
quinoa with, 90
salsa with corn, avocados and, 58
soup with pumpkin and, 103
Blackberries
lemon yogurt cake with mixed
berries, 200
muffins, banana-, 28
smoothie of blueberries and, 209
Black-eyed peas
chipotle turkey and bean chili, 106
kale with, 76
West African bean fritters, 147
Black rice
pudding, pumpkin-, 203
pudding with tart cherry sauce, 195

Blueberries
flax pancakes, banana-blueberry with
strawberry yogurt topping, 31
lemon smoothie with, 210
lemony cream cheese pancakes
with, 43
lemon yogurt cake with mixed
berries, 200
Malibu beach bum, 215
mini muffins, bran-, 30
smoothie of blackberries and, 209
yogurt tart, 190
Bok choy
satay with shrimp, peaches and, 144
tofu and, 179
Broccoli
Asian sesame salad with soba
noodles, 118
buckwheat with red bean sauce and, 77
Cajun catfish with brown rice and, 151
crustless quiche, salmon and, 38
halibut with tomatoes and, 150
Italian pasta salad, 84
miso soup with udon noodles, 112
soup with leeks and, 104
Butternut squash
risotto with arugula, 95
shiitake mushroom risotto and, 78
turkey and winter vegetable stew, 114

C

Cabbage
Japanese miso salad with, 122
slaw, carrot and, 79
vegetarian pad thai, 182
vegetarian vegetable soup, 115
Cannellini beans
bean salad with creamy herb
dressing, 75
chicken and navy-bean salad, 119
fontina fusilli with broccoli rabe and, 184
See also **White beans**
Carrots
aromatic chicken stew, 101
Asian sesame salad with soba
noodles, 118
beef stew with sun-dried tomatoes, 102
chickpea and sunflower tahini
burgers, 134
chipotle turkey and bean chili, 106
cookies, walnut-, 192
flax muffins, 45
Italian pasta salad, 84
mango-ginger salad with, 124
miso soup with udon noodles, 112
oat muffins, apple-, 32
pasta with pesto of beets, kale and, 149
quinoa tabbouleh, 93
roasted parsnips and, 92
sautéed onion and pork sandwiches, 142
slaw, cabbage and, 79

soup, 108
tofu and bok choy, 179
vegetarian pad thai, 182
vegetarian vegetable soup, 115

Cashews
granola, chocolate-, 34
Japanese miso cabbage salad, 122
maple-nut granola, 44
spinach tofu with cashew-coconut
sauce, 175

Cauliflower
baked pepper, potatoes and, 80
soup with jarlsberg and, 105
vegetarian vegetable soup, 115

Celery
chicken and navy-bean salad, 119
chipotle turkey and bean chili, 106
cocoa-scented black bean chili, 107
Moroccan potato casserole, 88
polenta and roasted vegetables, 94
shrimp étouffée, 172
soup with almonds and, 100
turkey and winter vegetable stew, 114
vegetarian vegetable soup, 115
wild rice casserole, 96

Chard
fusilli with walnuts and, 155
gnocchi with greens and beans, 167

Cheddar cheese
black bean and sweet potato
enchiladas, 133-134
easy, speedy chicken tacos, 136

Cheese. *See specific varieties*

Cherries
avocado gelato with peach-cherry
sauce, 189
black rice pudding with tart cherry
sauce, 195
chocolate-almond biscotti, 193
oatmeal-cherry-chocolate chip
cookies, 202
smoothie, chocolate-, 211
smoothie of bananas and, 211
tilapia with cherry cilantro sauce, 178

Chicken
Angela's aromatic stew, 101
Dijon-pecan, 154
easy, speedy tacos, 136
green curry shiitake, 157
grilled wraps with cilantro dressing, 137
lychee braised, 163
navy-bean salad with, 119
quiche with spinach, mushrooms and, 33

Chickpeas
bean salad with creamy herb dressing, 75
lentil stew with, 110
Moroccan potato casserole, 88
sesame tofu with spinach and, 171
sunflower tahini burgers with, 134

Chipotle chiles
cocoa-scented black bean chili, 107
cornmeal-crusted scallops with
lime-chipotle vinaigrette, 152
turkey and bean chili, 106

Chocolate
biscotti, almond-, 193
cake, 201
cheesecake, hazelnut-, 194
cookies, oatmeal-cherry-chocolate
chip, 202
cream soda, 211
dark chocolate banana bread with
pecans, 39
dark chocolate chip-nut whole
wheat cookies, 207
dark hot, 213
granola, cashew-, 34
pancakes, pecan-, 35
shake, strawberry-banana-, 212
smoothie, cherry-, 211

Clams
mahi mahi fisherman's stew, 111
Spanish seafood paella, 174

Coconut
oatmeal-cherry-chocolate chip cookies,
202
pudding, 196

Coconut milk
black rice pudding with tart cherry
sauce, 195
green curry shiitake chicken, 157
spinach tofu with cashew-coconut
sauce, 175

Corn
easy, speedy chicken tacos, 136
green curry shiitake chicken, 157
quinoa with black beans, 90
salad with grilled shrimp and, 120
salsa with beans, avocados and, 58
vegetarian vegetable soup, 115

Cornmeal
crusted scallops with lime-chipotle
vinaigrette, 152
polenta and roasted vegetables, 94

Crabmeat
mahi mahi fisherman's stew, 111

Cranberries
bread pudding with apple-cranberry
sauce, 191
conserve, apple-pecan-, 59
granola cookies, 199
haricots verts with vinaigrette of
walnuts and, 82
oatmeal, pecan-, 36
oatmeal quick bread, apple-, 27
pancakes, walnut-, 37
quinoa tabbouleh, 93
smoothie of bananas and, 212
vegetable baked risotto with, 135

Cream cheese
chocolate-hazelnut cheesecake, 194
crumble of walnut and, 197
lemony cream cheese pancakes
with blueberries, 43

D

Dates
almond milk shake with, 209
scones with walnuts, fennel and, 49

E

Edamame
Italian pasta salad, 84
quinoa with, 91

Eggplant
lamb moussaka, 160
sauté with Italian herbs and shallots, 82

Eggs
Joe's Negri's frittata, 139

F

Fennel
scones with walnuts, dates and, 49

Feta cheese
roasted red pepper dip with, 61

Flaxseed meal
apple-nut cake, 187
blueberry-banana flax pancakes with
strawberry yogurt topping, 31
blueberry-bran mini muffins, 30
buttermilk pancakes with peaches
and pecan maple syrup, 40
carrot-walnut cookies, 192
Flaxseed oil and herbed olive oil
dressing, 64
Flaxseeds, muffins with, 45
Fontina cheese, white bean, broccoli
rabe fusilli, 184

G

Green beans
jicama and pomegranate-pecan
salad with, 123
Spanish seafood paella, 174

Green chiles
black bean and sweet potato
enchiladas, 133-134
green curry shiitake chicken, 157
mahi mahi fisherman's stew, 111
poblano pesto, 63

Greens
easy, speedy chicken tacos, 136
grilled salmon salad, 121
mango-ginger-carrot salad with, 124
papaya and mixed, salad with
cumin-lime vinaigrette, 125
roasted beets and walnut salad with, 129
sweet potatoes patties, 146
vegetarian cobb salad with citrus-miso
dressing, 131

H

Halibut
broccoli and tomato, 150
Italian sandwiches, 138
steamed Asian, with sesame kale, 176
walnut-crusted, with pear chutney, 183

Hazelnuts
chocolate-hazelnut cheesecake, 194
dip, almond-, 55
strawberry polenta with, 48

J

Jalapeño peppers
lemon-herb salmon with mango-
peach-avocado salsa, 161

The Anti–Breast Cancer Cookbook

walnut-crusted halibut with pear chutney, 183
white-bean and poblano chili, 116

K

Kale
black-eyed peas with, 76
hash with potatoes and, 85
pasta with pesto of beets, carrots and, 149
steamed Asian halibut with sesame, 176

Kidney beans
buckwheat with broccoli and red bean sauce, 77
chipotle turkey and bean chili, 106
cocoa-scented black bean chili, 107
vegetarian cobb salad with citrus-miso dressing, 131

L

Leeks
mushroom barley salad, 126
soup with broccoli and, 104

Lentils
burgers, 140
chickpea stew with, 110
curried salmon with, 153
red lentil soup, 109

M

Mangoes
ginger-carrot salad with, 124
lemon-herb salmon with mango-peach-avocado salsa, 161
salmon with nectarines and, 164
smoothie of oranges and, 215

Miso
Japanese cabbage salad with, 122
sauce, tahini-, 66
sesame beef, spinach and water cress salad, 130
soup with udon noodles, 112
vegetarian cobb salad with citrus-miso dressing, 131

Monterey Jack cheese
black bean and sweet potato enchiladas, 133-134

Mozzarella
herb-crusted Margherita and mushroom pan pizza, 158
lamb moussaka, 160
sole stuffed with spinach and, 165

Mung bean sprouts
vegetarian pad thai, 182

Mushrooms
barley salad with, 126
cranberry-vegetable baked risotto, 135
mozzarella and spinach-stuffed sole, 165
onion and spinach quesadillas with Manchego cheese and, 145
portobello burgers, 141
spicy turkey relleno burgers, 144
steamed Asian halibut with sesame kale, 176
wild rice casserole, 96
See also Shiitake mushrooms

Mussels
Spanish seafood paella, 174

N

Napa cabbage
steamed Asian halibut with sesame kale, 176

Navy beans
chicken salad with, 119

Nuts
carrot-apple oat muffins, 32
See also specific varieties

O

Oat bran
carrot-apple muffins, 32
pancakes, banana-, 29

Oats
apple-cranberry oatmeal quick bread, 27
carrot-walnut cookies, 192
cherry-chocolate chip cookies, 202
chocolate-cashew granola, 34
cranberry-pecan oatmeal, 36
granola cookies, 199
maple-nut granola, 44
whole-wheat dark chocolate chip-nut cookies, 207

Olives
sautéed swordfish Niçoise, 170

Oranges
Malibu beach bum, 215
smoothie of mangoes and, 215

P

Parsnips
roasted carrots and, 92
turkey and winter vegetable stew, 114

Peaches
avocado gelato with peach-cherry sauce, 189
buttermilk pancakes with pecan maple syrup and, 40
lemon-herb salmon with mango-peach-avocado salsa, 161
Malibu beach bum, 215
melon blend, 216
satay with shrimp, bok choy and, 144
smoothie of strawberries and, 217

Peanut butter
shrimp, peach and bok choy satay, 143
whole-wheat dark chocolate chip-nut cookies, 207

Pears
muffins, almond-, 26
walnut-crusted halibut with pear chutney, 183

Peas
aromatic chicken stew, 101
nutty salad, 127
Spanish seafood paella, 174

Pecans
blueberry yogurt tart, 190
buttermilk pancakes with pecan maple syrup and peaches, 40
chicken with Dijon-, 154

conserve, cranberry-apple, 59
dark chocolate banana bread with, 39
oatmeal, cranberry-, 36
oatmeal-cherry-chocolate chip cookies, 202
pancakes, chocolate-, 35
salad, jicama and pomegranate-, 123
sweet potatoes with apples and, 89
whole-wheat dark chocolate chip-nut cookies, 207
zucchini nut bread, 53

Poblano peppers
pesto, 63
spicy turkey relleno burgers, 144
white-bean and poblano chili, 116

Potatoes
baked pepper, cauliflower and, 80
hash with kale and, 85
Joe's Negri's frittata, 139
lentil and chickpea stew, 110
mashed rosemary yams and, 87
Moroccan casserole, 88
roasted brussels sprouts and, 83
vegetarian vegetable soup, 115

Pumpkin
gingerbread Belgian waffles, 41
orange blast, 216
pudding, black rice-, 203
soup with black beans and, 103
spiced soup, 113
whole-wheat pancakes, 51
Pumpkin seed pesto, 71

Q

Quinoa
with black beans, 90
with edamame, 91
tabbouleh, 93

R

Raspberries
iced sun tea, 214
muffins, whole-wheat apple-, 50
pudding, 205
smoothie of cherries and, 217
tart of walnuts and, 206
vinaigrette, 67
yogurt tart with strawberries, lime and, 204

Red peppers, roasted
buckwheat with broccoli and red bean sauce, 77
grilled salmon salad, 121
sautéed swordfish Niçoise, 170
sesame beef, spinach and water cress salad, 130
Ricotta cheese, raspberry pudding, 205

S

Salmon
crustless quiche, broccoli and, 38
curried, with lentils, 153
grilled, salad, 121
herb horseradish-crusted, 159
lemon-herb, with mango-peach-avocado salsa, 161
mango-nectarine, 164

roasted barbecued wild, 169
Salsa verde–Italian style, 69
Scallops
  cornmeal-crusted, with lime-chipotle
    vinaigrette, 152
  garlic shrimp and, 156
Shiitake mushrooms
  green curry chicken, 157
  herb-crusted Margherita and mush
    room pan pizza, 158
  miso soup with udon noodles, 112
  risotto with butternut squash and, 78
Shrimp
  étouffée, 172
  garlic scallops and, 156
  mahi mahi fisherman's stew, 111
  salad with grilled corn and, 120
  satay with peach, bok choy and, 144
  Spanish seafood paella, 174
Snow peas
  miso soup with udon noodles, 112
Sole
  amandine, 173
  mozzarella and spinach-stuffed, 165
Spinach
  black bean and sweet potato
    enchiladas, 133-134
  easy, speedy chicken tacos, 136
  gnocchi with greens and beans, 167
  lentil and chickpea stew, 110
  linguine with arugula and, 162
  mango-ginger-carrot salad with, 124
  onion and mushroom quesadillas with
    Manchego cheese, and, 145
  quiche with chicken, mushrooms and, 33
  red lentil soup, 109
  sesame beef, watercress salad with, 130
  sesame tofu with chickpeas and, 171
  sole stuffed with mozzarella and, 165
  spicy turkey relleno burgers, 144
  swordfish florentine, 177
  tofu with cashew-coconut sauce, 175
Squash. *See specific varieties*
Squid
  Spanish seafood paella, 174
Strawberries
  banana-oat bran pancakes, 29
  blueberry-banana flax pancakes
    with strawberry yogurt topping, 31
  chocolate shake with bananas and, 212
  lemon yogurt cake with mixed berries, 200
  pie, apple-, 188
  polenta, hazelnut-, 48
  smoothie of peaches and, 217
  yogurt tart, raspberry-lime-, 204
Summer squash. *See* **Zucchini**
Sweet potatoes
  enchiladas with black beans and, 133-134
  patties, 146
  pecan-apple, 89
Swiss cheese
  chicken, spinach, and mushroom
    quiche, 33
Swordfish
  florentine, 177
  sautéed Niçoise-style, 170

T

Thai eggplant
  green curry shiitake chicken, 157
Tilapia
  with cherry cilantro sauce, 178
  tomato walnut, 181
Tofu
  bok choy and, 179
  coconut pudding, 196
  creamy avocado dressing, 60
  Japanese miso cabbage salad, 122
  sesame, with spinach and chickpeas, 171
  silken berry smoothie, 217
  spinach, with cashew-coconut sauce, 175
Tomatillos
  salsa with avocados and, 56
  white-bean and poblano chili, 116
Tomatoes
  black bean and pumpkin soup, 103
  chipotle turkey and bean chili, 106
  cocoa-scented black bean chili, 107
  dipping sauce, ginger-, 62
  easy, speedy chicken tacos, 136
  gnocchi with greens and beans, 167
  grilled corn and shrimp salad, 120
  halibut with broccoli and, 150
  herb-crusted Margherita and mushroom
    pan pizza, 158
  lamb moussaka, 160
  mahi mahi fisherman's stew, 111
  mango-nectarine salmon, 164
  meatloaf, bacon turkey and, 180
  Moroccan potato casserole, 88
  panzanella bread salad, 128
  polenta and roasted vegetables, 94
  shrimp étouffée, 172
  Spanish seafood paella, 174
  tilapia with walnuts and, 181
  vegetarian vegetable soup, 115
Tomatoes, grape/cherry
  Italian pasta salad, 84
  quinoa tabbouleh, 93
  vegetarian cobb salad with citrus-miso
    dressing, 131
Tomatoes, Roma/plum
  arugula and white-bean salad, 117
  spicy turkey relleno burgers, 144
  sweet potatoes patties, 146
Tomatoes, sun-dried
  beef stew with, 102
  chicken and navy-bean salad, 119
  tomato and bacon turkey meatloaf, 180
Turkey, ground
  chipotle turkey and bean chili, 106
  spicy turkey relleno burgers, 144
  tomato and bacon turkey meatloaf, 180
  white-bean and poblano chili, 116
Turkey sausage
  Joe's Negri's frittata, 139

U

Udon noodles
  miso soup with, 112
  tofu and bok choy, 179

W

Walnuts
  apple-nut cake with, 187
  cookies, carrot-, 192
  crumble of cream cheese and, 197
  flax muffins, 45
  fusilli with Swiss chard and, 155
  granola cookies, 199
  halibut crusted with, and pear chutney, 183
  haricots verts with vinaigrette of
    cranberries and, 82
  oatmeal-cherry-chocolate chip cookies,
    202
  pancakes, cranberry-, 37
  quinoa tabbouleh, 93
  scones with dates, fennel and, 49
  tart of raspberries and, 206
  tilapia with tomatoes and, 181
  vinaigrette, 72
White beans
  broccoli rabe, fontina fusilli and, 184
  gnocchi with greens and, 167
  poblano chili with, 116
  salad with arugula and, 117
  See also Cannellini beans

Y

Yams
  mashed rosemary potatoes and, 87
  turkey and winter vegetable stew, 114
Yogurt
  almond-date shake, 209
  banana-oat bran pancakes, 29
  blackberry-banana muffins, 28
  blueberry-banana flax pancakes with
    strawberry yogurt topping, 31
  blueberry-lemon smoothie, 210
  blueberry tart, 190
  carrot-apple oat muffins, 32
  chocolate-cherry smoothie, 211
  coffee frozen, 196
  cranberry-banana smoothie, 212
  creamy carrot soup, 108
  lamb moussaka, 160
  lemon yogurt cake with mixed berries,
    200
  orange-mango smoothie, 215
  orange–poppy seed muffins, 46
  raspberry-cherry smoothie, 217
  raspberry-strawberry-lime yogurt tart, 204
  silken berry smoothie, 217
  strawberry-hazelnut polenta, 48
  strawberry-peach smoothie, 217
  white-bean and poblano chili, 116

Z

Zucchini
  bread with nuts, 53
  chicken and navy-bean salad, 119
  grilled chicken wraps with cilantro
    dressing, 137
  Italian pasta salad, 84
  penne with sugar snap peas and, 168
  polenta and roasted vegetables, 94
  vegetarian vegetable soup, 115

Also Available from Sunrise River Press

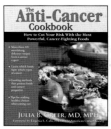

The Anti-Cancer Cookbook
How to Cut Your Risk with the Most Powerful, Cancer-Fighting Foods

Julia B. Greer, MD, MPH Dr. Julia Greer—a physician, cancer researcher, and food enthusiast—explains what cancer is and how antioxidants work to prevent pre-cancerous mutations in your body's cells, and then describes in detail which foods have been scientifically shown to help prevent which types of cancer. She shares her collection of more than 220 scrumptious recipes for soups, sauces, main courses, vegetarian dishes, sandwiches, breads, desserts, and beverages, all loaded with nutritious ingredients chock-full of powerful antioxidants that may significantly slash your risk of a broad range of cancer types, including lung, colon, breast, prostate, pancreatic, bladder, stomach, leukemia, and others. Dr. Greer even includes tips on how to cook foods to protect their valuable antioxidants and nutrients and how to make healthy anti-cancer choices when eating out. Softbound, 7.5 x 9 inches, 224 pages. Item # SRP149

The Thin In 10 Weight-Loss Plan
Transform Your Body (and Life!) in Minutes a Day

Jessica Smith and Liz Neporent Best-selling exercise DVD star and certified fitness and lifestyle expert Jessica Smith, along with award-winning health and fitness writer Liz Neporent, break down weight loss into 10-minute, easy-to-follow workouts that fit your busy schedule. Step-by-step photos and instructions, along with an exciting, fast-paced DVD with six 10-minute workouts, make this a simple, fun, and sustainable program for anyone, whether you're just starting out or have been at it for a while. High- and low-intensity fat-burning and muscle-building exercises, along with healthful, easy (and quick) recipes, numerous tips and tricks to burning more calories throughout the day, and a bonus DVD, make this the essential fitness and weight-loss kit! Softbound, 6 x 9 inches, 224 pages. Item # SRP635

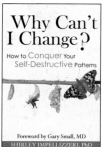

Why Can't I Change?
How to Conquer Your Self-Destructive Patterns

Shirley Impellizzeri, PhD This book is a psychological self-help manual to improve self-esteem and overall well-being. It is for anyone who feels stuck repeating patterns in their lives that don't work—a series of dead end jobs, bad relationships, or even self-sabotaging behaviors. *Why Can't I Change?* incorporates the latest research on brain science to see how your identity is not defined by your behavior but is a reaction to your early programming. Dr. Shirley Impellizzeri identifies four categories of attachment styles we adopt as children based on our perceptions of how those most influential in our lives perceive us. Softbound, 6 x 9 inches, 240 pages. Item # SRP637